ANCIENT IRAN

IN THE ISAC MUSEUM

ANCIENT IRAN

IN THE ISAC MUSEUM

From Prehistory to the Achaemenid Period

Abbas Alizadeh

INSTITUTE FOR THE STUDY OF ANCIENT CULTURES
OF THE UNIVERSITY OF CHICAGO
ISAC MUSEUM PUBLICATIONS • NUMBER 3

Library of Congress Control Number: 2026931563
ISBN (hardcover): 978-1-61491-138-8
ISBN (Adobe PDF): 978-1-61491-139-5
ISBN (Adobe Digital Editions): 978-1-61491-140-1

Institute for the Study of Ancient Cultures, Chicago

Printed in the United States of America.

ISAC Museum Publications 3

Series Editor
Andrew Baumann

with the assistance of
Connie Gundry Tappy

Cover Illustration
Colossal bull head from the Hall of a Hundred Columns at Persepolis.
Limestone, Achaemenid period. ISACM A24065.

Cover Design
Joshua Tulisiak

Layout
PerfecType, Nashville, TN

The paper used in this publication meets the minimum requirements of American National Standard for Information Services—Permanence of Paper for Printed Library Materials, ANSI Z39.48-1992. ♾

MIX
Paper | Supporting responsible forestry
FSC® C005010

Contents

Foreword

Timothy P. Harrison
Director, Institute for the Study of Ancient Cultures—West Asia & North Africa

Ancient Iran, the third in a series of catalogs that feature the extraordinary collections of the Institute for the Study of Ancient Cultures (ISAC) at the University of Chicago, celebrates the Institute's pioneering research on the cultures and history of ancient Persia and Iran. The catalog highlights the astonishing monumental sculptures and cultural artifacts in the collection, one of the largest and most comprehensive cultural assemblages on ancient Iran in existence and beautifully displayed in the Robert and Deborah Aliber Persian Gallery of the ISAC Museum. Recovered as part of carefully controlled and systematically recorded excavations at sites encompassing the full geographical and historical scope of ancient Iran's bountiful cultural legacy—ranging from Sarab and Surkh Dum-i-Luri in the northwest to Chogha Mish and Tall-e Geser in lowland Khuzestan and Tall-e Bakun, Istakhar, and Persepolis in the Fars imperial heartland—the Institute's ancient Iran collection holds exceptional cultural and historical value, and it represents an unparalleled resource for scholars and the broader public alike.

The objects displayed in this catalog, which have been carefully selected and described by Abbas Alizadeh, research associate professor of Iranian archaeology and director of ISAC's Iranian Prehistoric Project, provide a beautifully illustrated account of the rich cultural history of this ancient land. The presentation begins with the ceramic cultures of the early Neolithic through the early urban Protoliterate period, best preserved on the vast Khuzestan plain at Chogha Mish and in highland Fars at Tall-e Bakun with its aesthetically breathtaking ceramic industry, and in the ensuing Proto-Elamite period at Tall-e Geser. The narrative continues with the Elamite cultures of the Bronze Age, notably the Luristan bronzes of Surkh Dum-i-Luri in west-central Iran—crafted with astounding metallurgical skill and stylistic sophistication, and possibly the work of itinerant metalsmiths—and culminates with the imperial art and architecture of Achaemenid Persia, best represented in the ISAC collections by the awe-inspriring colossal bull's head and composite capitals but also by the Achaemenids' masterfully crafted jewelry and luxurious fine arts, notably the exquisite gold winged-lion roundel, all on display in the Robert and Deborah Aliber Persian Gallery.

The catalog is prefaced by introductory chapters that provide helpful overviews of the archaeological and cultural history of ancient Iran, from its earliest manifestations in the form of small agricultural communities in the Neolithic to the great imperial ambitions and expanse of the Persian Achaemenid dynasty, and of the Institute's central role in the exploration and study of this long and glorious history. *Ancient Iran* represents both a wonderful testament to the pioneering work of almost a century of distinguished ISAC scholarship and a beautiful introduction to one of the great civilizations of the ancient Near East.

Preface

Marc Maillot
Director and Chief Curator, Institute for the Study of Ancient Cultures Museum

Ancient Iran is the third in a series of books designed to present outstanding artifacts from the collection of the Institute for the Study of Ancient Cultures (ISAC) Museum. This catalog features highlights of one of the museum's most prominent galleries—the Robert and Deborah Aliber Persian Gallery. The aesthetically extraordinary objects in this space hold exceptional scientific value, as most of them come from carefully recorded excavations conducted by ISAC in Iran—at sites as varied as Persepolis, Naqsh-e Rustam, Istakhr, Tall-e Bakun, and Surkh Dum-i-Luri, among others—from as early as 1931, only twelve years after ISAC's founding and the same year the ISAC Museum opened to the public, until 1972, the year the UNESCO convention ratification protecting the world's cultural heritage entered into force. This collection, apart from serving as an unparalleled resource for scholars, is thus deeply rooted in the history of our institution. It constitutes the largest and most comprehensive group of artifacts from ancient Iran in the United States.

Among the masterpieces of the collection, the painted bowl from Tall-e Bakun A (ISACM A20136; **cat. no. 20)** is one of the finest examples of the prehistoric potter's craft in Iran. The disk-headed pin from the Surkh Dum-i-Luri sanctuary (ISACM A25293; **cat. no. 54**) demonstrates the expertise of nomadic populations in metalworking and casting. Beyond such small finds, the limestone column with a double-bull capital (ISACM A24069–70; **cat. no. 66**), originally a component of the southern portico at Persepolis, is a tour de force mixing Egyptian, Phoenician, and Greek influences with pure Achaemenid style in a single architectonic gesture. The colossal bull's head (ISACM A24065; **cat. no. 68**), embedded in the wall opposite the gallery entrance, is one of the most iconic pieces in the ISAC Museum's collection. Its missing ears and horns were manufactured separately, and probably gilded, prior to being attached to the head.

These incomparable masterpieces are merely a glimpse of the Persian gallery's remarkable holdings, carefully gathered in this catalog authored by Dr. Abbas Alizadeh, research associate professor of Iranian archaeology at the University of Chicago. Notably, this catalog not only presents the collection but also sheds personal light on Dr. Alizadeh's scholarly path. His long-standing passion for Persian archaeology has inspired new generations of scholars studying at the University of Chicago, where he earned his doctorate in 1987, as well as at Harvard University, where he has taught a course on ancient nomadism. Sponsored by a grant from the University of Chicago, Dr. Alizadeh has taken a modern approach to the field by undertaking an ethnoarchaeological survey in the southern Iranian province of Fars, where for one month in 1995 he traveled with a nomadic tribe, gathering data for future publications. He pursued work in areas such as Elam, on the border with Iraq in the region north of Khuzestan province, and he undertook the enormous endeavor of classifying and documenting the pottery collection of the Iran Bastan Museum in Tehran. Thanks to Dr. Alizadeh, that museum houses today an impressive collection of nearly one million sherds, cataloged according to region and type, allowing scholarly access to an unparalleled archaeological resource.

That the ISAC Museum's Persian collection is exhibited in the Robert and Deborah Aliber Persian Gallery gives me the welcome opportunity to pay tribute to this cherished couple. Married on September 9, 1955, in Charleston, South Carolina, Deborah and Robert moved to Chicago's Hyde Park neighborhood in 1965. There, they became greatly engaged in and committed to education at ISAC, where they both served as docents and Deborah as the first librarian of the docent library. Their enthusiasm for the history and cultures of the ancient Middle East led them to take numerous study trips to Egypt, Syria, Turkey, Iran, India, and other areas in the eastern Mediterranean. We have treasured their warm friendship and honor their commitment to ISAC as their legacy continues to bear fruit throughout this catalog and the gallery bearing their names.

Finally, my deep thanks go to curator Kiersten Neumann and associate registrar Susan Allison of the ISAC Museum and to managing editor Andrew Baumann in the ISAC publications office for their dedication and expertise in producing a catalog that meets the reputation for excellence that our institution has earned worldwide in the field of the humanities.

Acknowledgments

Abbas Alizadeh
Research Associate Professor, Institute for the Study of Ancient Cultures—West Asia & North Africa

This guide to the Robert and Deborah Aliber Persian Gallery of the Institute for the Study of Ancient Cultures (ISAC) Museum was created to fill a long-standing gap, as no such resource previously existed. I first presented plans for a comprehensive and up-to-date guidebook during the tenure of the ISAC Museum's former chief curator, Jean M. Evans. The manuscript was in its initial stages when she left ISAC in March 2022. In 2023 her successor, current chief curator and Museum director Marc Maillot, enthusiastically championed the project and encouraged its completion.

A book of this nature requires the collaboration of many people. ISAC Museum registrar Helen McDonald and associate registrar Susan Allison provided essential field and museum registration information for every object presented in the catalog. Many of the objects featured in this volume also had to be photographed, a task that Ms. Allison graciously carried out alongside her regular duties, and I thank her for the excellent images that appear throughout. Once the manuscript was completed, ISAC curator Kiersten Neumann undertook the time-consuming tasks of checking (and rechecking) the detailed data and reorganizing much of the content. Assisted by freelance editor Connie Gundry Tappy, ISAC publications managing editor Andrew Baumann carefully edited the manuscript and proofread the typeset version, making many valuable suggestions and recommendations in the process. Finally, ISAC senior designer Josh Tulisiak designed the cover. I am grateful for the collective efforts of my ISAC colleagues and thank them for their valuable assistance in producing this volume.

I also wish to extend my appreciation to Dr. Jebreil Nokandeh, director of the National Museum of Iran in Tehran, for granting permission to publish images of selected objects from that museum's collection. My thanks also go to Dr. Farzin Rezaeian, author of several books and documentary films on ancient Iran, who generously provided high-resolution images of Persepolis and digital reconstructions of Chogha Mish. I am grateful to Mr. Kourosh Afhami of Gambke Persepolis 3D for providing the digital reconstruction of Persepolis and giving me permission to publish it here.

My sincere thanks go to François Desset of the University of Liège in Belgium and of Tehran University for providing information about the proto-Elamite tablet from Tall-e Geser, and to Matthew Stolper at the University of Chicago for the images of and information about the Persepolis tablets. Sigourney Jacks of the National Gallery of Victoria in Melbourne, Australia, kindly provided the high-resolution image of Edwin Long's 1878 painting *Queen Esther* and granted permission to publish it. And finally, I am grateful to Dr. Arnulf Hausleiter of the German Archaeological Institute, who kindly provided permission to publish an image of the Uruk jar sealing.

PART I

Background

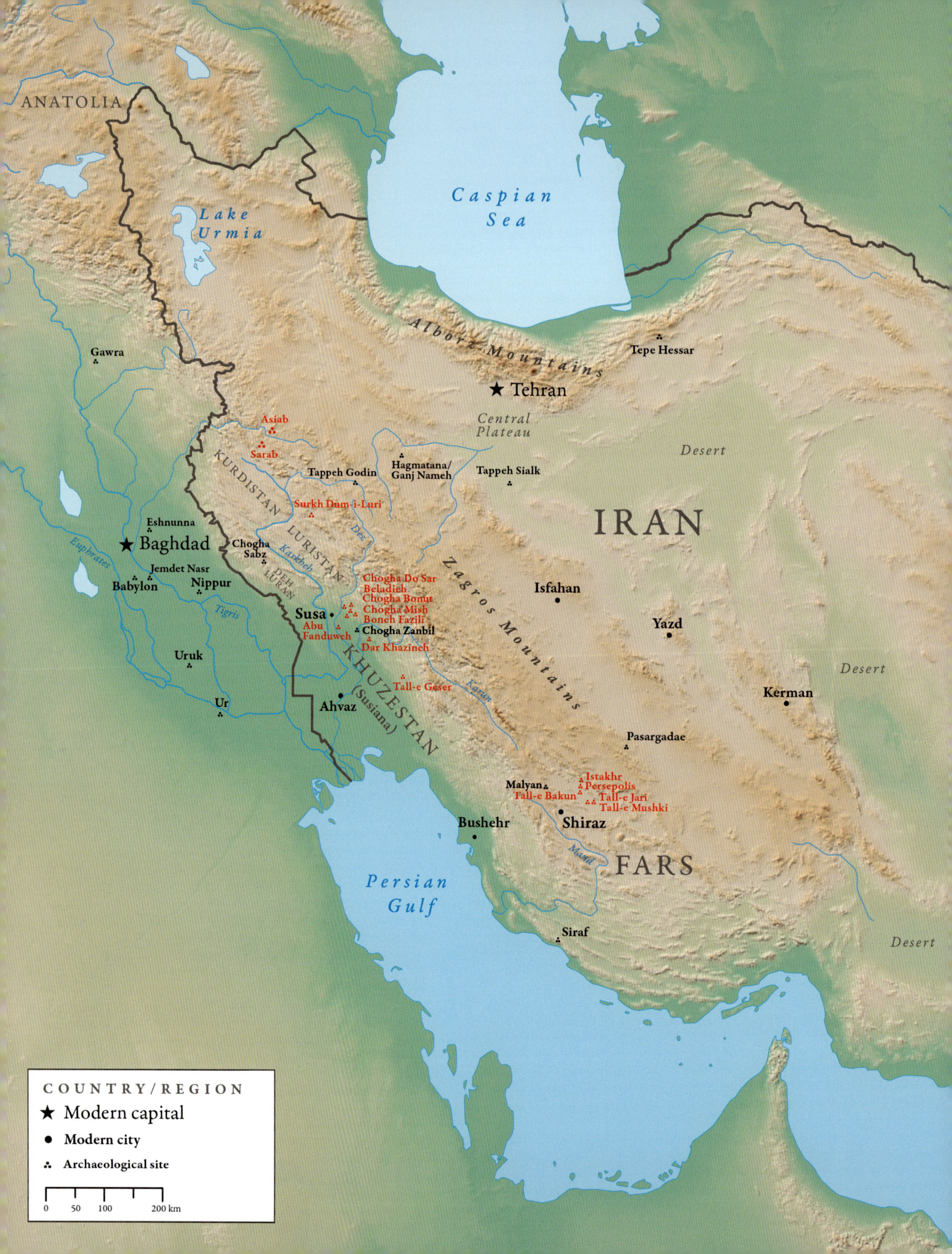

ANATOLIA
Caspian Sea
Lake Urmia
Alborz Mountains
Tepe Hessar
Tehran
Central Plateau
Desert
Gawra
Asiab
Sarab
KURDISTAN
Hagmatana/ Ganj Nameh
Tappeh Godin
Tappeh Sialk
Surkh Dum-i-Luri
LURISTAN
Dez
IRAN
Eshnunna
Baghdad
Euphrates
Chogha Sabz
Karkheh
DEH LURAN
Jemdet Nasr
Babylon
Nippur
Tigris
Chogha Do Sar
Beladieh
Chogha Bonut
Chogha Mish
Boneh Fazili
Susa
Abu Fanduweh
Chogha Zanbil
Dar Khazineh
Zagros Mountains
Isfahan
Yazd
Desert
Uruk
Ur
KHUZESTAN (Susiana)
Tall-e Geser
Karun
Ahvaz
Kerman
Pasargadae
Istakhr
Persepolis
Malyan
Tall-e Bakun
Tall-e Jari
Tall-e Mushki
Bushehr
Shiraz
Mand
FARS
Persian Gulf
Siraf
Desert
COUNTRY/REGION
Modern capital
Modern city
Archaeological site
0 50 100 200 km

1

Iran: An Archaeological and Historical Overview

Iran was a major contributor to the cultural heritage of the ancient Near East and thus to Western civilization. Before 1935, when *Iran* became its official name, the country was commonly known in the West as Persia, a name given to the country by the Greeks. Persia proper was the mainland of the Achaemenids, a ruling dynasty founded by Cyrus II (Cyrus the Great) in 550 BCE, with Persepolis as its ceremonial capital.

Iran (or *Eran*) means "the land of the Aryans," a branch of the Indo-European peoples who emigrated from the steppes of Central Asia to Europe and the Near East in the early first millennium BCE. The geographical name Iran derives from *Airyanem Vaeja* ("expanse/territory of the Aryans"), an ancient expression found in the Avesta (early Iranian religious texts). The Aryans were close relatives of the Indo-Aryans; both peoples were, linguistically and culturally, part of the extensive family of Indo-Europeans. Their languages were varieties of the same tongue, which is also believed to be the parent of Greek, Latin, and Celtic, Slavic, and Teutonic languages—including English.

The land of Iran has a varied geography that includes rugged mountains, vast stretches of desert, high plateau plains, and fertile lowlands. Covered by rocky terrain and unsuitable for agriculture as a primary subsistence economy, the valleys of the Zagros Mountains provide excellent seasonal pastures and have been used by pastoral nomadic tribes since prehistoric times. The Iranian central plateau (flanked by the Zagros Mountains to the west and the Alborz range to the north), Fars, and Khuzestan (ancient Susiana) are Iran's major cultural provinces, each with a distinct culture but related to the others.

Village life in these regions began in the initial stage of the Neolithic period (ca. 7500–7000 BCE). Excavations at Tappeh Sialk in the central plateau have revealed an early period (ca. 6000 BCE) when the inhabitants of the site used stone tools, employed shell and bone for decoration, and created pottery with decorative designs that imitated basketry. In a later period (ca. 5000 BCE), the pottery was even more decorative: black paint was applied on a dark-red surface in floral and faunal motifs. Somewhat later (ca. 4000 BCE), the pottery shows a

Map of Iran, with archaeological sites excavated by the Institute for the Study of Ancient Cultures indicated in red.

Relative Chronology of Iran and Mesopotamia

Date BCE	Susiana	Geser (Ram Hormuz)	Fars	Mesopotamia
550–330	Achaemenid	Geser IX	Achaemenid	Achaemenid
				Neo-Babylonian / Neo-Assyrian
1000–550	Neo-Elamite	Geser VIII	Shogha / Teimuran	
1400–1000	Middle Elamite	Geser VII		Kassite / Middle Assyrian
1600–1400	Transitional		↑	
1900–1600	Sukkalmah	Geser VI	Qaleh	Old Babylonian / Isin-Larsa
2350–1900	Shimashki		↓	Ur III
		(gap)	Kaftari	
2600–2350	Awan			Akkadian
			↓	Early Dynastic
3100–2600	Proto-Elamite (Susa III)	Geser V	Late Banesh	Jemdet Nasr
			Middle Banesh	
			Early Banesh	Uruk
3900–3100	Susa II	Geser IV		
4000–3900	Terminal Susa		Lapui	Terminal Ubaid
4400–4000	Late Susiana 2 (Susa I)	Geser III	Bakun A	Ubaid 4
4700–4400	Late Susiana 1	Geser II	Tall-e Gap II	
5200–4700	Late Middle Susiana	Geser I	Bakun B2 / Tall-e Gap I	Ubaid 3
5700–5200	Early Middle Susiana	?	Bakun B1	Ubaid 2
6000–5700	Early Susiana		Jari B Jari A (III)	Ubaid 1
6200–6000	Archaic Susiana 3			Ubaid 0 / Samarra
6300–6200	Archaic Susiana 2		Mushki	Hassuna
6500–6300	Archaic Susiana 1		Aceramic Fars	Jarmo

greater variety of shapes and stylized animal motifs, and around this time the potter's wheel seems to have been invented there. Copper smelting and casting were developed as a result of increasing interregional commerce with Fars and Susiana.

Fars was a major cultural province in Iran and also a major Elamite and Achaemenid Persian center. Here the prehistoric artistic traditions are best represented by the archaeological materials from Tall-e Bakun, near Persepolis, excavated by the University of Chicago's Institute for the Study of Ancient Cultures (ISAC) in 1932, 1937, and 2004. The painted pottery from this small prehistoric mound is arguably the highest manifestation of prehistoric ceramic art. It exhibits mastery in the organic relationship between the shape of the vessel and its decorative design. The artists employed a vast repertoire of designs and created a harmonic relationship between painted and unpainted areas. Excavations at Tall-e Bakun have also revealed evidence of planned architecture, the separation of residential and industrial quarters, and the earliest evidence of administrative technology in the use of door sealings—conical lumps of clay stamped with a seal, used to secure storeroom doors against unauthorized entry.

The third and most important major cultural center, Susiana, in the modern province of Khuzestan, lies in the lowlands of southwestern Iran. Susiana occupies an important place in the history and archaeology of the Near East. In prehistoric times, it was a breeding ground for highly developed cultures and civilizations. In historical periods, Susiana retained its importance as both a major administrative center and the breadbasket of the Achaemenid, Parthian, and Sasanian empires.

The artistic achievements of Susiana's prehistoric inhabitants are shown by their fine painted pottery. Many prehistoric and protohistoric materials from Susiana come from Chogha Mish, a major regional center excavated by ISAC for eleven seasons between 1961 and 1978. Excavations at this important site documented the development of a simple village community into a large town with complex social and economic institutions. Chogha Mish also yielded evidence of the development of prehistoric pottery from the earliest coarse ware to the highly decorated vessels of fine shapes and elegant designs of the Late Susiana 1 period (ca. 4700–4400 BCE), as well as evidence of craft specialization and administrative technology. Chogha Mish and Susa in Khuzestan were the only settlements in the region where early state organizations developed between 3500 and 3000 BCE.

Around 2500 BCE, the Elamite kingdom—the only pre-Achaemenid Persian state with indigenous written documents—emerged in the lowlands and highlands of southwestern Iran. The name *Elam* has been generally associated with southwestern Iran and its inhabitants. Numerous studies have indicated that the Elamites were by no means a homogeneous people and that the land of Elam constituted only part of what may have been a loose federation of several polities in the Zagros Mountains, lowland Susiana, Fars, and possibly Kerman in the southeast.

The various Elamite dynasties dominated the country well into the first half of the first millennium BCE, when their power gradually eroded due to the penetration and establishment of Median and Persian tribes in western and south-central Iran. The control of most of the highlands by these tribes must have contributed to the erosion of Elam's influence as a regional power and to its political fragmentation. Archaeological data are the primary evidence we have on the early history of the Medes and Persians. These data are complemented by outside (Assyrian and Babylonian) written sources until the advent of Cyrus II, founder of the Achaemenid Persian Empire, in the mid-sixth century BCE.

From the mid-ninth century BCE, both the Medes and the Persians appear prominently in the cuneiform sources from Assyria and Babylonia. The Medes, closely related to the Persians, became the prominent ruling tribe in Iran around the middle of the seventh century BCE. In 612 BCE, an alliance between the Medes and Babylonians overthrew the Neo-Assyrian Empire, and the Near East was divided between the two powers. In the meantime, the Persians were consolidating their power in Fars. In 550 BCE, Cyrus II defeated the Medes and, in a series of campaigns, forged the largest empire in the region. It was not, however, until the time of Darius I (Darius the Great) (522–486 BCE) that Persia united all the Near Eastern nations, including Egypt, under its umbrella. From the mid-sixth century BCE, indigenous written sources and the accounts of Greek historians constitute the main sources for the history of the Medes and Achaemenid Persians.

The overthrow of the Achaemenid Persian Empire by the Macedonian Greeks in 330 BCE made a profound impact on Near Eastern cultural trends and traditions. Like their predecessors (the Elamites, Assyrians, and Babylonians), the Persians had preserved major Near Eastern cultural trends and successfully incorporated them into the matrix of their own cultural heritage. As best exemplified at Persepolis—excavated by ISAC's Persian Expedition from 1931 to 1939 (fig. 1.1)—they successfully created an artistic and architectural style that, though composed of several regional elements of their empire, is distinctively and unmistakably Persian in character. But the new Macedonian masters of the region ignored this tradition of preserving and developing the rich cultural, architectural, and artistic heritage of the ancient Near East. Thus the millennia-old continuity of ancient Near Eastern art, architecture, and cultural traditions took a different course of development around the third century BCE.

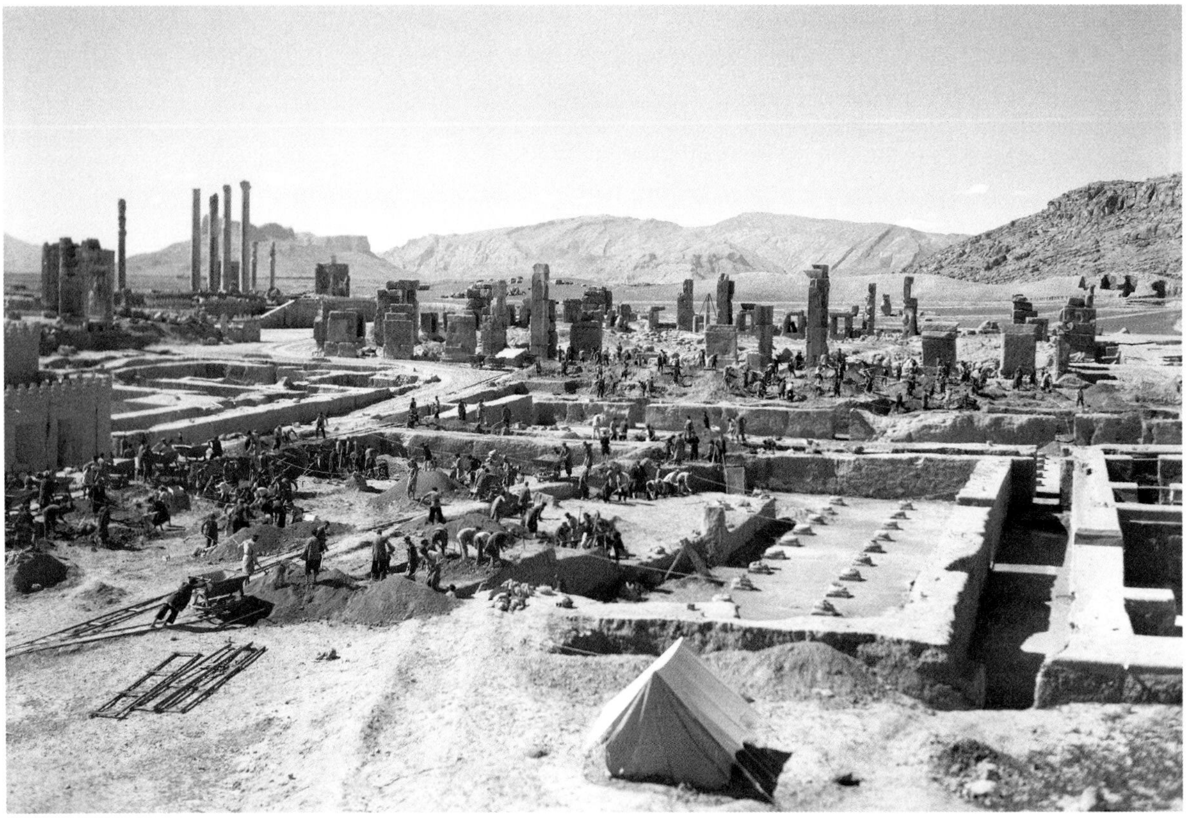

Figure 1.1. ISAC's Persian Expedition excavating the Treasury at Persepolis (ISACM P. 58336).

2 The Collection

Except for the Luristan bronzes and some Achaemenid gold pieces, the objects in the ISAC Museum's Persian collection came to the museum as ISAC's legal share following excavations it conducted in Iran until 1972, when the UNESCO Convention of 1970 prohibiting the illicit import, export, and transfer of cultural property took effect. No objects from excavations conducted after 1972 were brought to Chicago from Iran.

ISAC excavated at Persepolis and nearby Naqsh-e Rustam, Istakhr, Tall-e Bakun A and B, and Surkh Dum-i-Luri from 1931 to 1939. Work began at Persepolis, Naqsh-e Rustam, and Istakhr under Ernst Herzfeld and continued from 1935 onward under the direction of Erich Schmidt. Excavations in Iran halted temporarily with the advent of World War II. In 1947–1948 and 1949, Donald McCown, seeking the origins of urbanism, excavated Tall-e Geser (formerly Ghazir) in the Ram Hormuz region in the southeastern province of Khuzestan, ancient Susiana.

In the late 1950s, ISAC resumed its pioneering scientific and interdisciplinary research on the early stages of the domestication of plants and animals in Iranian Kurdistan, a project directed by Robert and Linda Braidwood. Following the Braidwoods' work, Robert McCormick Adams conducted the first comprehensive and systematic regional survey in Khuzestan.

After Adams's survey, Helene Kantor and Pinhas Delougaz headed work at the Susiana sites of Chogha Mish, Boneh Fazili, and Chogha Bonut from 1961 to 1979 that contributed greatly to our understanding of early cultural development in the region. Through a generous division of finds granted by the government of Iran, they added more than 15,000 objects to the ISAC Museum's collection.

In 1996, Abbas Alizadeh resumed ISAC's research in Iran by conducting surveys in Fars and Khuzestan and by excavating Chogha Bonut, Dar Khazineh, Chogha Do Sar, Beladieh, and Abu Fanduweh in Khuzestan, as well as Tall-e Bakun A and B, Tall-e Jari A and B, and Tall-e Mushki in Fars.

PART II

Catalog

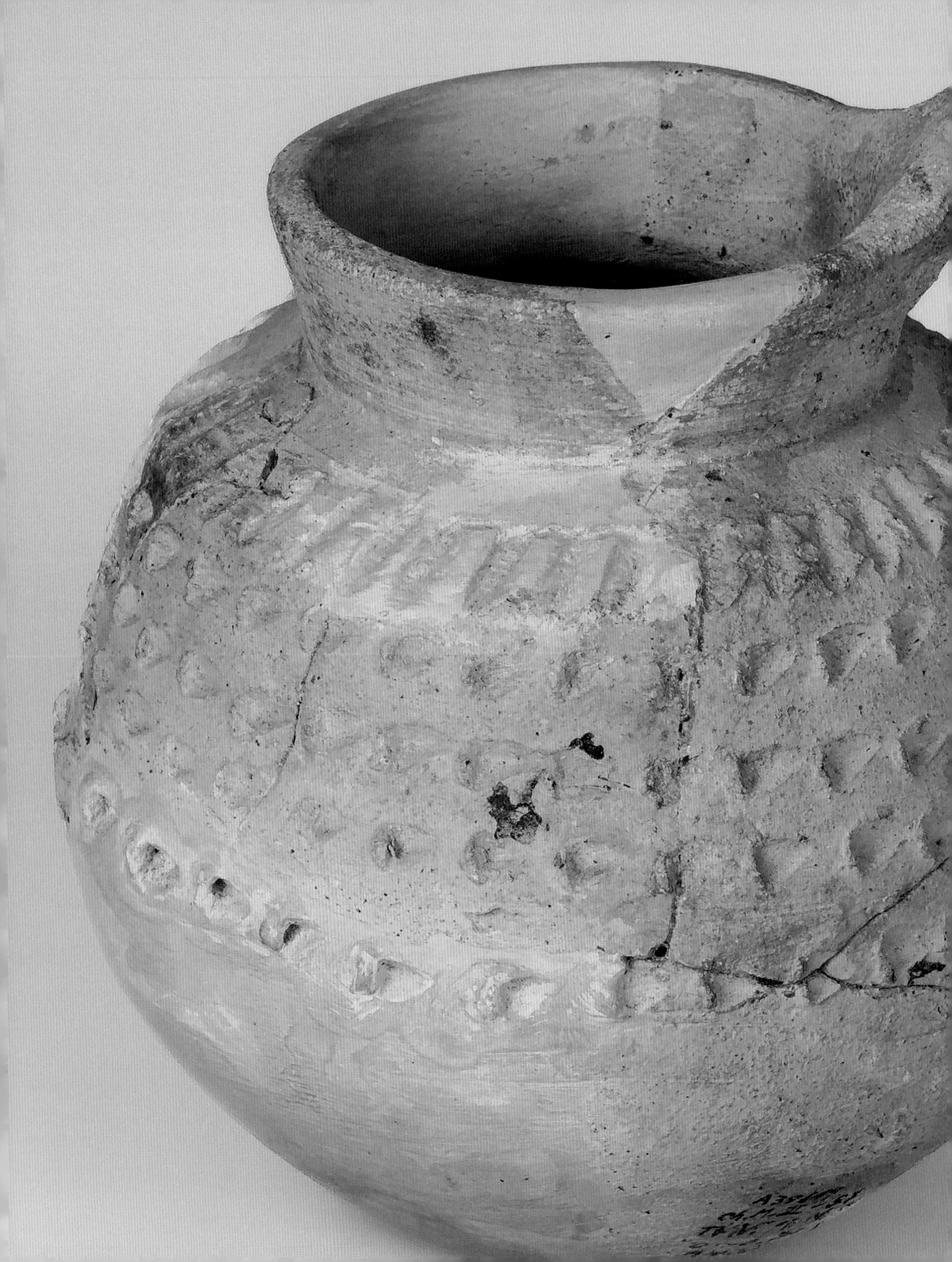

3 Prehistoric Chogha Mish

The prehistoric mound of Chogha Mish is among the few sites in Khuzestan that were occupied in early Neolithic times, around 6800 BCE (fig. 3.1). Excavations at the site (fig. 3.2) provided evidence of social and economic evolution from a simple village society to a nascent urban center for an uninterrupted period of three thousand years. The site also yielded evidence of administrative technology and craft production and specialization, especially the art of pottery.

The longevity of the settlement of Chogha Mish allows us to see the evolution from modest, single-family residential units to large, multifamily residences surrounding a monumental, multichambered house probably belonging to the leader of the community. This late prehistoric, proto-urban center, which developed in the eastern part of lowland Susiana, competed with Susa, another nascent urban center in the west.

Of the urban center of Chogha Mish we have only stumps of the walls of many buildings that once stood there. The town was planned with straight streets, winding alleys, and a sewage system made of baked bricks. The elaborate and detailed computer-generated images shown in figure 3.3 are based on excavation plans and the images of buildings found on seal impressions discovered

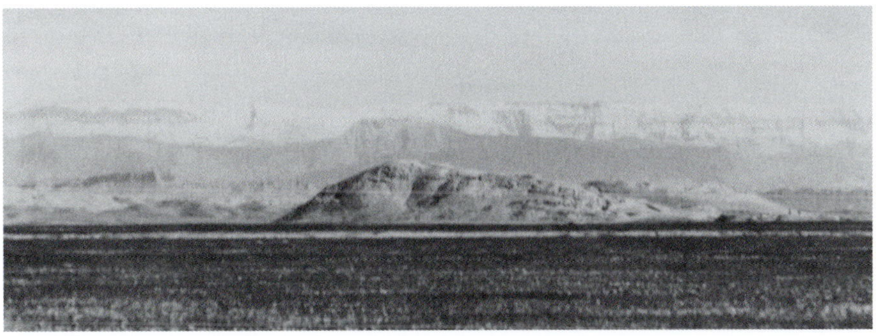

Figure 3.1. Panoramic view of Chogha Mish in lowland Khuzestan, with the Zagros Mountains in the background, 1962. Photo by H. Kantor.

Baked-clay cup with twisted handle from Chogha Mish, Iran. **Cat. no. 11**.

at Chogha Mish. Many painted, baked-clay cones found around one of the buildings—which, judging from its layout, must have been a temple and thus the center of public life in the city—decorated the structure.

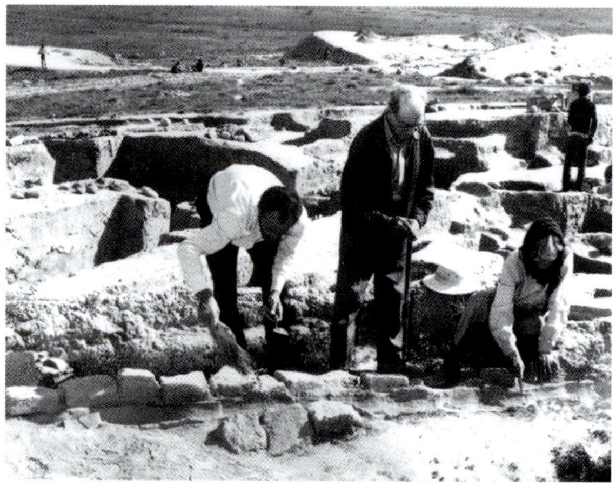

Figure 3.2. Pinhas Delougaz (center) and Helene Kantor (seated, right) at Chogha Mish, 1974. Photo by C. Adelman.

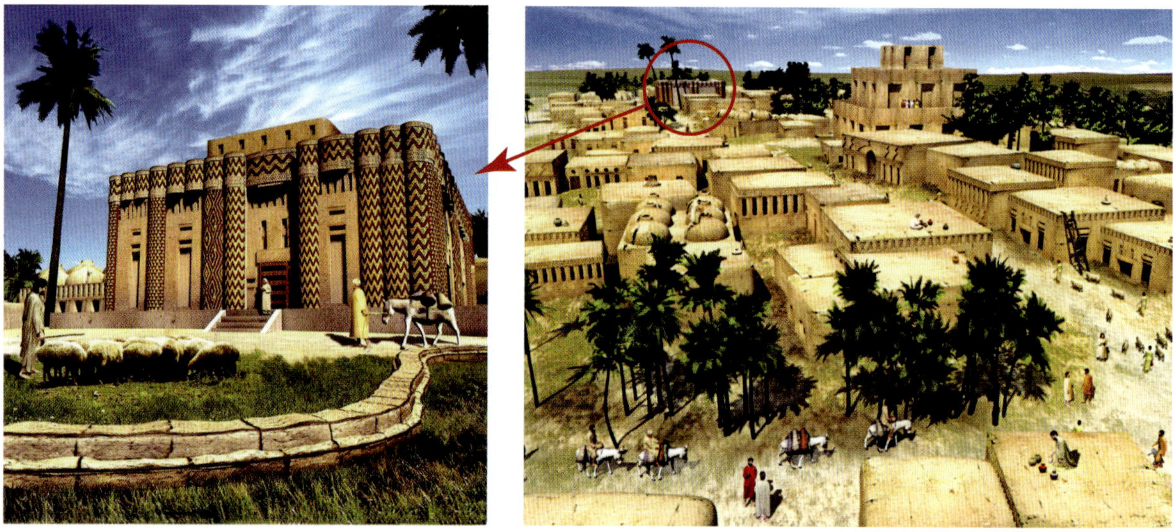

Figure 3.3. Digital reconstructions of Chogha Mish and its temple as they appeared around 3400 BCE. Images courtesy of F. Rezaeian.

Ceramics

Aside from its artistic qualities, pottery is arguably the most important tool for determining archaeological chronology and for studying interregional contacts and the diffusion of ceramic traits from one region to another. Painted pottery represents the principal material artistic activity of village communities in the ancient world. Pottery appeared in Iran in the early Neolithic period (ca. 7000 BCE); prior to the invention and development of pottery vessels, stone vessels and perishable wood and skin containers were primarily used. But clay, which was cheap and readily available, and which could be formed into a variety of shapes, was soon discovered to be the best material for making a wide variety of vessels. The vessels also provided excellent surfaces upon which an unlimited repertoire of designs could be painted.

At first, many vessels were simply utilitarian, with thick walls and little or no decoration. But from the very beginning, some vessels were embellished with simple geometric decorations. Soon a whole range of fine pottery with local styles of decoration and manufacturing techniques developed. Originally, vessels were shaped by hand or were formed around a mold, but a decisive forward step came with the invention of the potter's wheel, now known to have been used in Iran by about 3800 BCE.

The initial phase of the early Neolithic period includes pottery with geometric painted and incised decorations that resemble basketry. As the regional populations grew and contact among various regions increased (ca. 5000 BCE), well-cultivated styles of ceramic decoration were developed.

The examples of Archaic Susiana pottery from Chogha Mish included in this catalog represent the evolution of painted pottery with simple geometric painted patterns (**cat. nos. 1–3**). After the initial stage of pottery decoration, exemplified by **cat. no. 1**, the decoration became more sophisticated, with interrupted and continuous zigzags suggesting that the artist was attempting to create a sense of movement around the circumference of the vessel.

From about 6000 BCE, potters in Susiana and Mesopotamia shared a common artistic tradition. But by 5400 BCE, the two traditions diverged; whereas the decorative patterns and shapes in Susiana became more complex, with many representational motifs, in Mesopotamia they were reduced and simplified.

As village life evolved and the population increased, social life became more complex. Rituals for social cohesion developed, and material culture, primarily painted pottery, was used to express social rank. Around 5500 BCE, a variety of pottery vessels with sophisticated artistic and symbolic designs were produced.

The defining features of tortoise vessels are their lentoid bodies, hole mouths, and large, flaring spouts that issue from near the base (**cat. no. 4**; fig. 3.4). Such tortoise-shaped vessels appeared in Iran and Mesopotamia in the mid-sixth

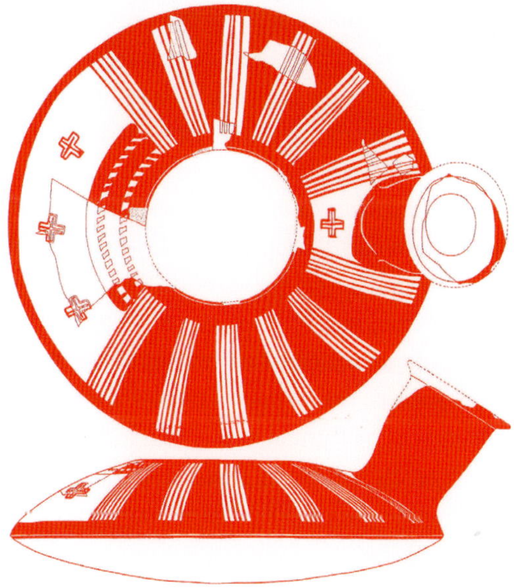

Figure 3.4. Tortoise-shaped ritual vessel from Chogha Bonut (ca. 5500 BCE) (diameter 22 cm, height 8 cm), National Museum of Iran, Tehran. Drawings by A. Alizadeh.

millennium BCE. They were not common household items and are found only in major population centers and certain archaeological contexts in both regions. Such vessels were probably used in rituals, the nature of which we can only surmise.

Large, deep bowls became popular beginning in the late sixth millennium BCE, perhaps reflecting a social development in which communal feasting became important (**cat. no. 5**). The surfaces of these impressive bowls are often decorated with a variety of geometric designs and highly stylized depictions of animals. The most outstanding of such decorations is a panel of stylized ibexes with soaring horns. These figures are boldly yet simply painted, the artist using only a small number of sweeping brush strokes. This attractive and minimalist decoration exhibits the sophistication of the ancient potter in prehistoric Iran.

Another material clue to the social complexity of village life in ancient Susiana is found in the depiction on pottery of dancers and dance masks. **Cat. no. 6** is an early example of the sophistication of the pottery craft. This delicately hand-shaped pottery vessel with thin walls is decorated with a series of what appear to be masks, probably worn by performers in a ritual dance or ceremony.

The pottery of the mid-fifth millennium BCE represents the zenith of ceramic artistic achievement in Susiana. Three potsherds in the ISAC Museum's collection derive from examples of the world-renowned Late Susiana 2–period goblets found primarily in the massive prehistoric Susa cemetery (**cat. no. 7**). Such vessels have been found intact only as funerary objects in graves (fig. 3.5). These goblets are prime examples of the artistic achievement of Iranian potters in ancient Susiana. The correlation between figure and design on these fine examples constitutes a major characteristic of Iranian prehistoric pottery. Although the overall design of the vessel shown here includes both representational and nonrepresentational elements, their relationship and spatial distribution have created an arrangement in which the elements seem tightly woven together to create a balance rarely achieved by ancient potters elsewhere. For example, the row of cranes just below the rim accentuates the height of the vessel, while the interrupted vertical lines that frame the highly stylized mountain goat emphasize its slender, tapering shape.

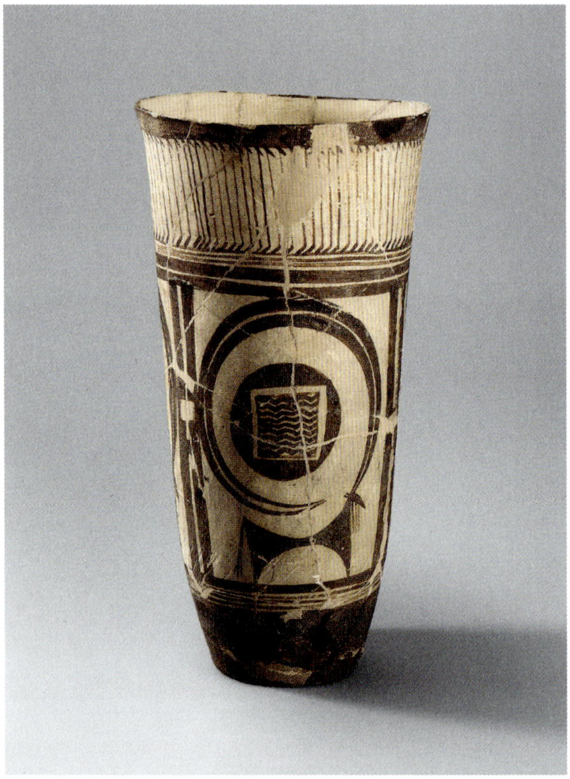

Figure 3.5. Funerary goblet from the Susa cemetery (ca. 4200 BCE) (diameter 16 cm, height 38 cm), National Museum of Iran, Tehran. Photo by N. Fakurzadeh.

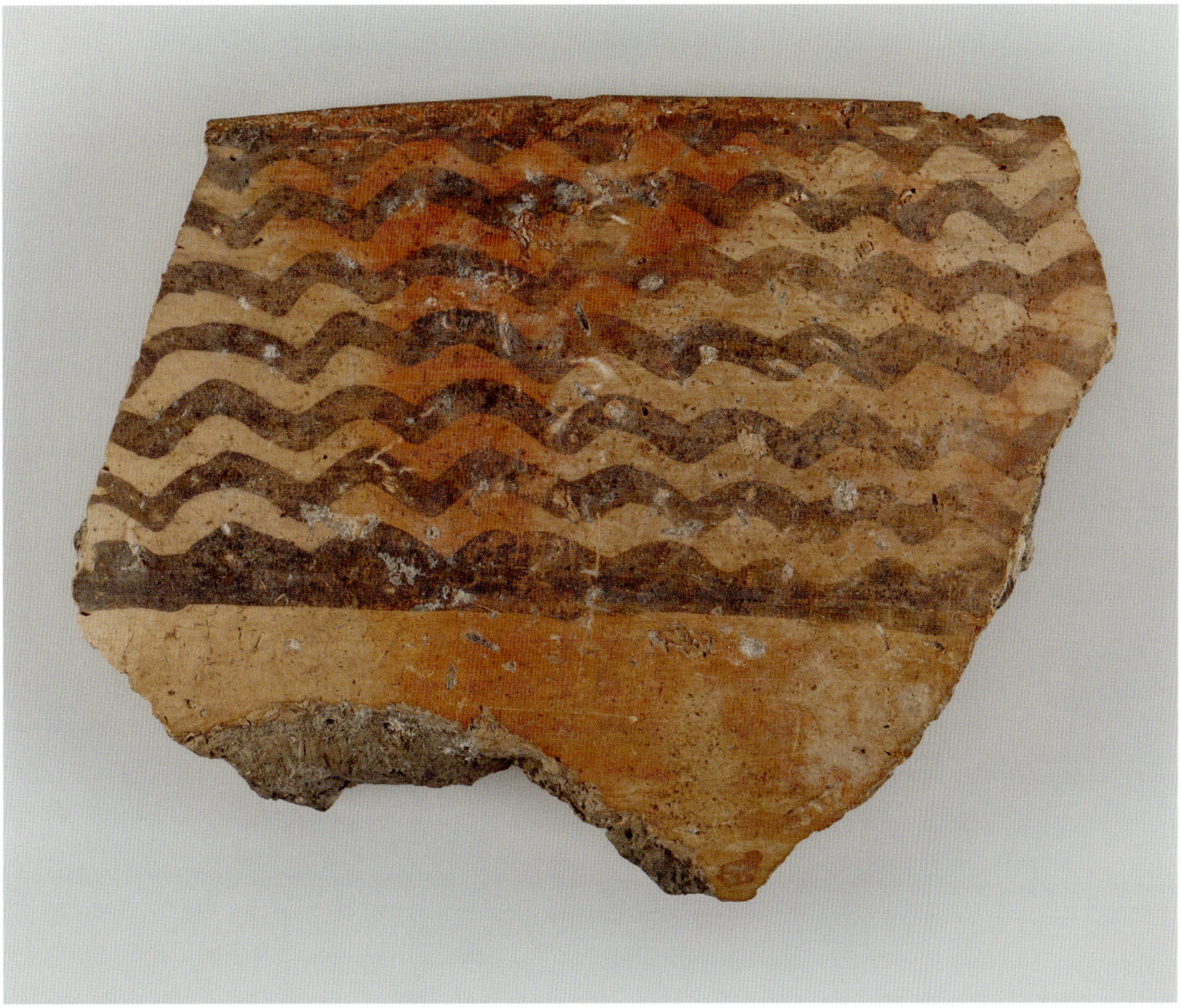

1. Sherd

Baked clay, paint

Iran, Chogha Mish

Archaic Susiana 1 period (ca. 6300 BCE)

Excavated in 1965–1966

ISACM A51141

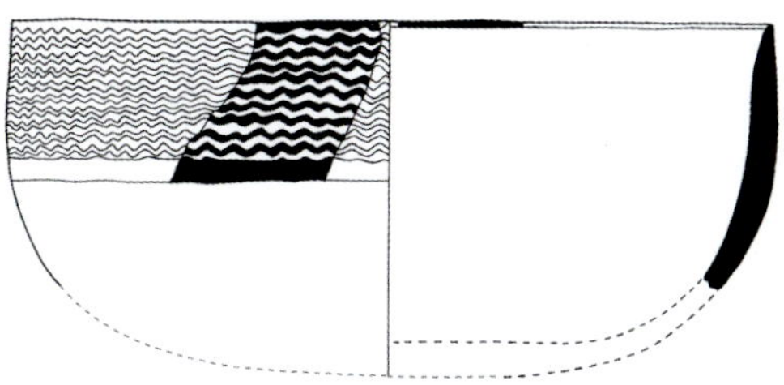

Drawing by A. Alizadeh.

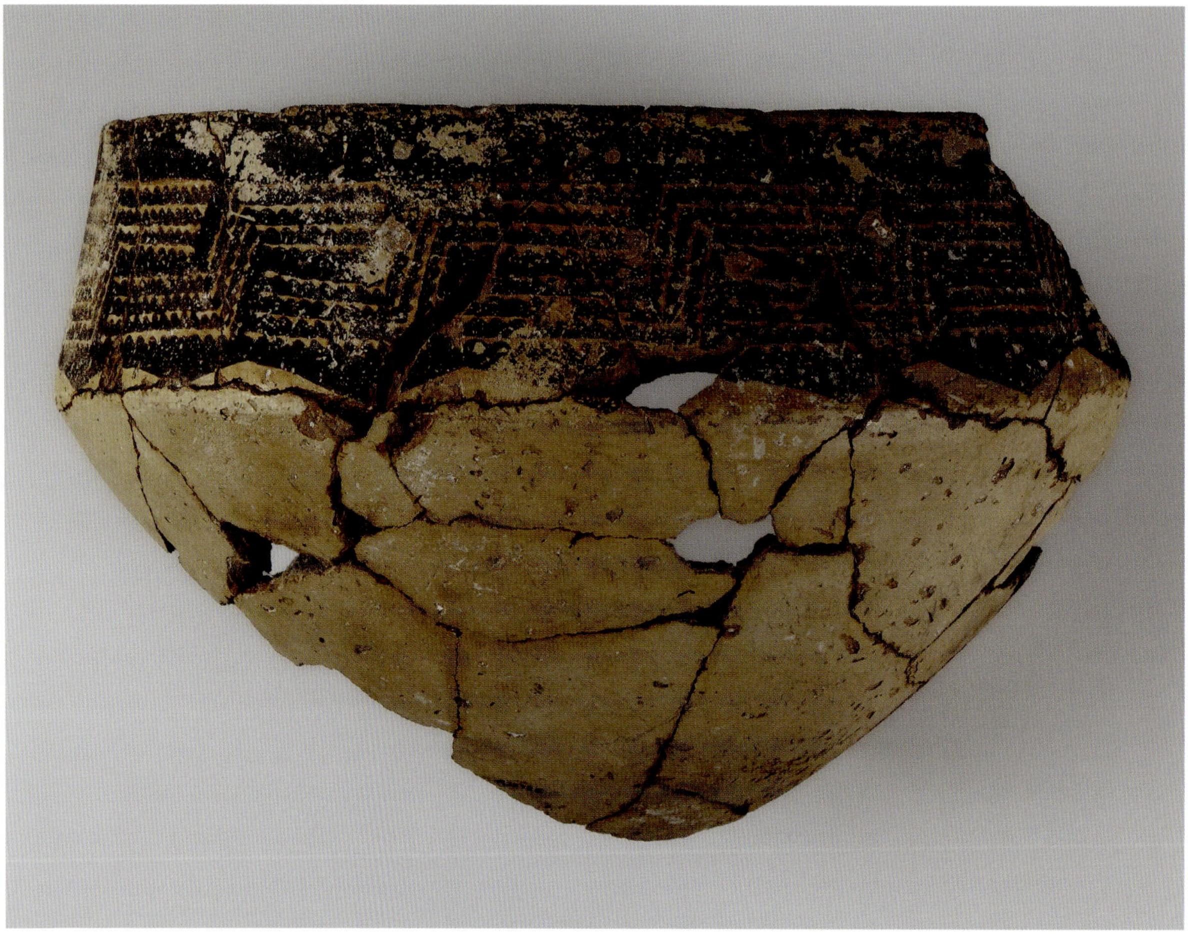

2. Fragmentary Bowl

Baked clay, paint

Iran, Chogha Mish

Archaic Susiana 1 period (ca. 6300 BCE)

Excavated in 1971

ISACM A34785

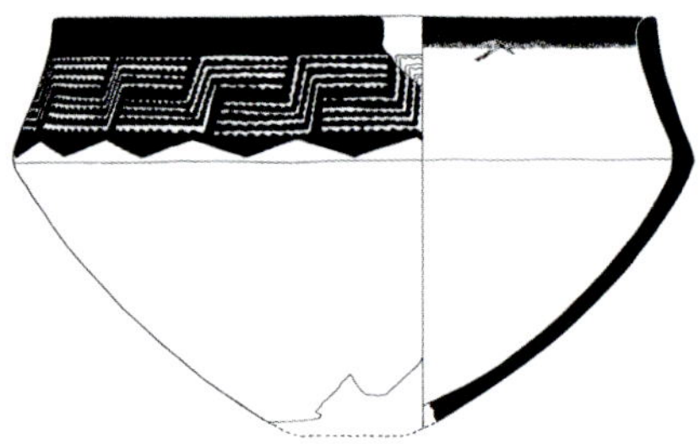

Drawing by A. Alizadeh.

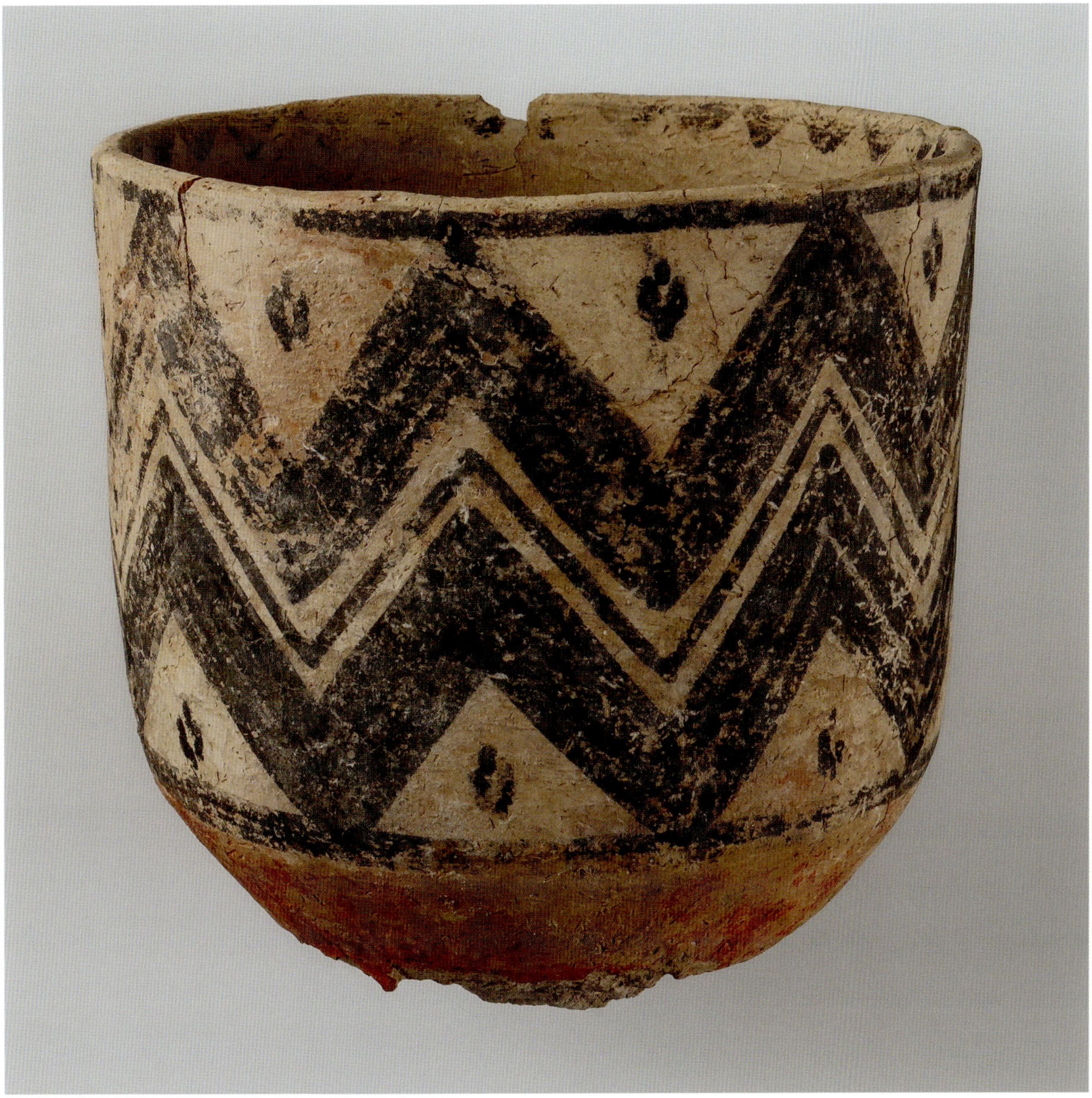

3. Cylindrical Bowl

Baked clay, paint

Iran, Chogha Mish

Archaic Susiana 2 period (ca. 6200 BCE)

Excavated in 1972

ISACM A34802

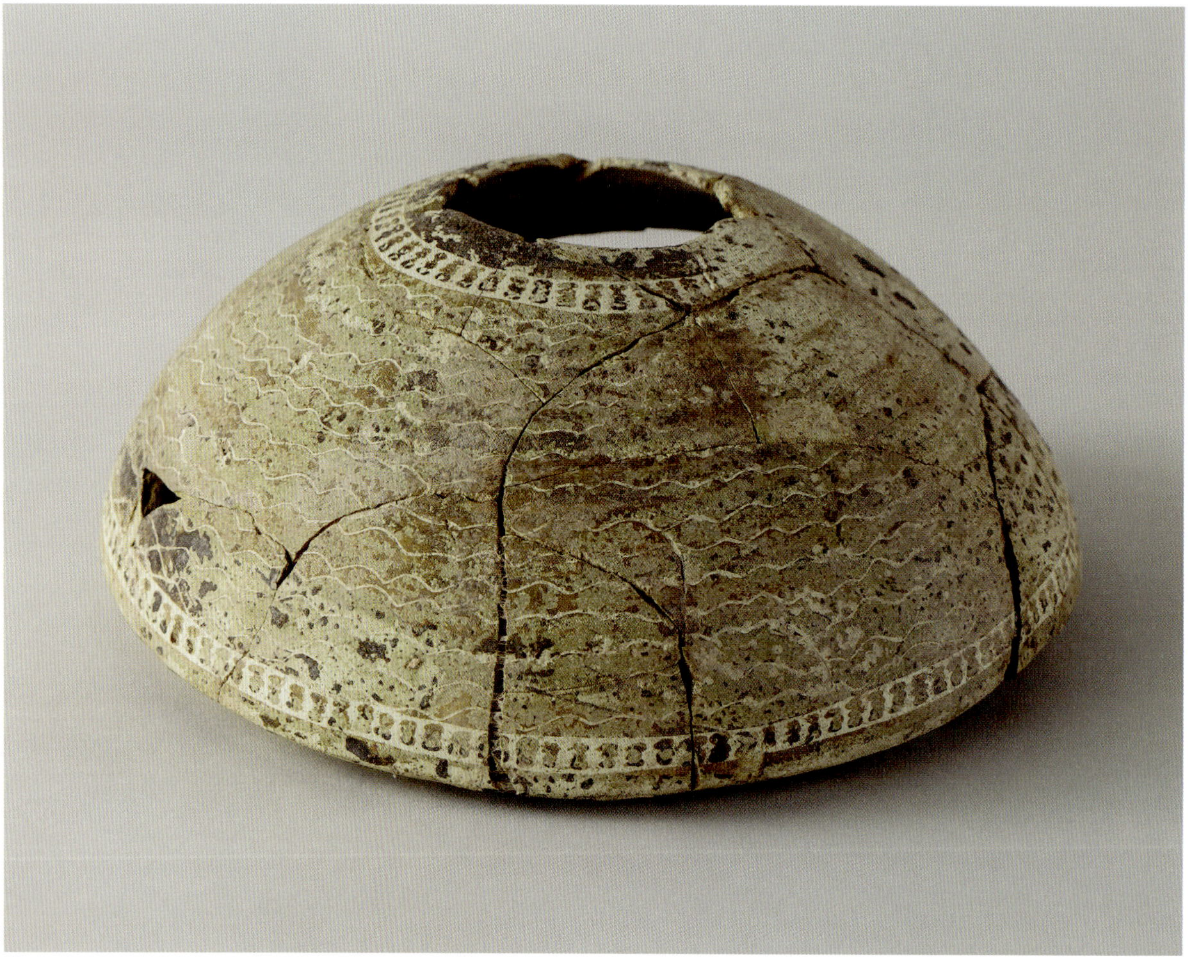

4. Tortoise-Shaped Ritual Vessel

Baked clay, paint

Iran, Chogha Mish

Early Middle Susiana period (ca. 5700–5200 BCE)

Excavated in 1972

ISACM A64641

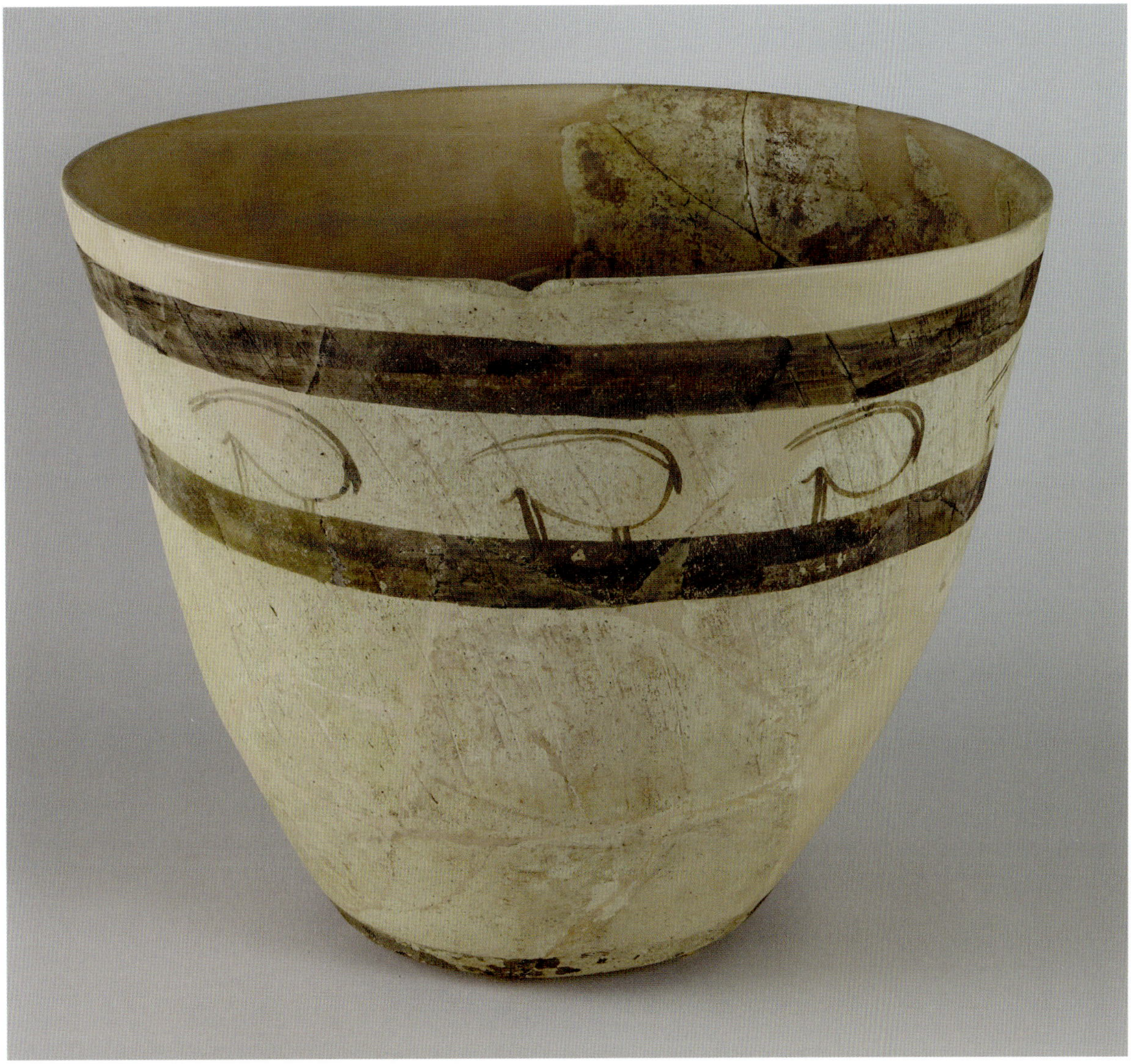

5. Deep Bowl with Ibexes

Baked clay, paint

Iran, Chogha Mish

Late Middle Susiana period (ca. 5200–4700 BCE)

Excavated in 1965–1966

ISACM A35278

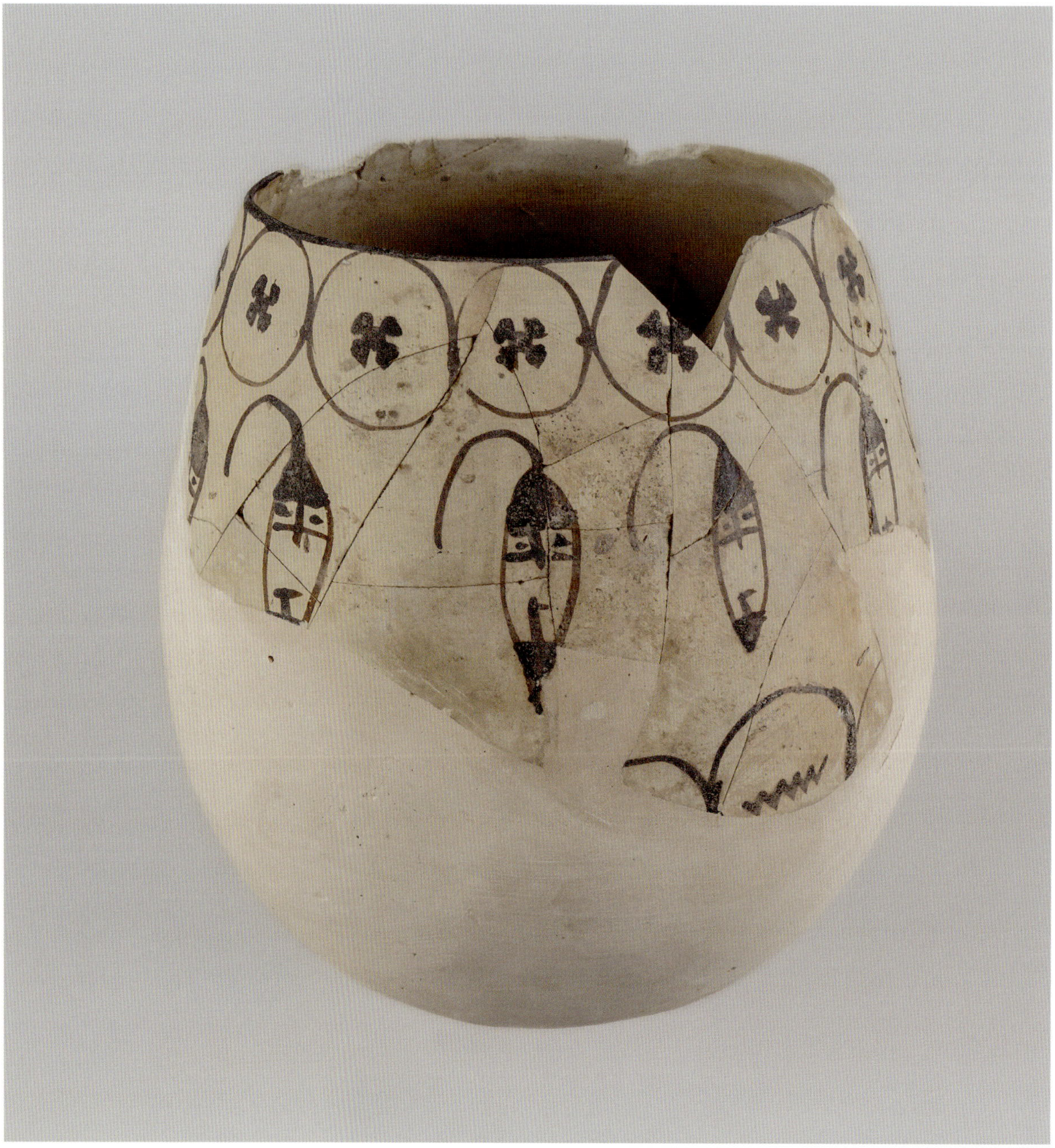

6. Jar

Baked clay, paint

Iran, Chogha Mish

Late Middle Susiana period (ca. 5200–4700 BCE)

Excavated in 1965–1966

ISACM A58299

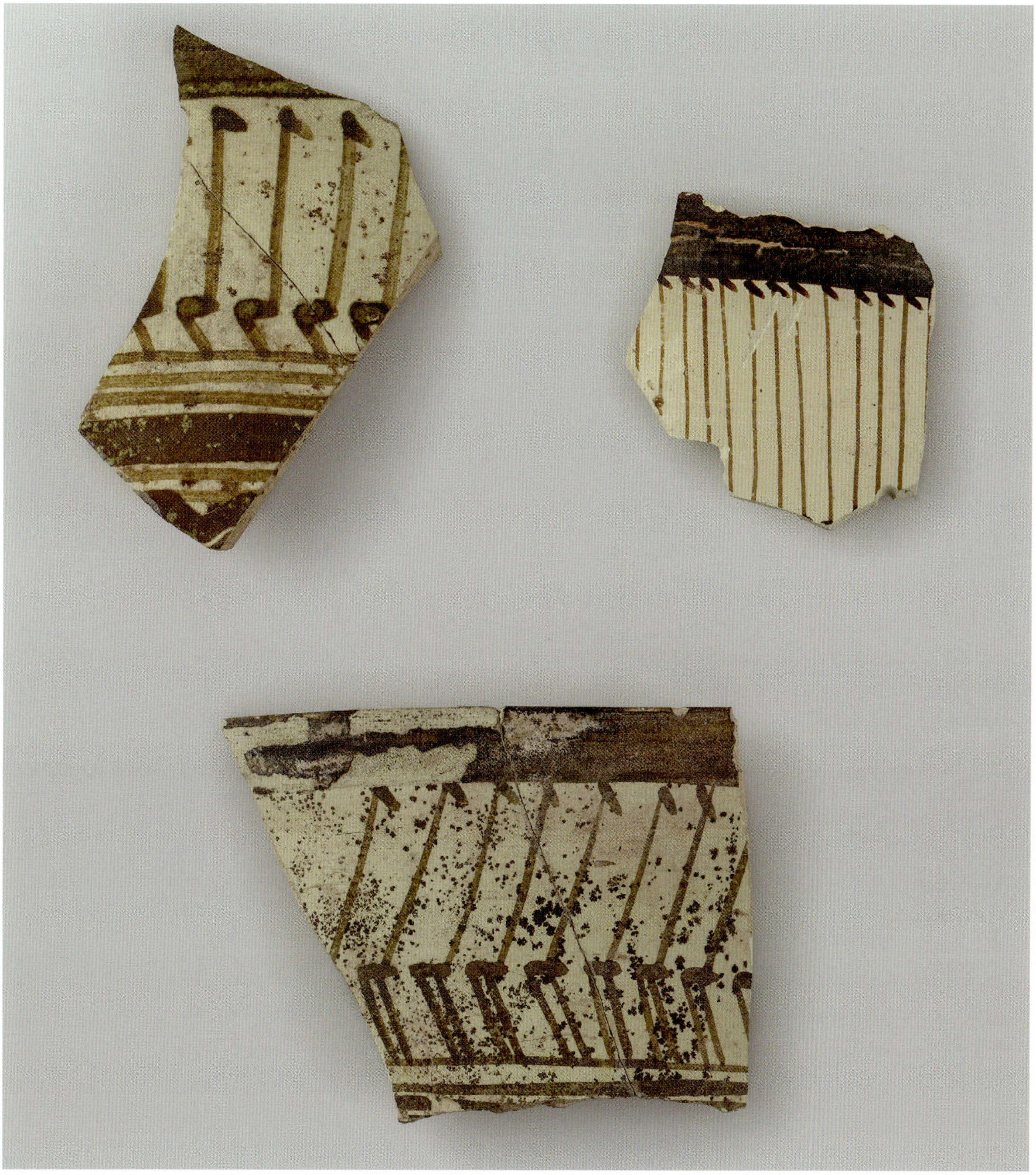

7. Sherds from Goblets

Baked clay, paint

Iran, Chogha Mish

Late Susiana 2 period (ca. 4400–4000 BCE)

Excavated in 1963–1966

ISACM A51208, A51205, A51210
(clockwise from top left)

Human Figurines and Labrets

Clay and stone figurines representing humans and animals are as old as the Paleolithic period. They may represent deities, mythological characters, ancestors, and even individuals. While animal figures are shaped in a more or less naturalistic (if stylized) fashion, human figures are highly abstract and stylized and only rarely take naturalistic forms. In historical periods, the sacred and ritualistic nature of human figurines may be suggested by the archaeological contexts in which they are deposited, but we can only guess at their meaning and function in prehistoric times.

Cat. no. 8 is the head of a figurine severed in antiquity, perhaps in a ritual, as most extant prehistoric figurines are found with severed heads or limbs (or both), and many severed heads are found without a matching body. This head has a notch on top—presumably an indication of parted hair—and a black-painted border, nose, eyes, nostrils, and lips. A pair of low knobs indicate the ears. The preserved eyebrow is raised and painted, and the eyes, as in many Mesopotamian and Iranian figurines from the southwest, are shaped like coffee beans.

The composite drawing of a female figurine shown in figure 3.6 has facial features similar to those on **cat. no. 8**. It is based on a head, torso, and lower body that were found separately and have been reconstructed to suggest the shape of a complete figurine, though the three pieces were found in different locations and do not necessarily belong to the same figurine. The head must have represented a person with an elongated skull, a sign of high status. The upper body is bare, and the tops of the breasts are tattooed. Whether the broad, horizontal and vertical bands represent clothes, body tattoos, or mere decoration is unknown. But the prominent genital area, indicated by an incised triangle, and the vertical line articulating the legs suggest a naked figure.

Around ten thousand years ago, when humans in the ancient Near East began to live in permanent villages, private ownership developed. People owned their houses, farmland, and a few animals and tools. As time passed, social life became more complex—some individuals became wealthier than others and gained higher economic and social status, achieved in different ways in different regions of the ancient Near East. In Iran, such social and economic status was expressed through the acquisition of sophisticated pottery vessels, cranial elongation, and personal ornamentation of the face or body with colorful semiprecious stones, copper, tattoos, or labrets (lip ornaments) (**cat. no. 9**; fig. 3.7). This mode of social expression is still practiced in parts of Africa today and has even reached modern Western societies (fig. 3.8), though in the latter case labrets are perhaps considered more rebellious than in ancient and African societies.

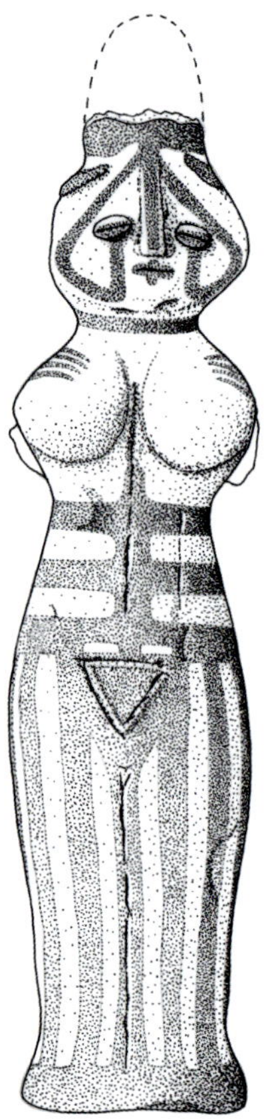

Figure 3.6. Composite drawing of three fragments of an Early Susiana female figurine by A. Alizadeh.

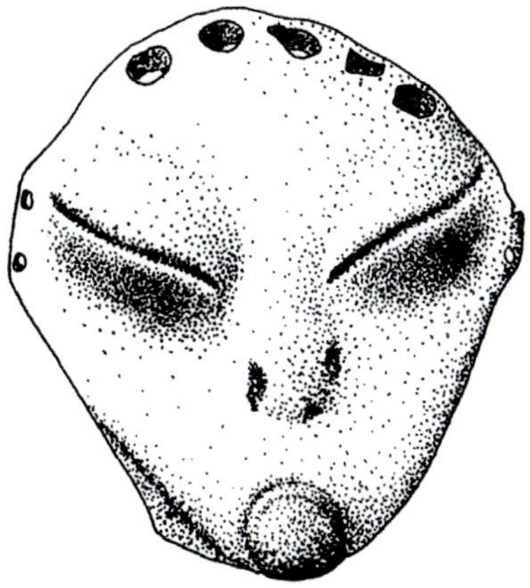

Figure 3.7. Early Susiana figurine head with labret from Chogha Mish (ca. 5800 BCE) (height 4.6 cm, diameter 4.7 cm), National Museum of Iran, Tehran. Drawing by A. Alizadeh.

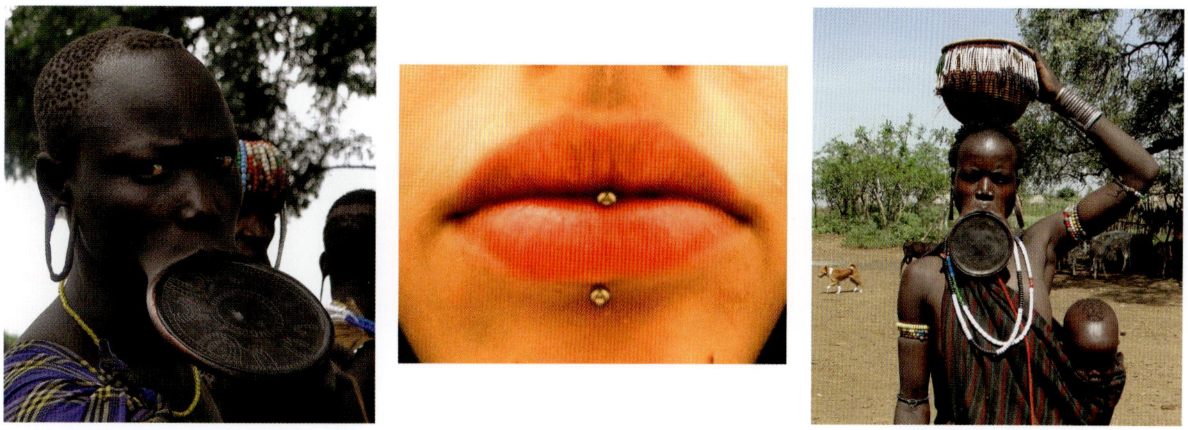

Figure 3.8. Left and right: African tribeswomen with huge labrets. Middle: A labret in Western urban society. Photos (from left to right) by R. Waddington, GorillaWarfare, and B. Gagnon, Wikimedia Commons.

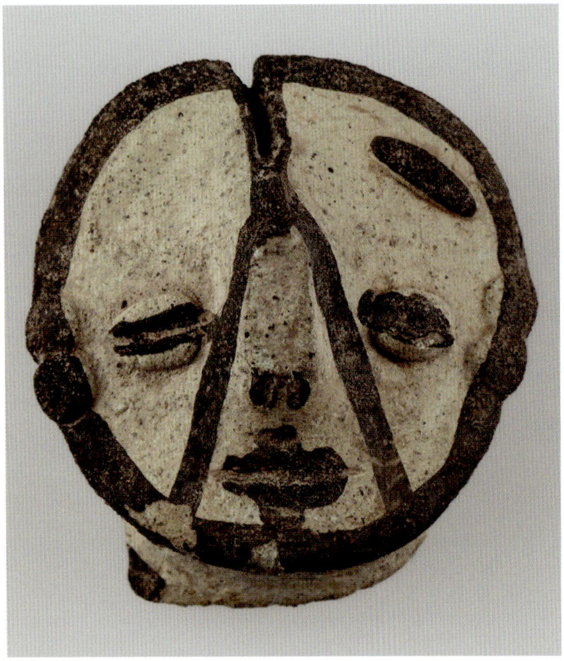
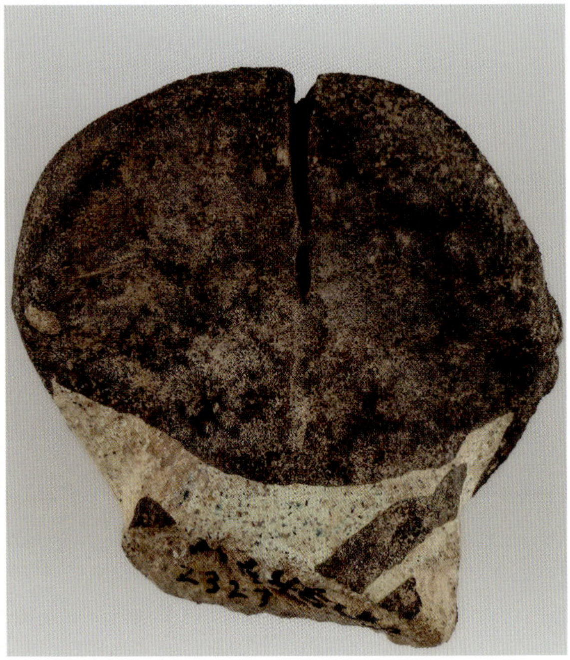

8. Figurine Fragment

Baked clay, paint

Iran, Chogha Mish

Early Susiana period (ca. 6000–5700 BCE)

Excavated in 1963

ISACM A64643

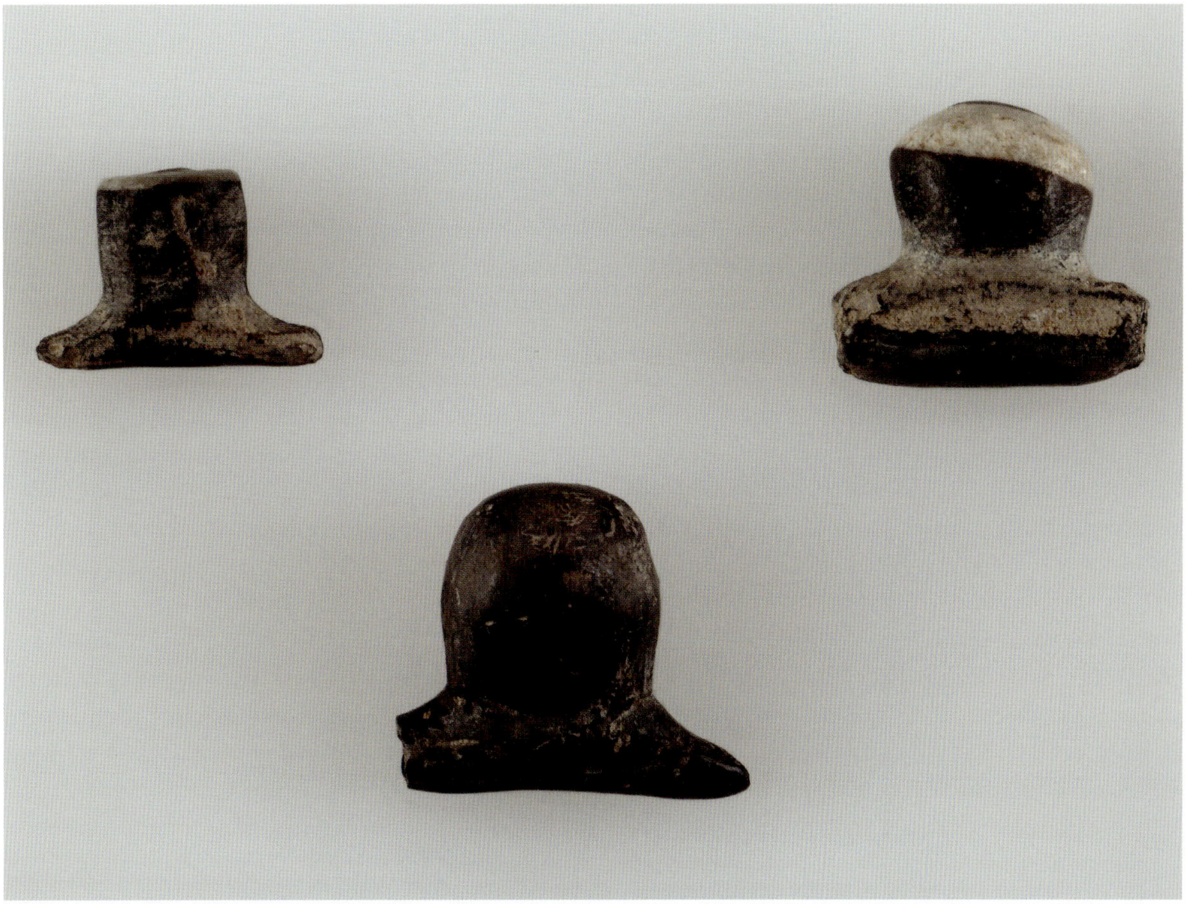

9. Lip or Ear Studs

Stone

Iran, Chogha Mish

Early and Middle Susiana periods
(ca. 6000–4700 BCE)

Excavated in 1963–1966, 1969–1970

ISACM A32494, A33008, A64642
(clockwise from top left)

Protoliterate/Urban Period

The second half of the fourth millennium BCE witnessed a series of socioeconomic developments second only to those of the era of animal domestication, farming, and village life four thousand years earlier. This period saw the formation of early states, urbanism, and initial steps in the invention of writing.

Chogha Mish was one of the early towns in southwestern Iran's province of Khuzestan. It was here, along with Susa, that urbanism and early state organizations took root and developed. A major feature of urban Chogha Mish was its administrative technology: clay envelopes impressed with cylinder seals to ensure authenticity.

Another major development involved the rapid disappearance of handmade painted pottery. The practice of elaborately decorating pottery with painted patterns could no longer be sustained. Instead, pottery was mass produced on fast wheels and was primarily plain, except for occasional incised or appliqué decorations.

The exigencies of commerce and daily life in the nascent urban centers of this period necessitated the manufacture of an unprecedented variety of ceramic vessels, including those for storing goods and transporting them within and between regions (**cat. nos. 10–15**). Many such vessels were sealed with jar stoppers, some of which were themselves sealed and stamped using cylinder seals.

With the development of state organizations came the control of labor, production, and commerce by nascent urban institutions. Commodities such as grain, dairy products, and oil were either stored in towns or shipped to other places and were sealed against tampering. When sealing a jar, the mouth of the jar was first covered with a piece of cloth that was secured around its neck by a string. Then either the entire cloth or the circumference of the neck was covered with clay and stamped with a cylinder seal (**cat. no. 16**; fig. 3.9).

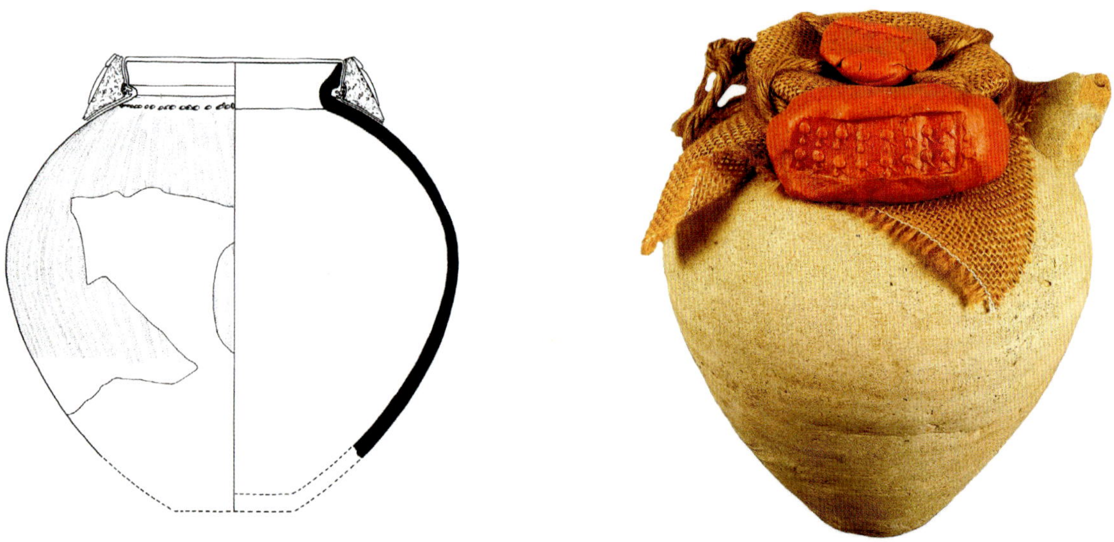

Figure 3.9. Left: Reconstruction of a sealed jar from Chogha Mish. Drawing by A. Alizadeh. Right: Reconstruction of a jar sealing on an actual jar from Uruk. After Feller 2013.

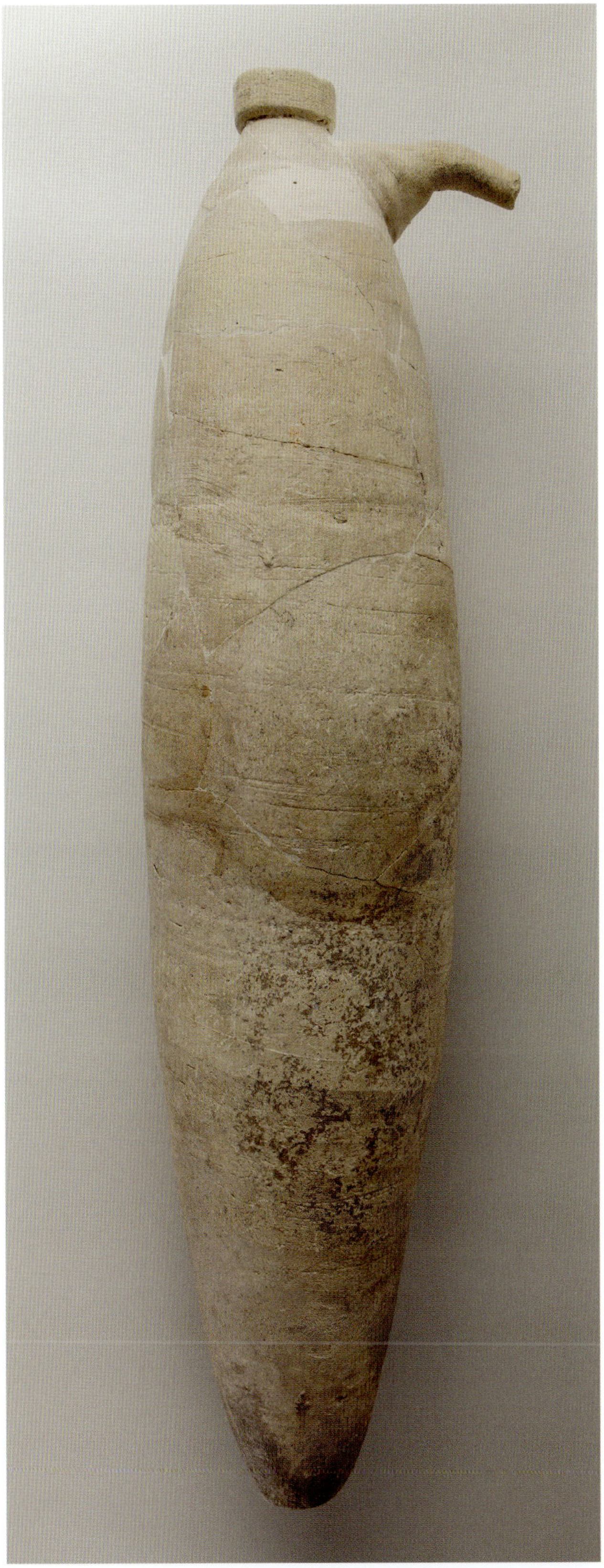

10. Bottle with Drooping Spout

Baked clay

Iran, Chogha Mish

Late Susa II period (ca. 3500–3100 BCE)

Excavated in 1965–1966

ISACM A33157

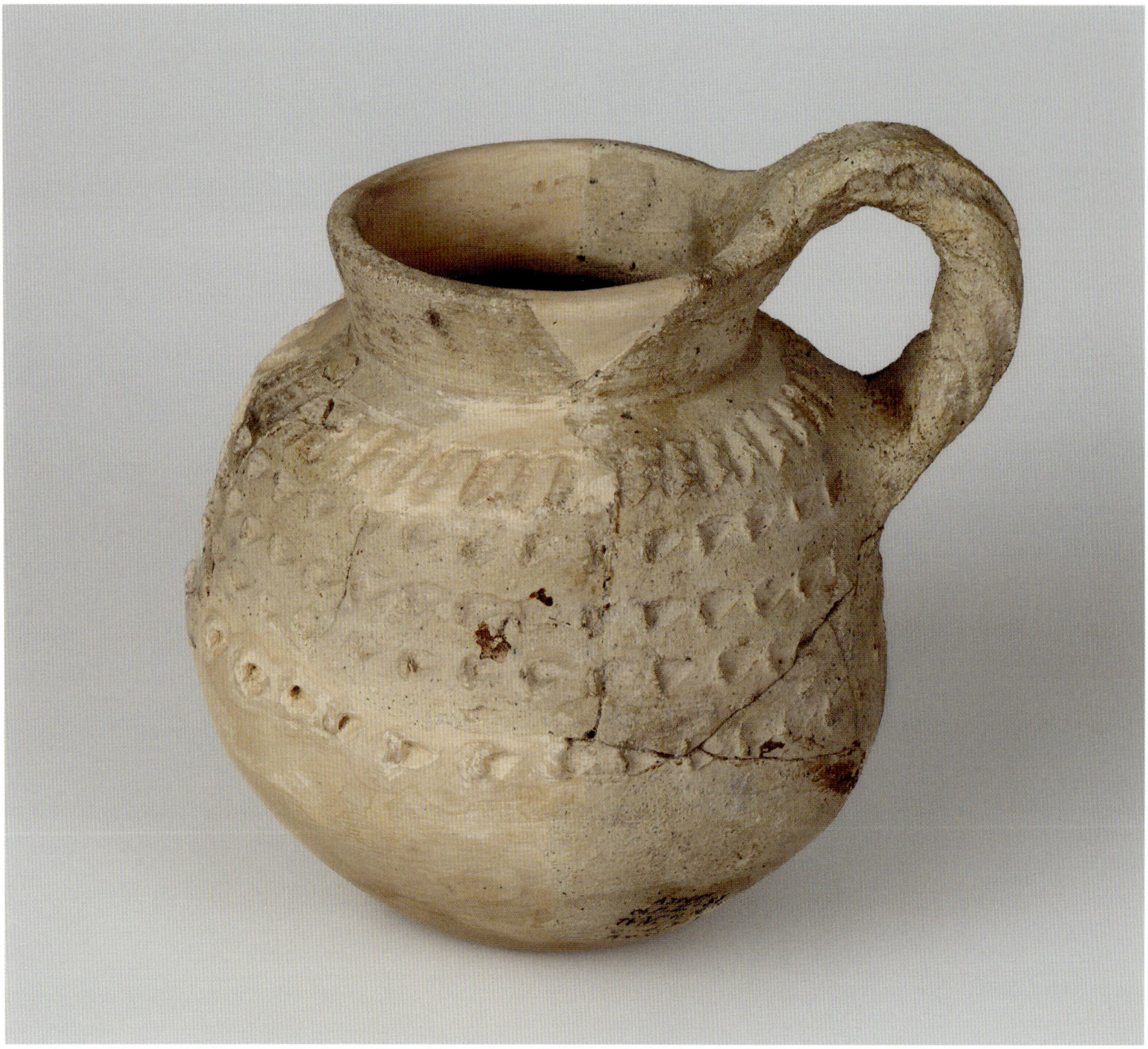

11. Cup with Twisted Handle

Baked clay

Iran, Chogha Mish

Late Susa II period (ca. 3500–3100 BCE)

Excavated in 1963

ISACM A38699

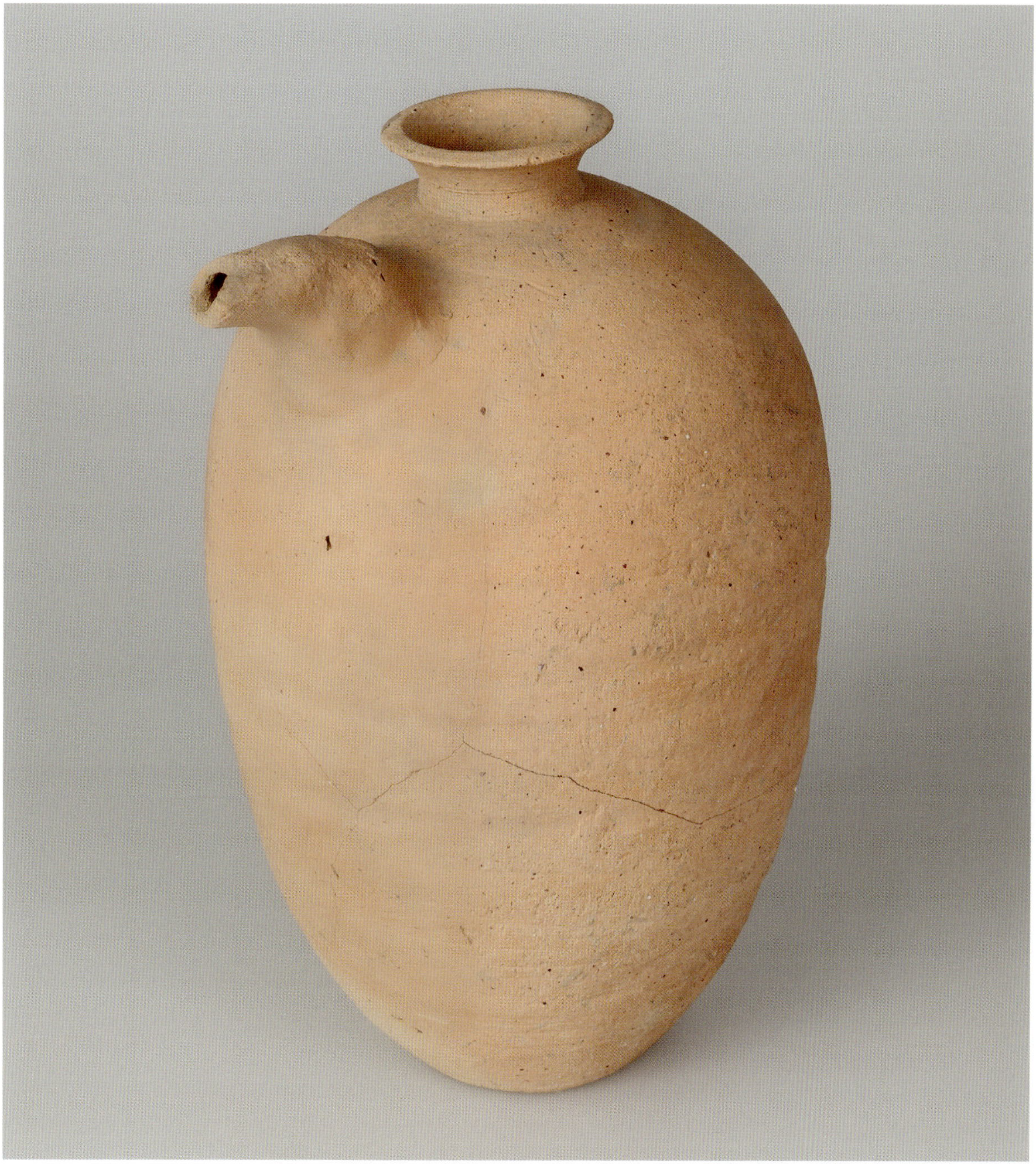

12. Spouted Jar

Baked clay

Iran, Chogha Mish

Late Susa II period (ca. 3500–3100 BCE)

Excavated in 1963–1966

ISACM A32412

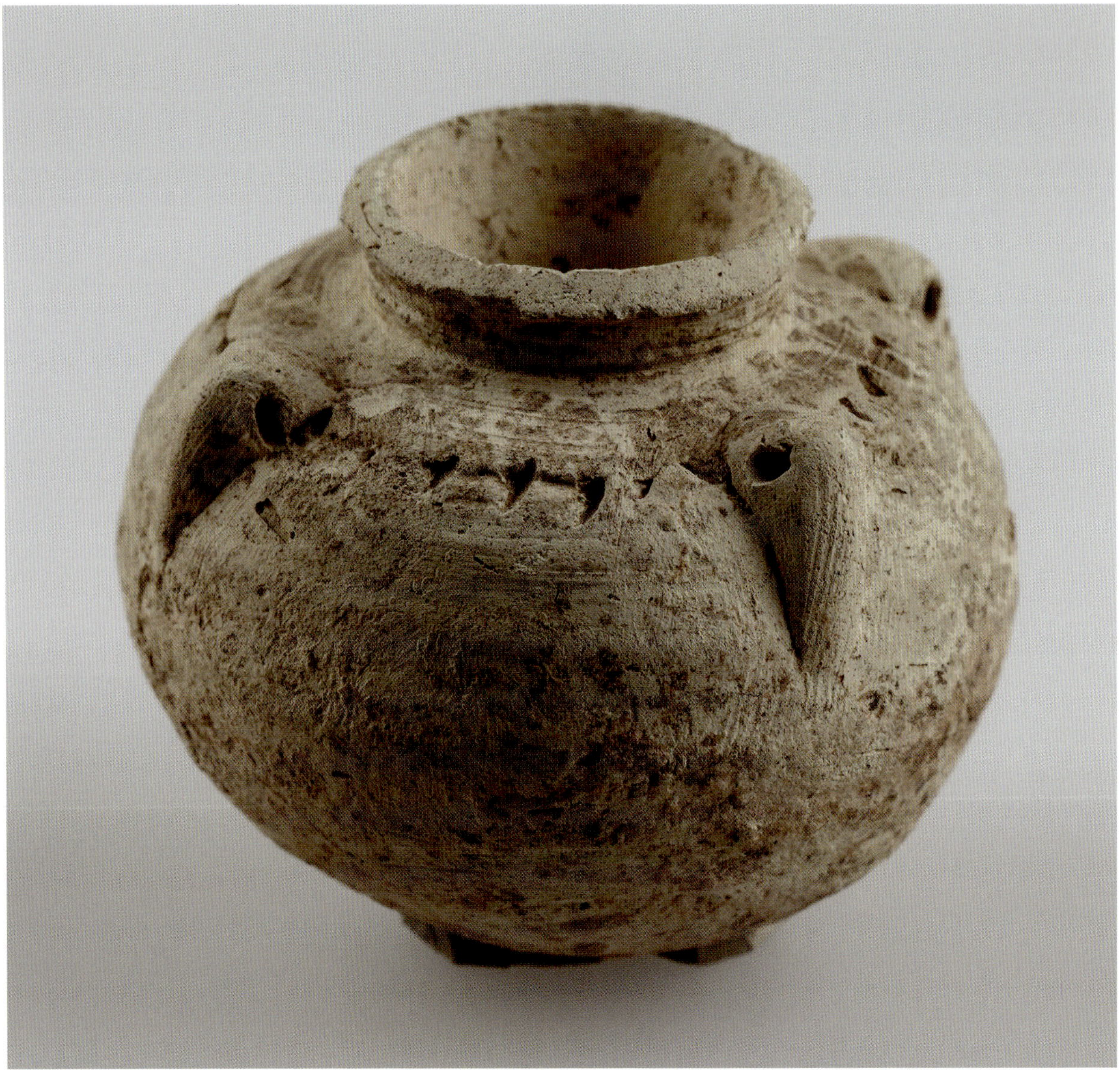

13. Miniature Jar

Baked clay

Iran, Chogha Mish

Late Susa II period (ca. 3500–3100 BCE)

Excavated in 1965–1966

ISACM A33062

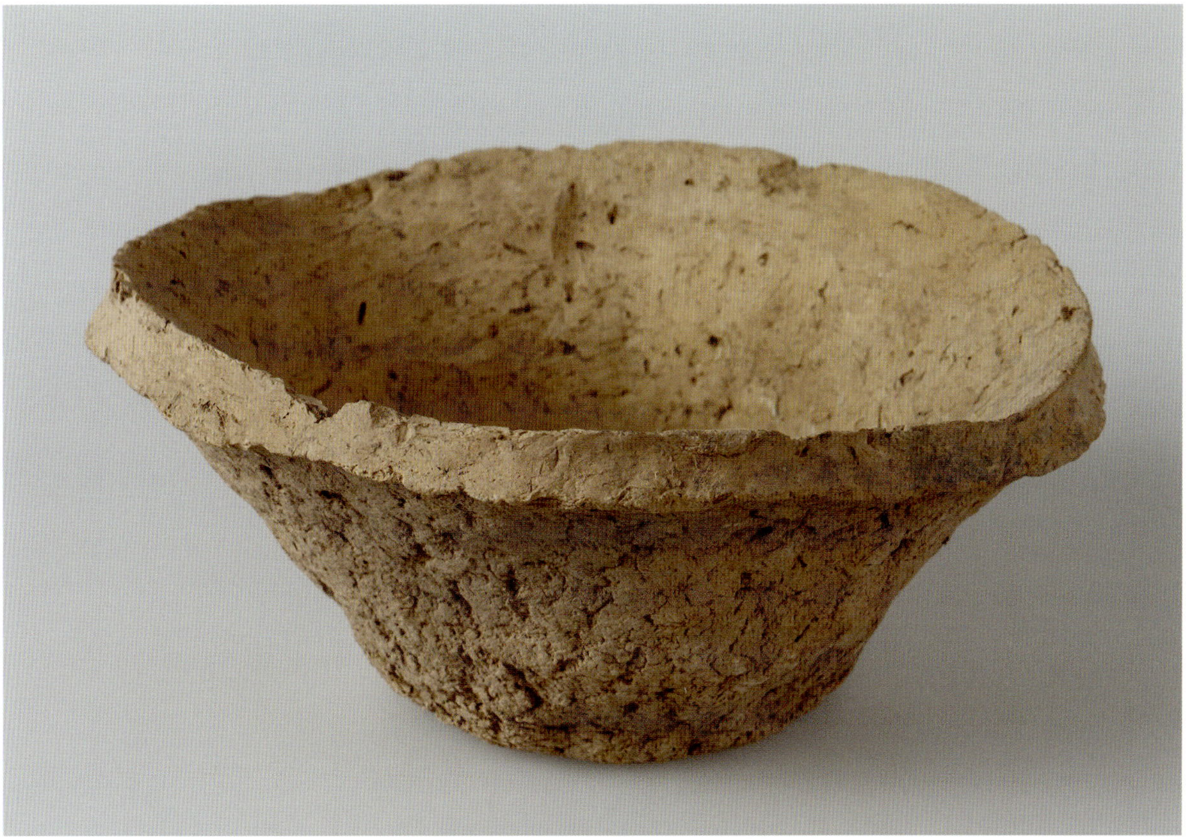

14. Beveled-Rim Bowl

Baked clay

Iran, Chogha Mish

Late Susa II period (ca. 3500–3100 BCE)

Excavated in 1963

ISACM A32404

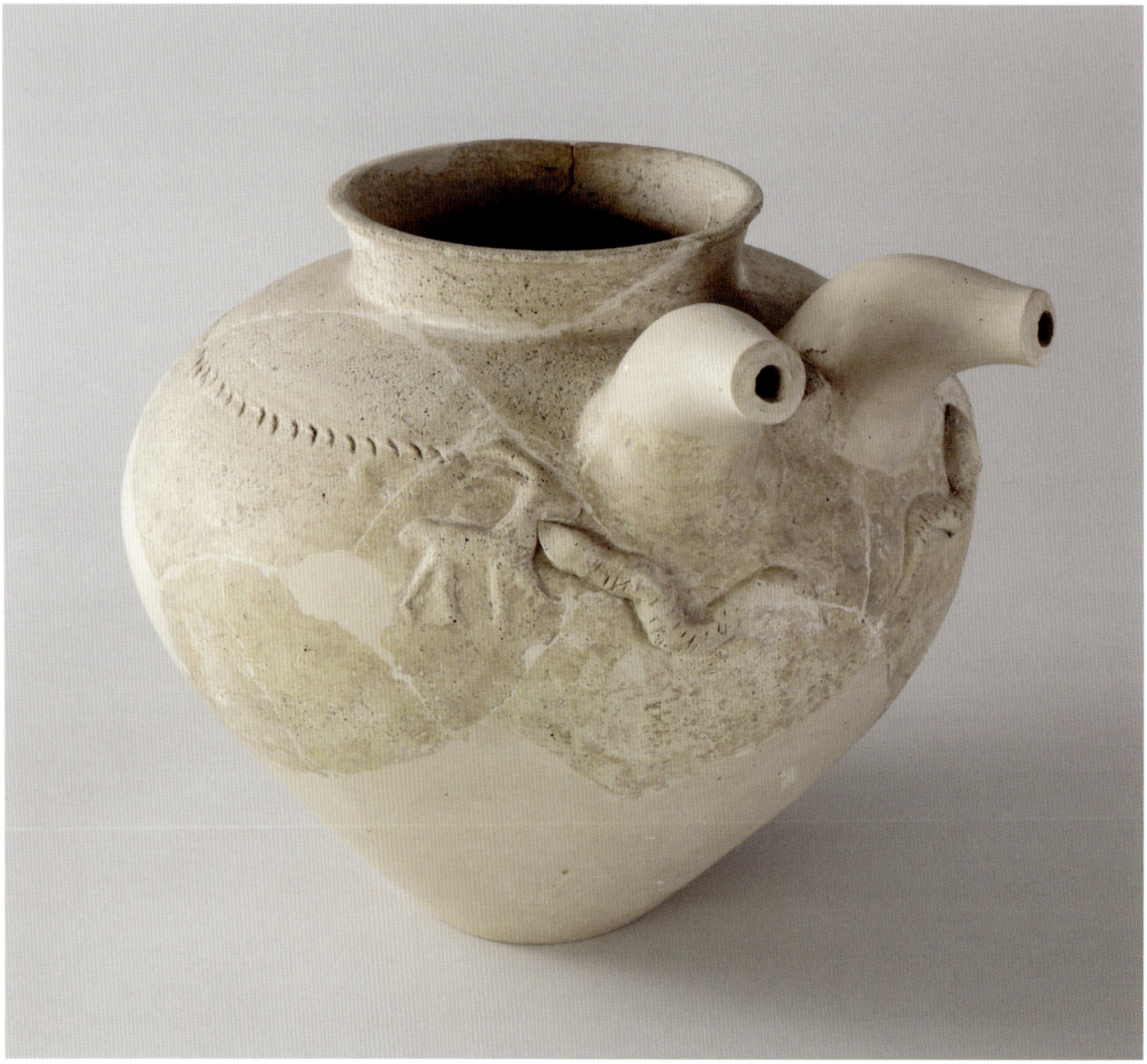

15. Double-Spouted Jar with Applied Decoration

Baked clay

Iran, Chogha Mish

Late Susa II period (ca. 3500–3100 BCE)

Excavated in 1965–1966

ISACM A32842

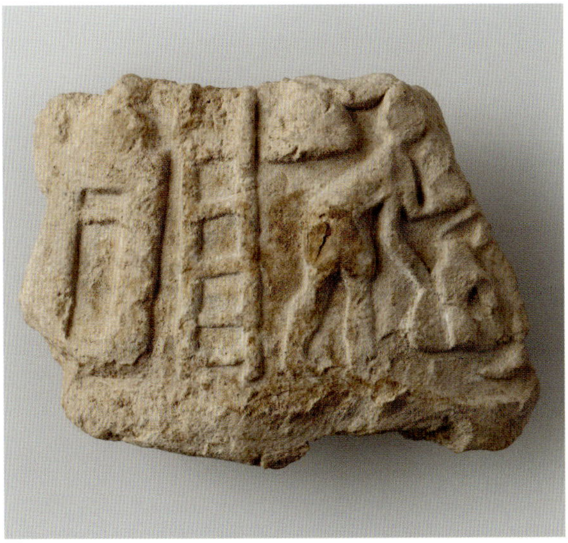

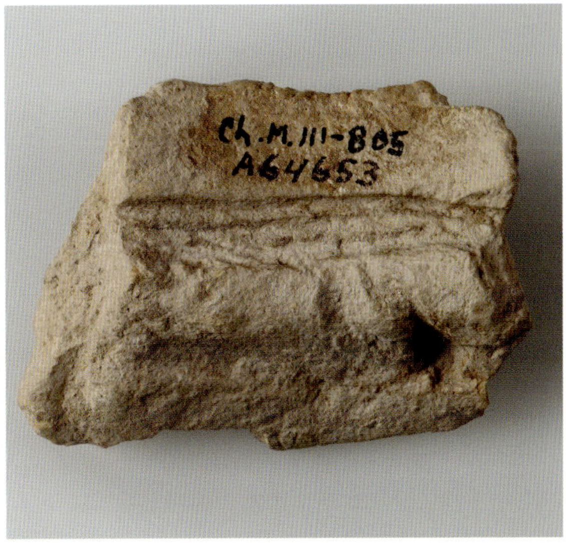

16. Jar Sealing Fragment

Clay

Iran, Chogha Mish

Late Susa II period
(ca. 3500–3100 BCE)

Excavated in 1969–1971

ISACM A64653

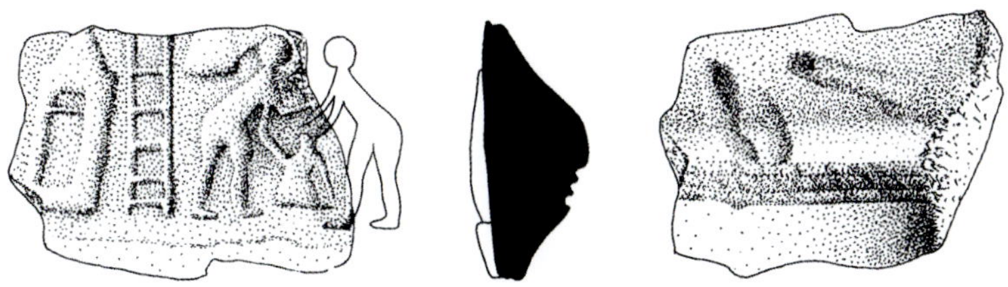

Drawings by A. Alizadeh.

Administrative Technology: Clay Tokens and Clay Envelopes

The crystallization of village life in the Near East in about 7000 BCE coincided with the appearance of a class of clay objects known as *numerical tokens*. Perhaps the new economic and social environment of early Neolithic farming villages presented a strong incentive for a personal, if not interpersonal, mnemonic notational system—an incentive not necessarily present in the fluid period of hunting and gathering in earlier (Upper Paleolithic) times. Such a system need not be formal, representing actual numbers; rather, it may be an informal tradition whose basic system is the accumulation of sets and subsets. The human brain is hardwired to seek patterns and organize them into a manageable form. This fact, coupled with the shared exigencies of daily life, may have led to the parallel development of simple mnemonic methods of recording numerical data—notches on a stick, a collection of pebbles, or a group of variously shaped clay objects that were easy to make, store, carry, and count.

Clay tokens of the early Neolithic period are simple in shape and show wide geographical distribution in the Near East. This type of counting device continued to develop into complex shapes, becoming an integral tool and a formal component of controlled administrative technology in the urban centers of the fourth millennium BCE. In this period, clay tokens were placed in clay envelopes that were then sealed (**cat. no. 17**). Complex tokens of this period represented not only numerical values but also types of commodities (**cat. no. 18**). These commodity-specific tokens are analogous—sometimes identical—to the signs found in the proto-cuneiform and Proto-Elamite writing systems, the earliest examples of writing.

Most clay envelopes bear more than one seal impression (fig. 3.10). The seals that made such impressions may have belonged to either the officials in charge of the transaction or the offices through which the transaction was handled. The pattern of the impressions suggests a hierarchy of such officials or offices. First the polar regions (top and bottom) would be impressed, and then the main, equatorial impression, which nearly always partially rolled over the other two impressions. The subject matter of the equatorial impression is typically more complex than that of the other two.

Clay envelopes containing clay tokens are the earliest administrative devices invented by ancient Near Eastern urban centers as accounting tools to control and monitor the flow of materials, commodities, and labor. But the manufacture of these envelopes was difficult and time-consuming, and they were awkward to store. Perhaps a few generations after the first appearance of clay envelopes, administrators simplified this accounting device by making a flat tablet instead and, after sealing it, impressing or scratching the shape of the token on it. **Cat. no. 19** from Chogha Mish is one of the earliest examples of such numerical tablets.

The next stage of urban development was groundbreaking and led to the invention of the proto-cuneiform and Proto-Elamite writing systems. Around this time, however, in about 3100 BCE, Chogha Mish was abandoned, and Susa survived as the only urban center in the entire Susiana plain.

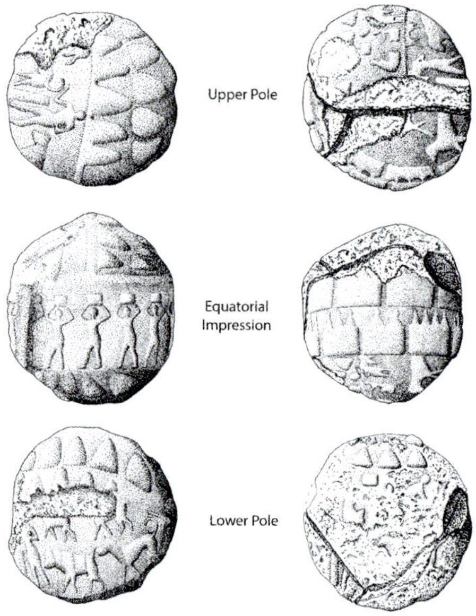

Figure 3.10. The sealings on two clay envelopes from Chogha Mish. Drawings by A. Alizadeh.

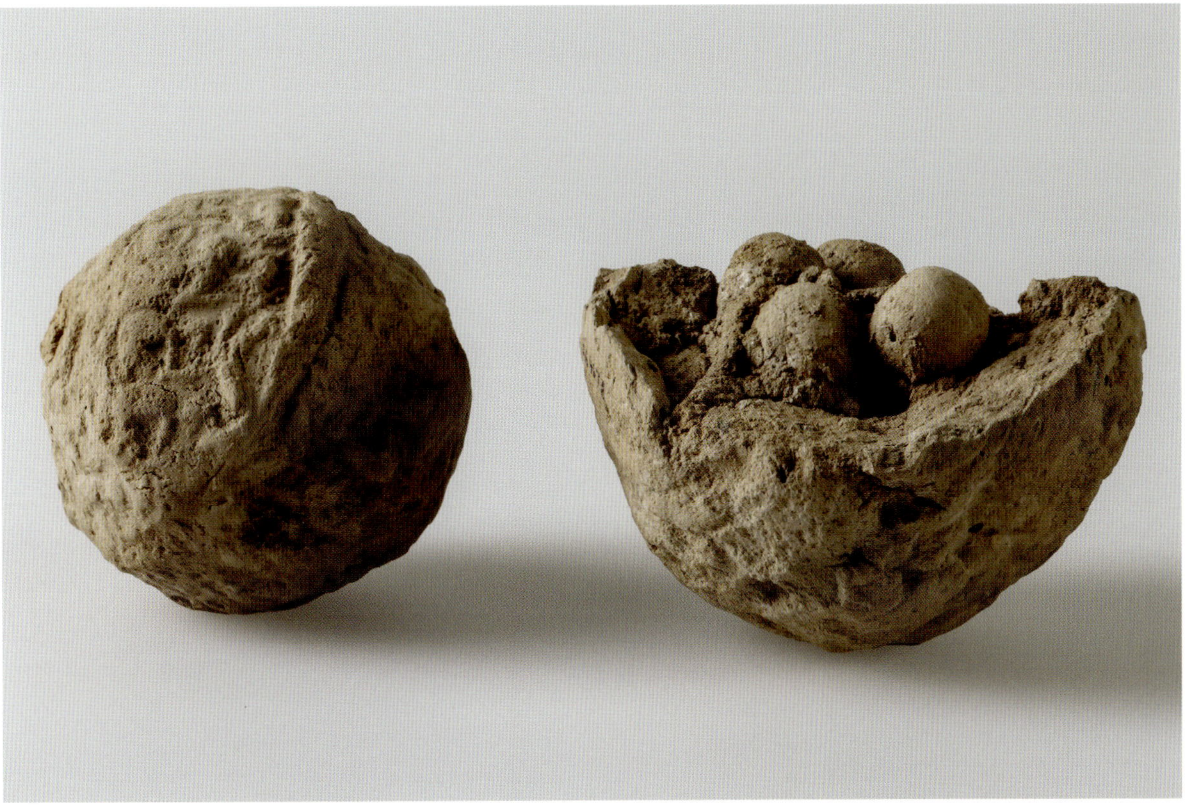

17. Envelopes

Clay

Iran, Chogha Mish

Late Susa II period (ca. 3500–3100 BCE)

Excavated in 1963–1966

ISACM A32566, A64606

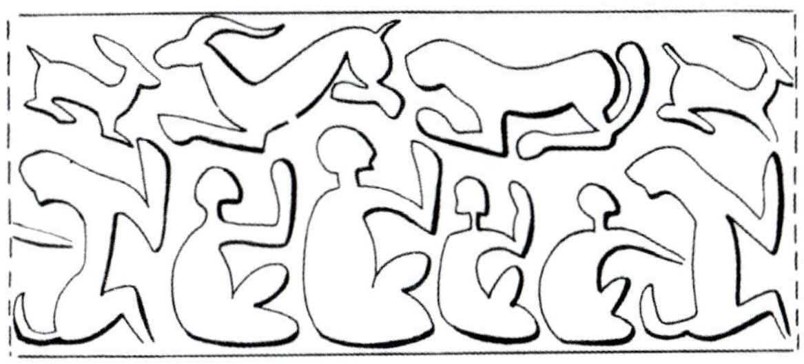

The seal design of ISACM A32566. Drawing by A. Alizadeh.

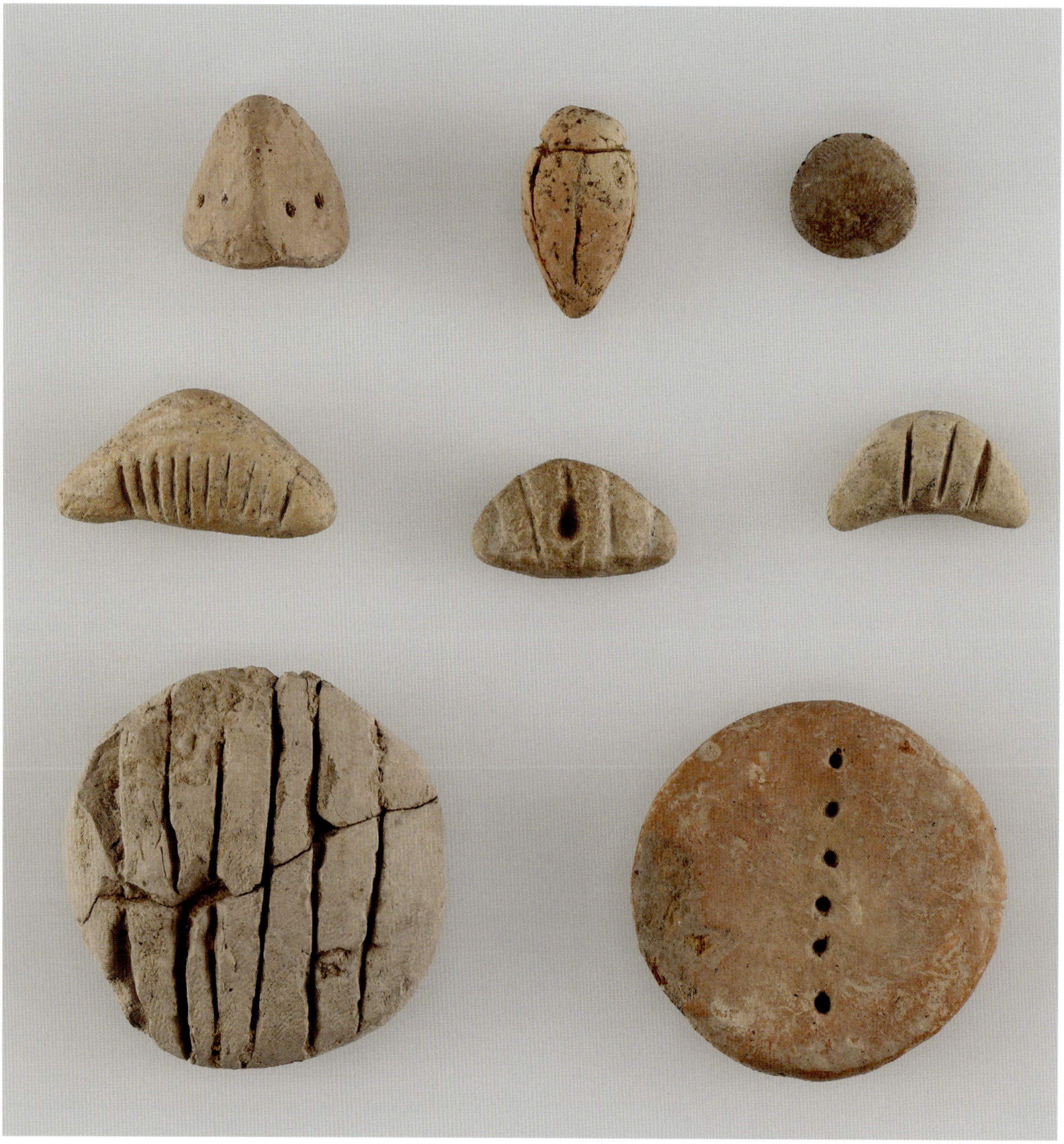

18. Complex Tokens

Clay, stone

Iran, Chogha Mish

Late Susa II period (ca. 3500–3100 BCE)

Excavated in 1963–1970

ISACM A64602, A64623, A64608, A64625, A64619, A32507, A181472, A64622 (top to bottom, left to right)

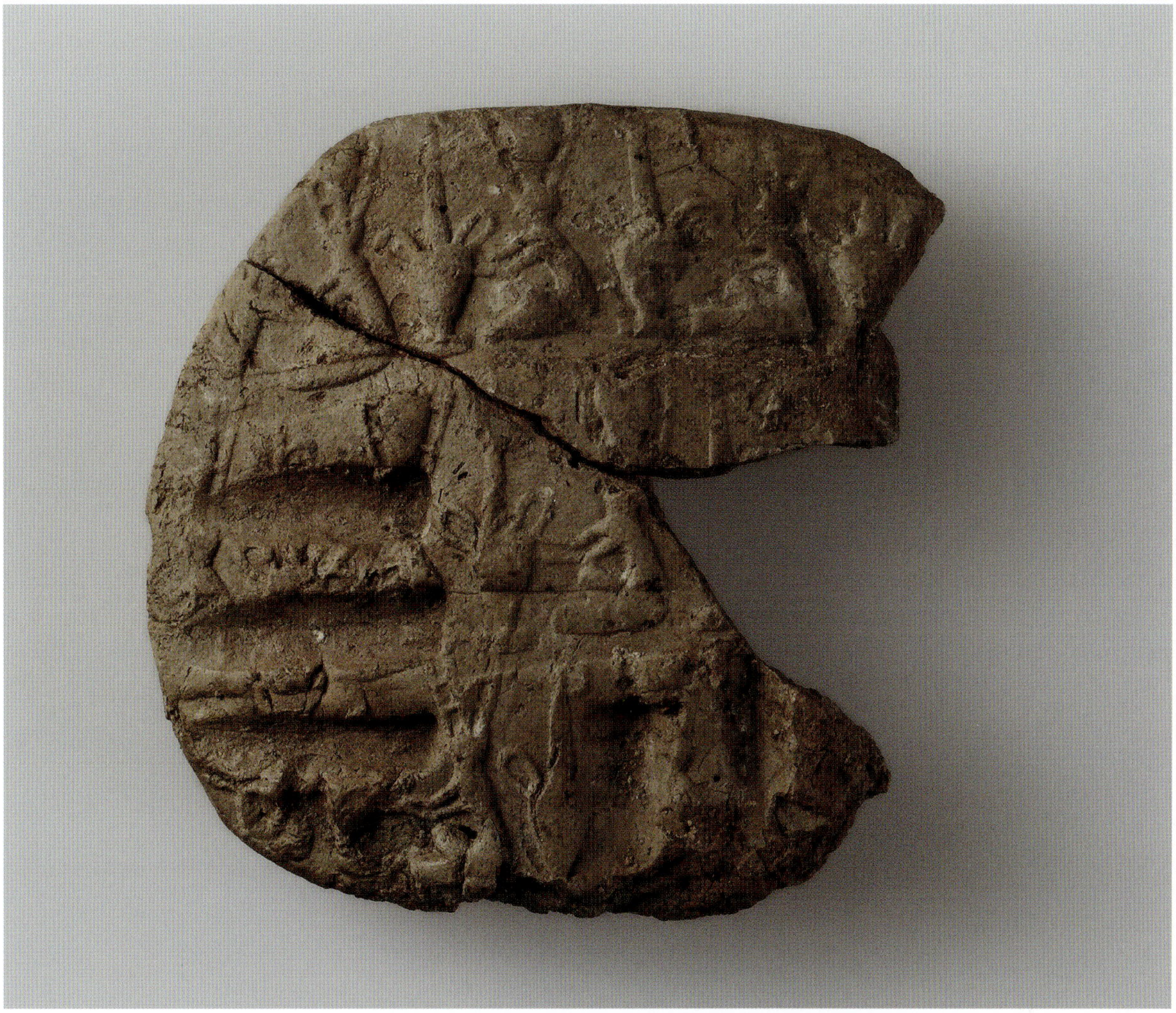

19. Numerical Tablet

Clay

Iran, Chogha Mish

Late Susa II period (ca. 3200–3100 BCE)

Excavated in 1963–1966

ISACM A32620A–B

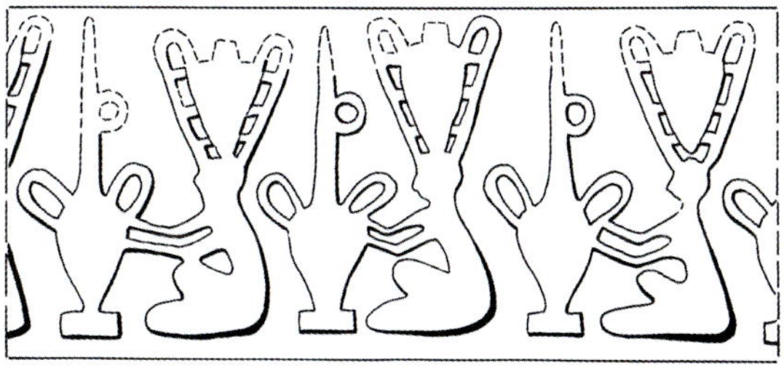

The seal design of ISACM A32620A–B. Drawing by A. Alizadeh.

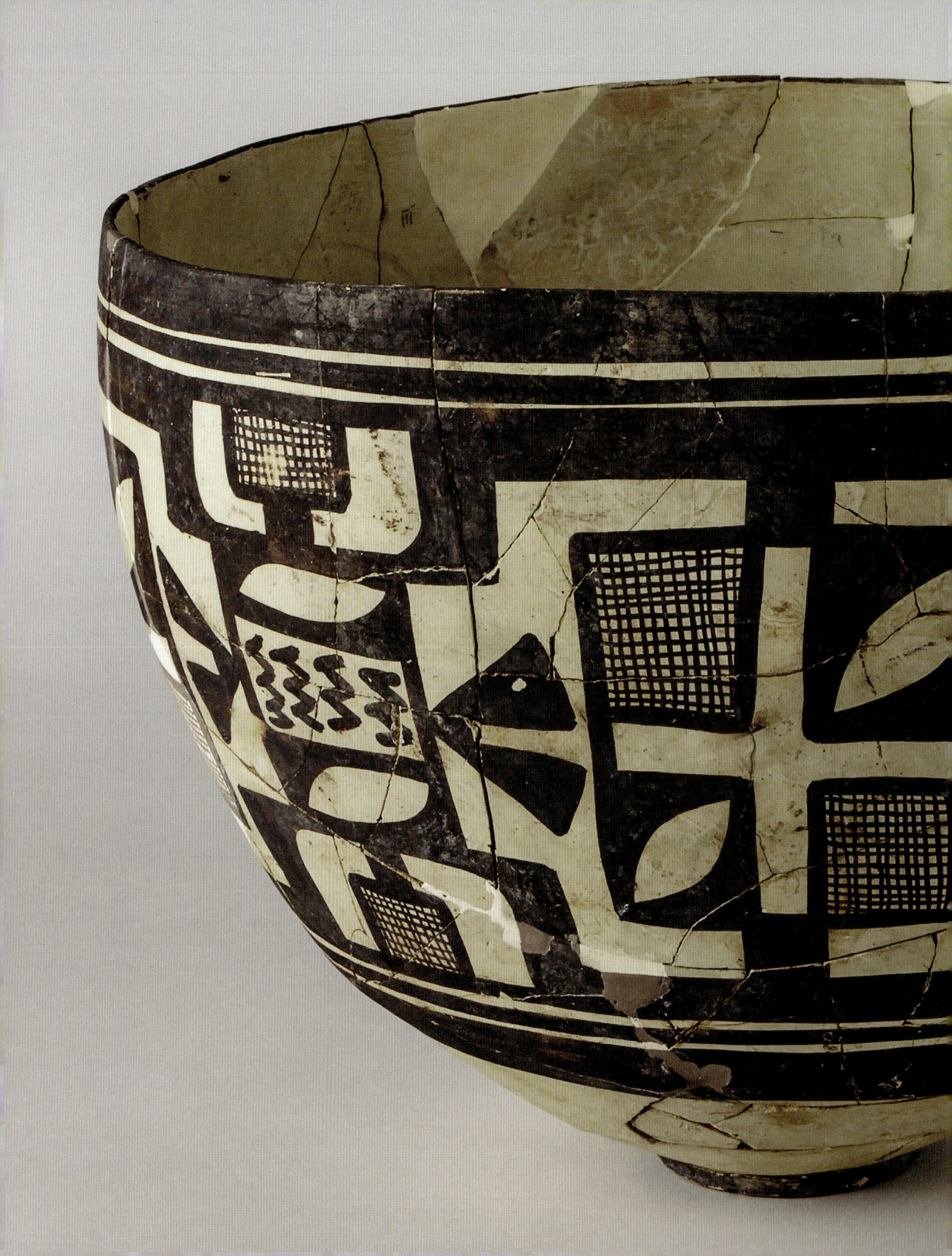

4 The Bakun Culture in Highland Fars

The Bakun culture (ca. 4700–4000 BCE) flourished in the highlands of the Iranian plateau at the same time as the Late Susiana 2 culture (also known as Susa I) in lowland Khuzestan and shared with it many features. The culture is known primarily from ISAC's excavations at Tall-e Bakun A, in the province of Fars near Persepolis. The ISAC Museum holds the largest collection of Bakun artifacts outside Iran.

The painted pottery of the contemporary Bakun culture of Fars is arguably the most sophisticated and aesthetically pleasing of all ancient Near Eastern painted ceramics. Most of the pottery bears elaborate painted designs of extraordinary beauty and sophistication. Additionally, Bakun artists produced naturalistic versions of animal forms. The depiction of principal subjects in reserved (unpainted) areas illustrates one of the outstanding and important characteristics of Bakun pottery—namely, the use of negative space in the creation of designs. This small settlement also yielded the earliest evidence of prehistoric administrative technology.

Baked-clay bowl from Tall-e Bakun, Iran. **Cat. no. 20**.

Ceramics

Conical bowls and cups of the Bakun culture are often decorated with figures of ibexes whose large, curved horns dwarf their bodies, often represented simply as a single triangle or a pair of opposed triangles. Other pieces make remarkable use of the vessel's surface, shown in reverse through the paint, to create floral patterns or to provide a backdrop for birds with outspread wings flying in a band encircling the pot. As in almost all prehistoric art, the rendering of human figures is highly stylized and abstract.

In Bakun pottery, the direction of the motif is easily suggested by connected elements such as zigzags, meanders, wavy lines, and rows of walking/running animals or wading birds. Bakun artists used the technique of pairing elements to produce a continuous frieze, thus linking an otherwise static design. Torsion, or the opposition of forces, is even more characteristic of Bakun pottery.

Cat. no. 20 is one of the finest examples known from Tall-e Bakun A. The mastery of the potter is exemplified by the excellent spacing and balance of the design elements on a curved surface. The scarcity of this type of pottery may indicate the special role these vessels played in rituals and feasts that enhanced the power or social status of their owners. The highly stylized and abstract invertible human figures on this bowl appear with square heads and arms raised, regardless of whether they are viewed right side up or upside down. In fact, every design element is rendered in this fashion. The painted pattern is so well balanced and spaced that even unpainted areas have become part of the decoration to be appreciated by the viewer.

Cat. no. 21, a now-fragmentary painted bowl, is decorated with a bold design consisting of a series of highly abstract flying birds shown sideways in such a way that the viewer may not notice them at first. The way the Bakun artist has embedded the birds in a field of curved geometric shapes makes the unpainted areas as pleasing to the eye as the painted elements.

Prehistoric dancing may seem an elusive subject. Dancing rituals enacted in celebrating a harvest, a successful hunt, or religious ceremonies, as well as the simple joy of rhythmic bodily movement so natural to human beings, do not often leave tangible evidence in the archaeological record. But beginning in the Neolithic period in the Levant, Anatolia, predynastic Egypt, northern Mesopotamia (Samarra and Halaf cultures), and especially Iran, dancing scenes were depicted on plaques, seals, walls, and pottery, indicating the importance of such ritual activity in human societies. In the archaeological record from Iran, these scenes first appear in Deh Luran and Susiana, in southwestern Iran, in the Archaic Susiana 3 period (ca. 6000 BCE).

Cat. no. 22, a potsherd from Tall-e Bakun A, shows a file of female dancers holding hands and what appear to be branches or ritual objects. A similar scene is depicted on the fragmentary bowl from ISAC's Chogha Sabz excavations, now housed at the National Museum of Iran (fig. 4.1). Again, as is usual in these scenes, the dancers are holding hands in such a way that they appear as though they are moving in a circle. Unlike the figures on the Bakun fragment, the dancers on the Chogha Sabz bowl have extremely stylized heads, which are indicated by simple sticks connected to the intricate frieze above. The dancers' broad hips suggest that they are women.

The narrow bases of beakers and conical cups (**cat. no. 23**) required some sort of stand in which to set the vessel upright. Decorated and plain hourglass-shaped and tapered cylindrical stands have been found at Bakun (**cat. no. 24**; fig. 4.2). But such supports could have been made of perishable wood as well (fig. 4.3).

Cone-shaped beakers represent one of the most outstanding classes of pottery vessels from Tall-e Bakun A. Such vessels are invariably decorated with geometric and floral designs. **Cat. no. 25** is decorated with four rectangular panels with floating

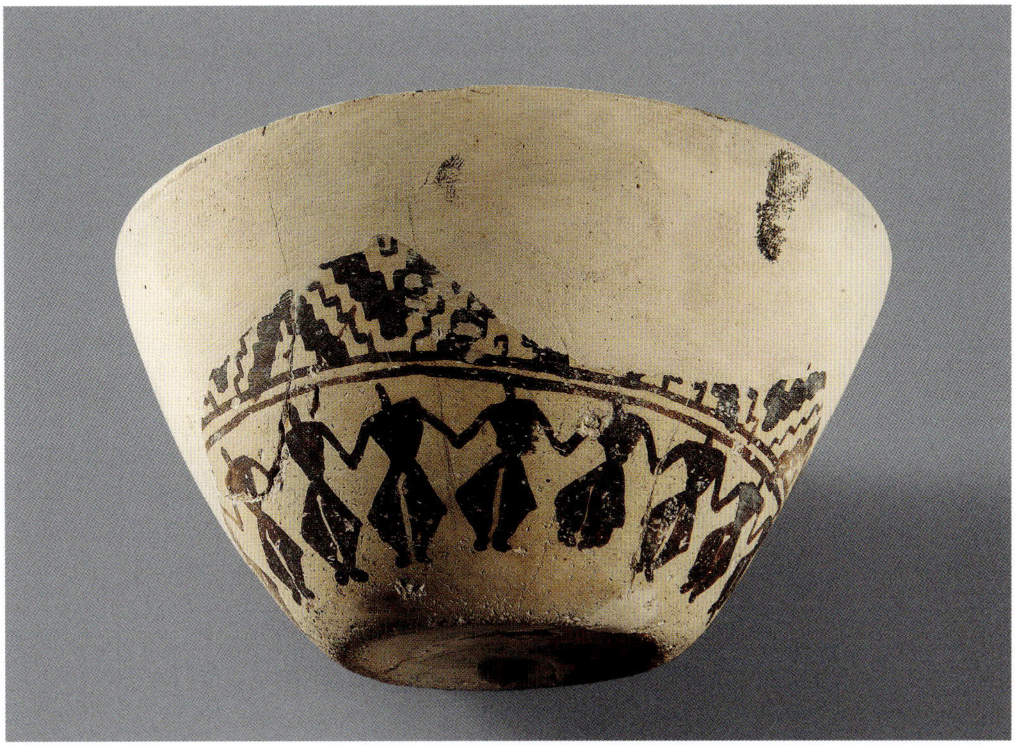

Figure 4.1. Painted bowl with dancing scene from Chogha Sabz, Luristan (ca. 5000 BCE) (diameter 25 cm), National Museum of Iran, Tehran. Photo by N. Fakurzadeh.

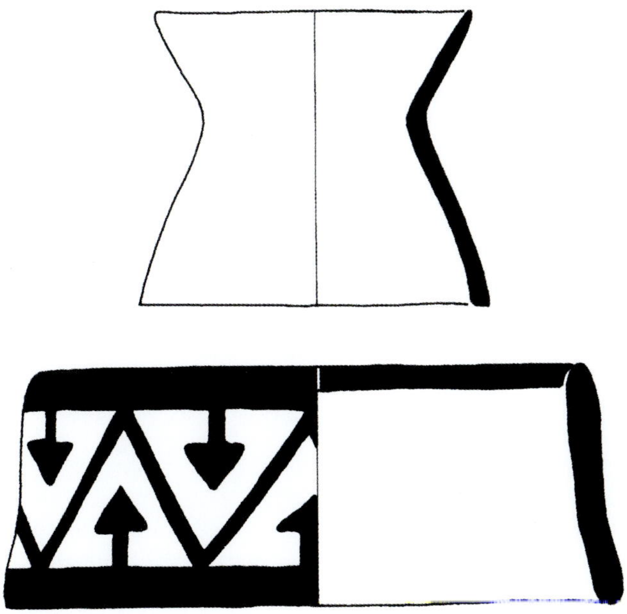

Figure 4.2. Plain and painted stands from Tall-e Bakun A (ca. 4300 BCE). Drawings by A. Alizadeh.

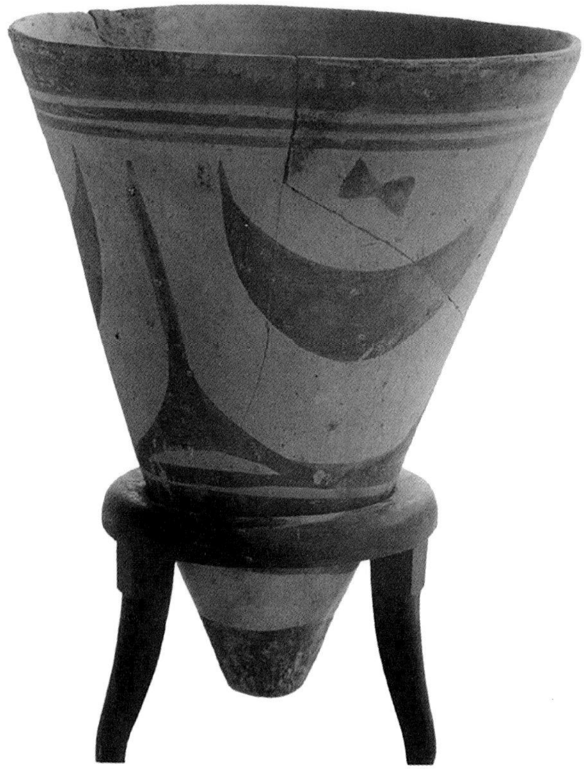

Figure 4.3. Beaker with modern stand, Tall-e Bakun A (ca. 4300 BCE), National Museum of Iran, Tehran. Photo by N. Fakurzadeh.

vertical dashes as a filler motif. The panels are separated by three sets of zigzagged lines in a reserved field. **Cat. no. 26** is decorated with three sets of large crescents, each of which encloses a butterfly as a filler motif.

Appreciation for such work increases when we note that such vessels with thin, even walls were, in the absence of a potter's wheel, made by hand. It has been assumed that vessels of this type were made using some type of mold; the discovery in 2014 of an actual mold in the storage facilities of the National Museum of Iran has provided solid evidence for this method of manufacture (fig. 4.4).

Conical cups decorated with images of mouflons (wild sheep) issuing from the base are the most characteristic component of the Bakun ceramic repertoire and have been found nowhere else. The animal images on such vessels are highly stylized, and the emphasis focuses on the swirling horns. On some examples only two mouflons appear, with their four horns placed high above the animals and expertly spaced on the vessel's curved and tapering surface (**cat. no. 27**). Other vessels, such as **cat. no. 28**, show three animals with extremely abbreviated bodies whose single horns circumscribe a floral motif.

Large, hemispherical bowls are decorated with a variety of animal, bird, floral, and geometric designs. The central motif on **cat. no. 29** is an ibex, the most popular animal depicted on Bakun pottery. Although the animal is stylized, anatomical

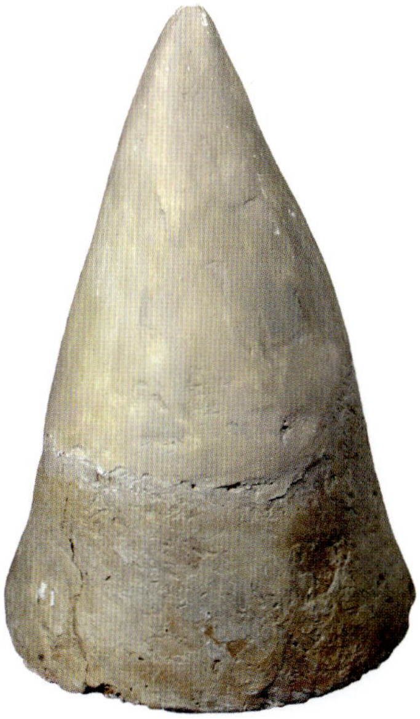

Figure 4.4. Beaker mold from Tall-e Bakun A (ca. 4300 BCE) (diameter 14 cm, height 20 cm), National Museum of Iran, Tehran. Photo by A. Alizadeh.

features such as knobbed horns, a beard, four legs, and a short tail are clearly indicated, thereby creating a naturalistic impression. The ibex is depicted twice on the vessel, once on each side. The images are separated by broad, rectangular panels formed by reverse triangles joined in such a way that the unpainted space between them has become its own independent decorative element.

Cat. no. 30 is decorated with a minimalistic yet vibrant pattern formed by a thick, continuous zigzag crossed by oblique Z-shapes. The Z-shapes are bordered on top by a single broad band and two thin lines, repeated in reverse below. A negative diamond is created at the crossing point. The opposing Z-shapes and zigzag create a torsion that makes this simple pattern dynamic.

The exterior of **cat. no. 31**, an elegant bowl from Tall-e Bakun, is decorated with three sets of design elements that consist of open rectangles with interior "hooks." Unusually, the sets are disconnected, separated by files of zigzags. The interior of the vessel is also decorated with an uncommon design pattern. Three sets of seven straight lines hanging from the rim are separated by three abstract, fringed designs that may or may not represent birds. Four solid butterfly shapes complete the pattern at the bottom of the bowl.

The interiors of some Bakun bowls are decorated exclusively with wavy parallel lines. On **cat. no. 32**, the bands radiate obliquely and divide the interior surface into two halves; the space between them is filled with additional pairs of wavy lines. Each group of wavy lines is bordered by a pair of straight lines, the outer line of which thickens into a solid triangle. The exterior design of linked, hatched lozenges in two rows is common and appears on a variety of vessels.

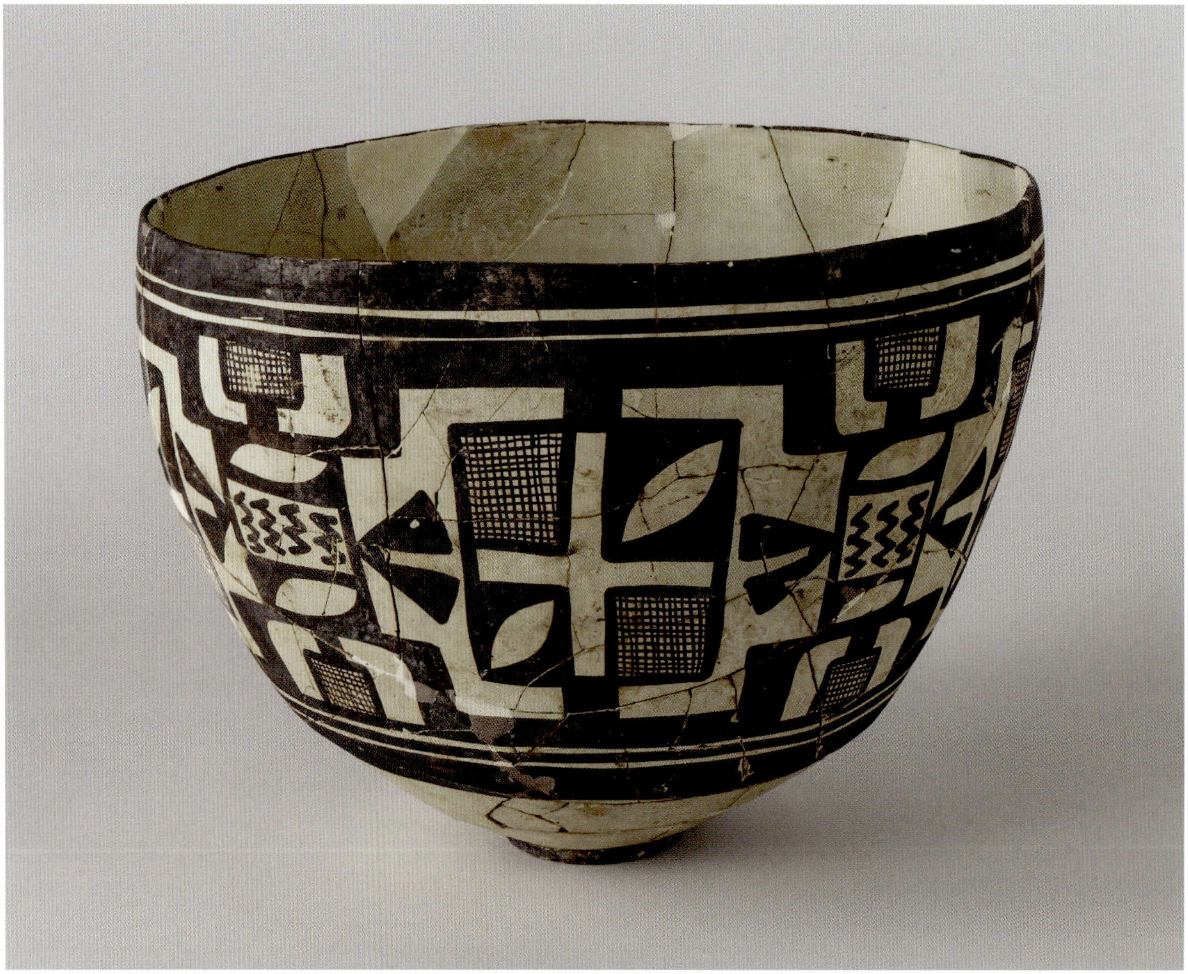

20. Bowl

Baked clay, paint

Iran, Tall-e Bakun A

Bakun A period (ca. 4400–4000 BCE)

Excavated in 1932–1934

ISACM A20136

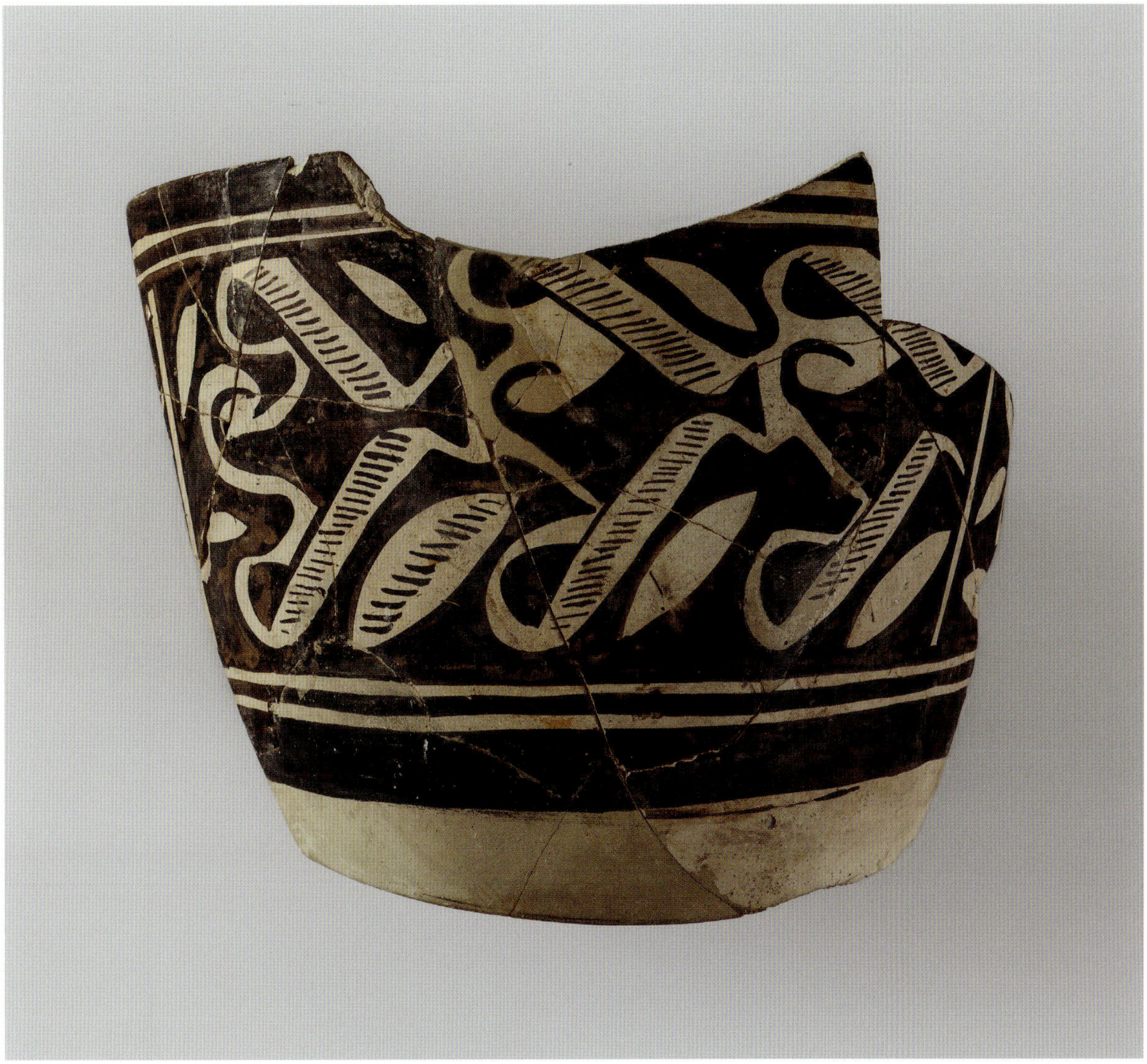

21. Fragmentary Bowl

Baked clay, paint

Iran, Tall-e Bakun A

Bakun A period (ca. 4400–4000 BCE)

Excavated in 1932

ISACM A39940

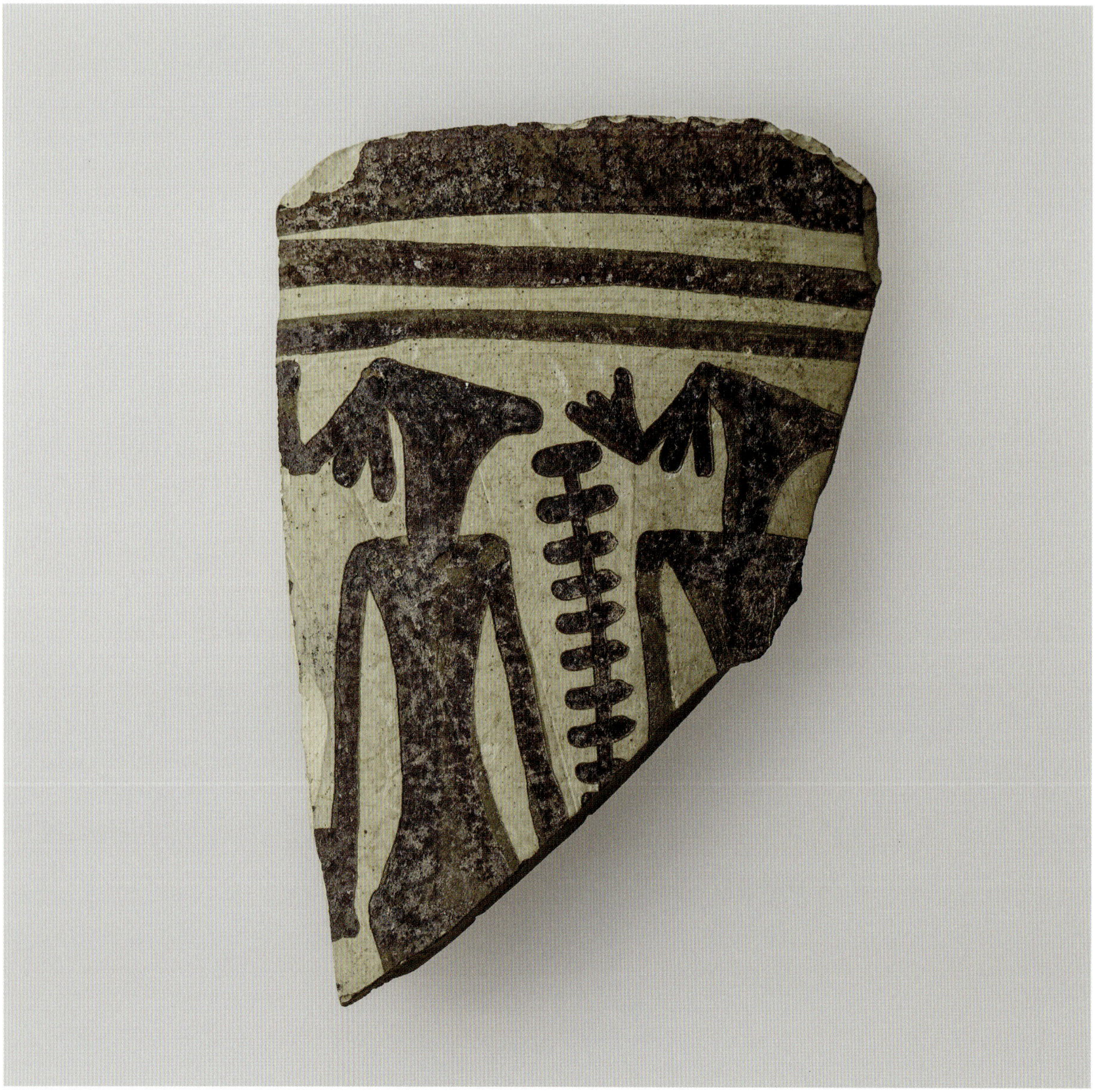

22. Sherd

Baked clay
Iran, Tall-e Bakun A
Bakun A period (ca. 4400–4000 BCE)
Excavated in 1932
ISACM A39941

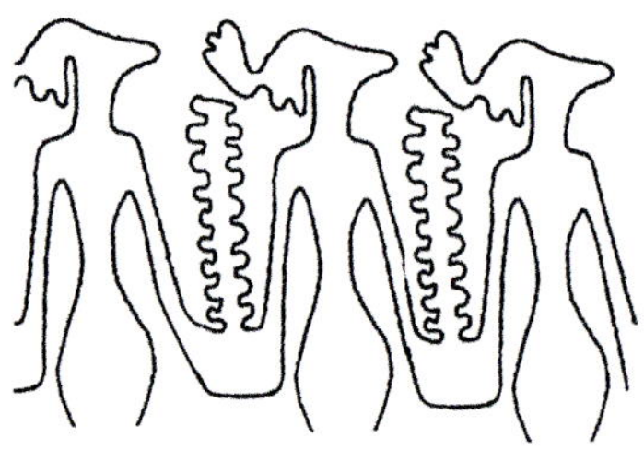

Drawing by A. Alizadeh.

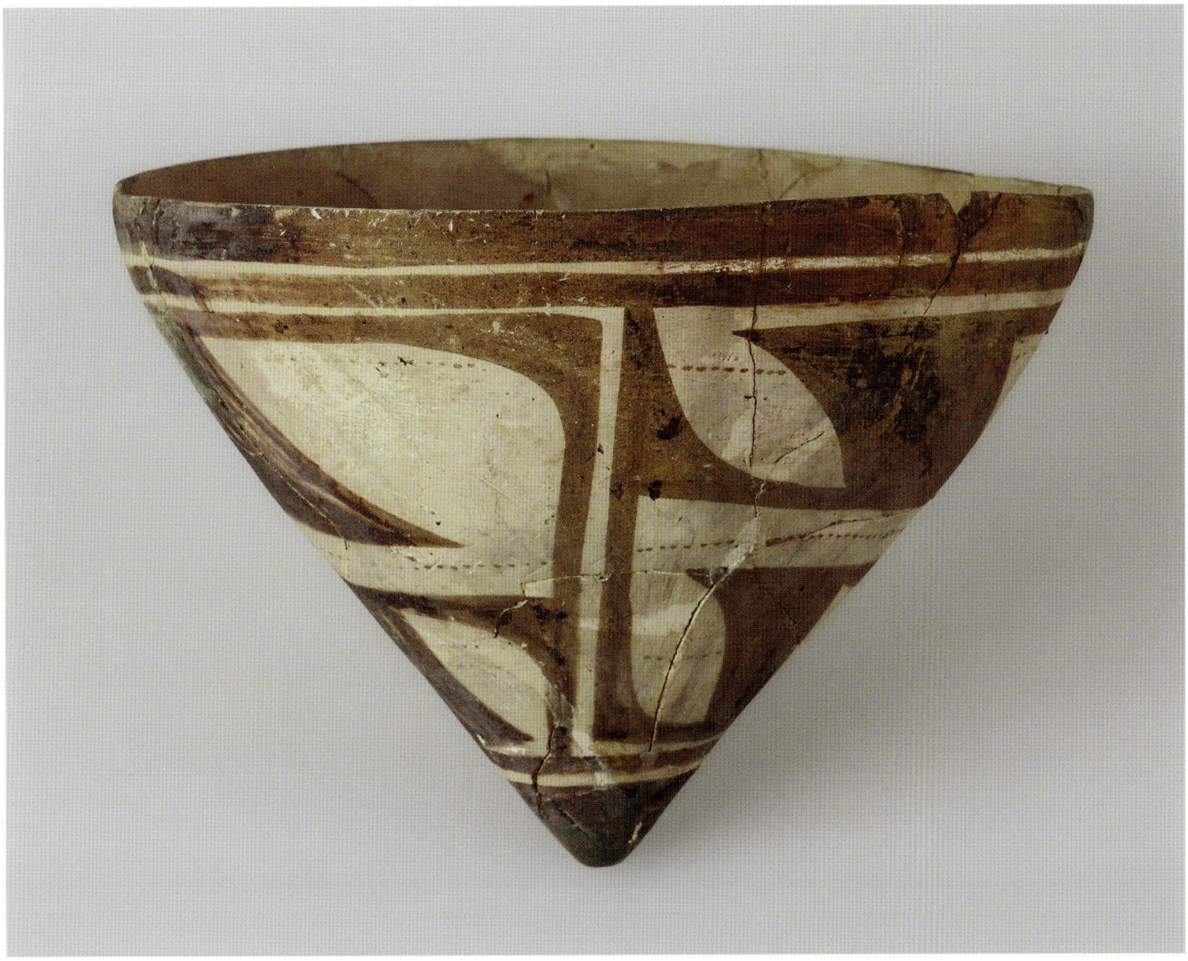

23. Conical Cup

Baked clay, paint

Iran, Tall-e Bakun A

Bakun A period (ca. 4400–4000 BCE)

Excavated in 1932–1934

ISACM A20116

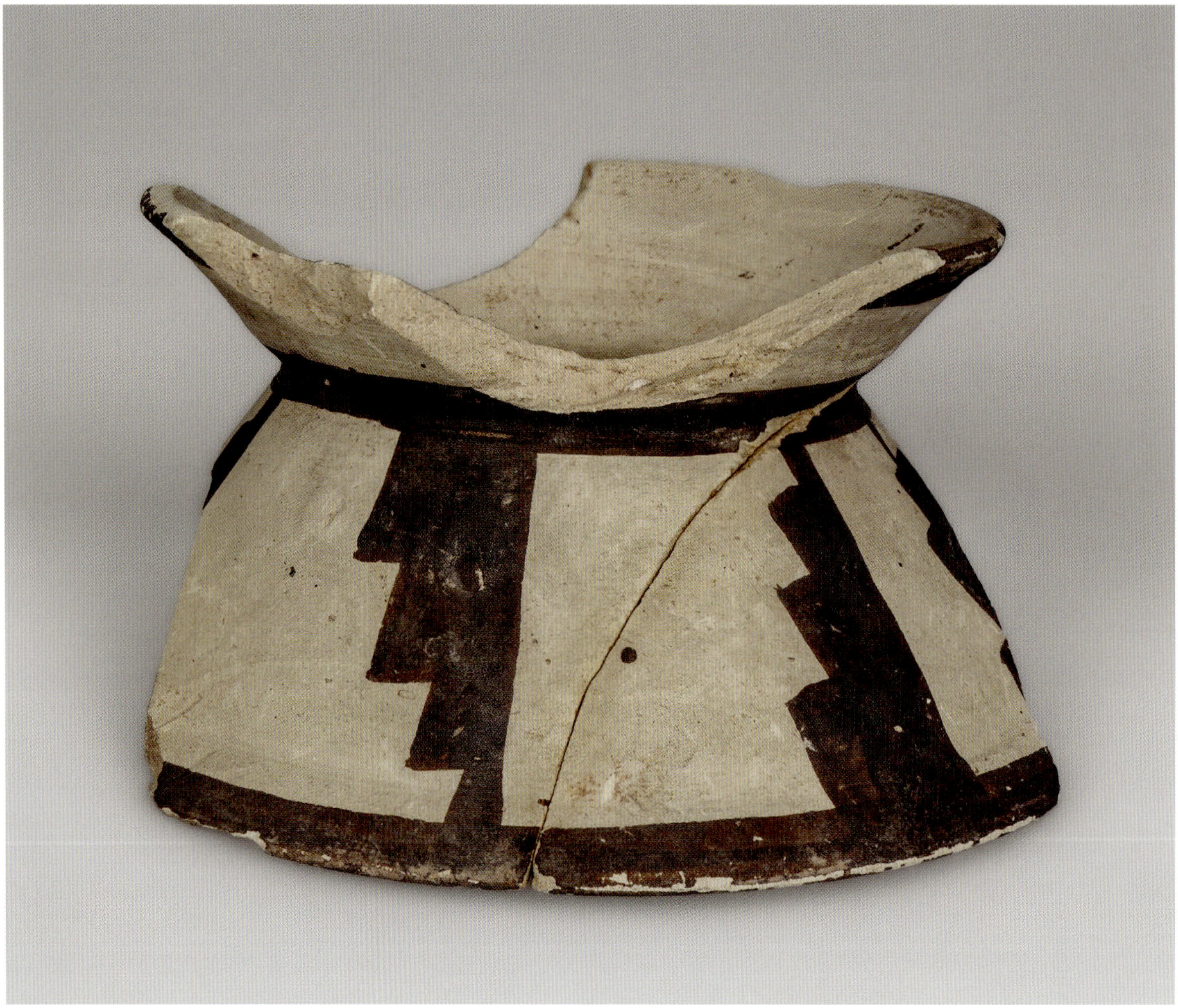

24. Fragmentary Stand

Baked clay, paint

Iran, Tall-e Bakun A

Bakun A period (ca. 4400–4000 BCE)

Excavated in 1932–1934

ISACM A20104

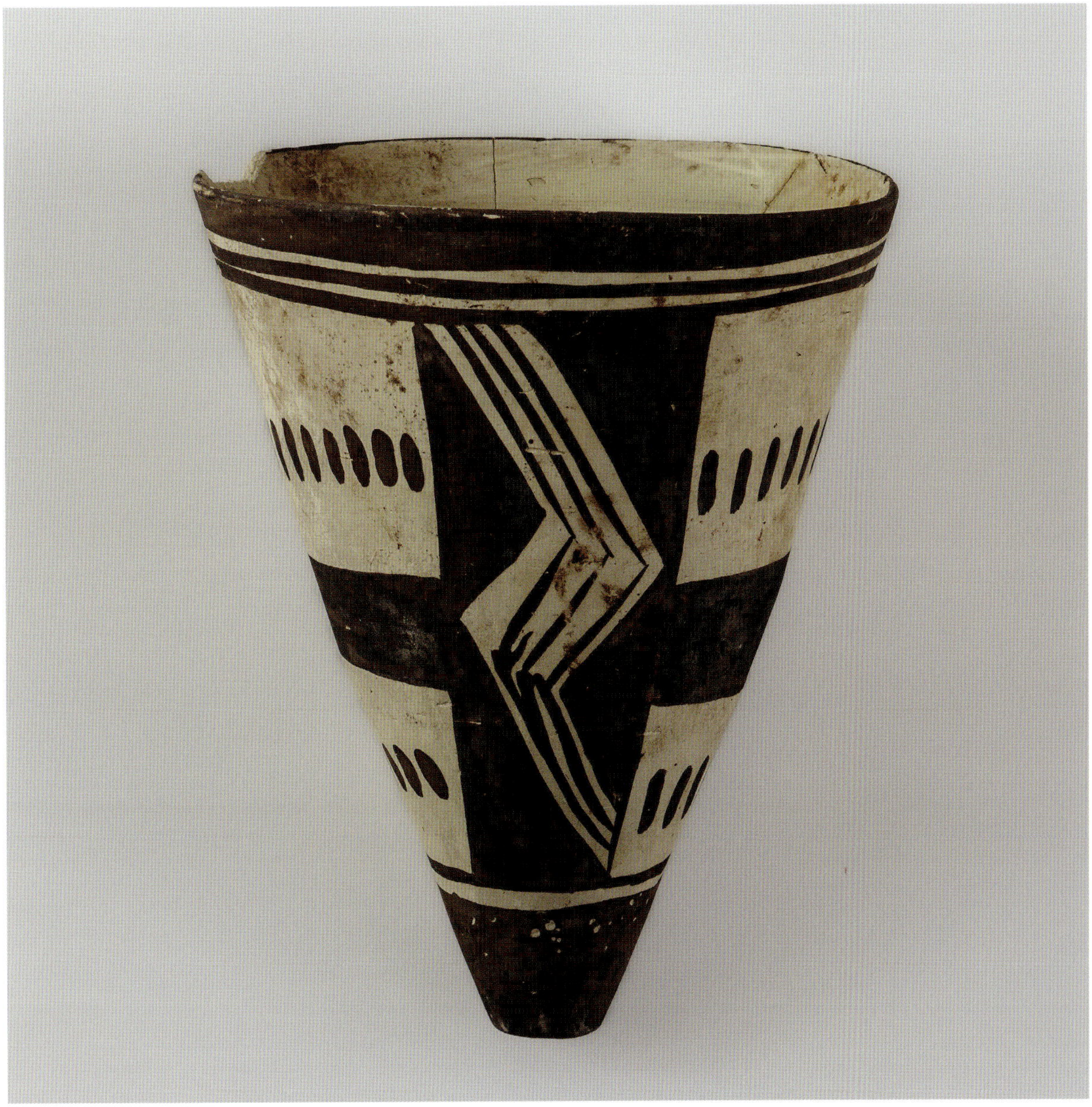

25. Beaker

Baked clay, paint
Iran, Tall-e Bakun A
Bakun A period (ca. 4400–4000 BCE)
Excavated in 1932–1934
ISACM A20097

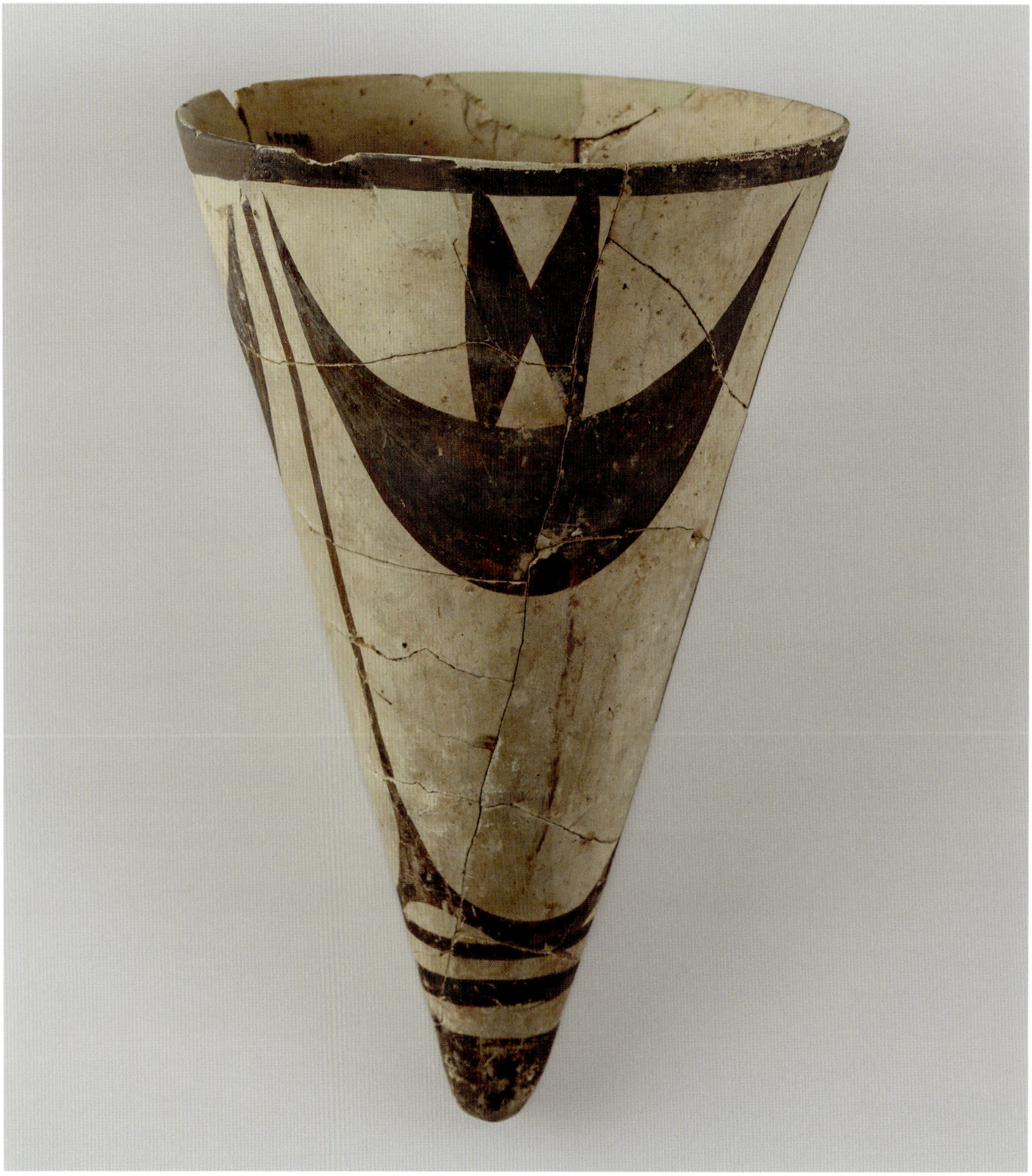

26. Beaker

Baked clay, paint

Iran, Tall-e Bakun A

Bakun A period (ca. 4400–4000 BCE)

Excavated in 1932–1934

ISACM A20164

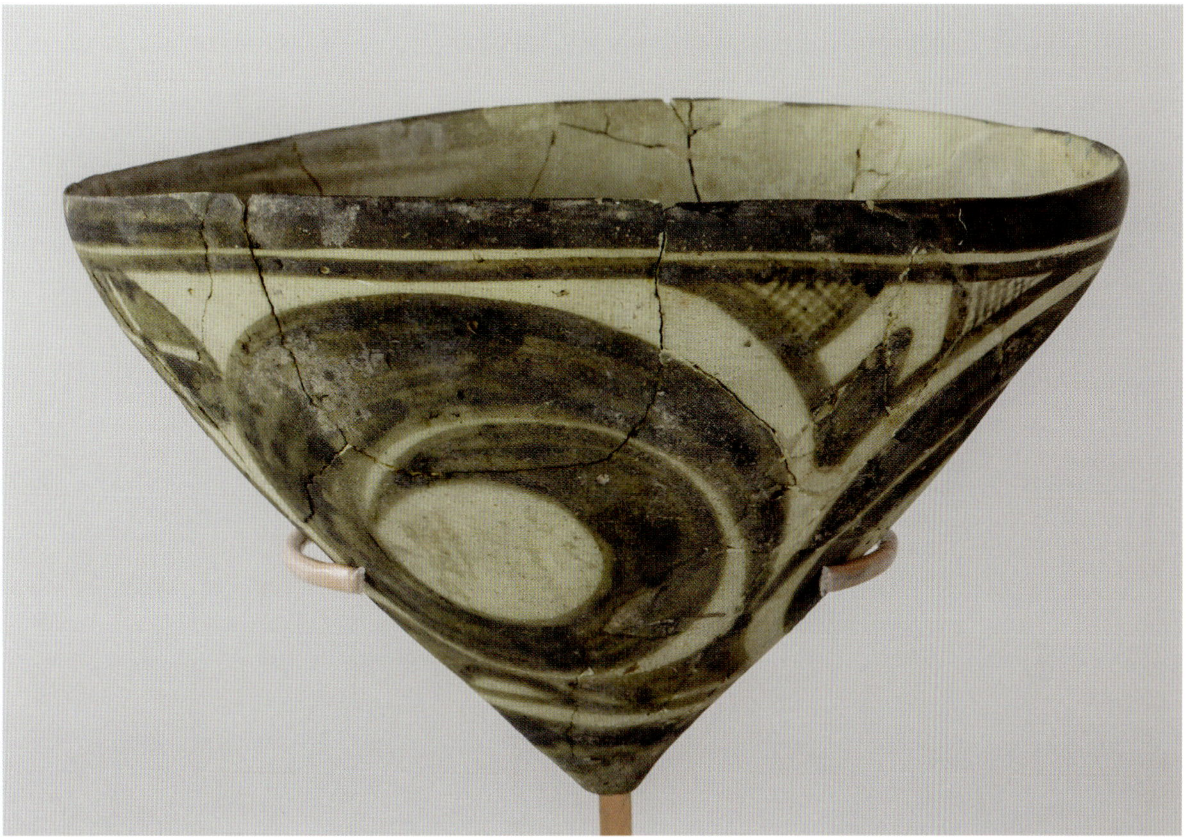

27. Conical Cup

Baked clay, paint
Iran, Tall-e Bakun A
Bakun A period (ca. 4400–4000 BCE)
Excavated in 1932–1934
ISACM A20089

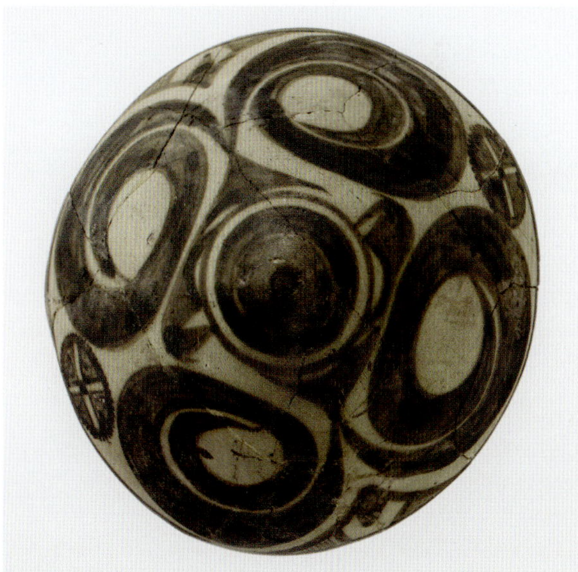

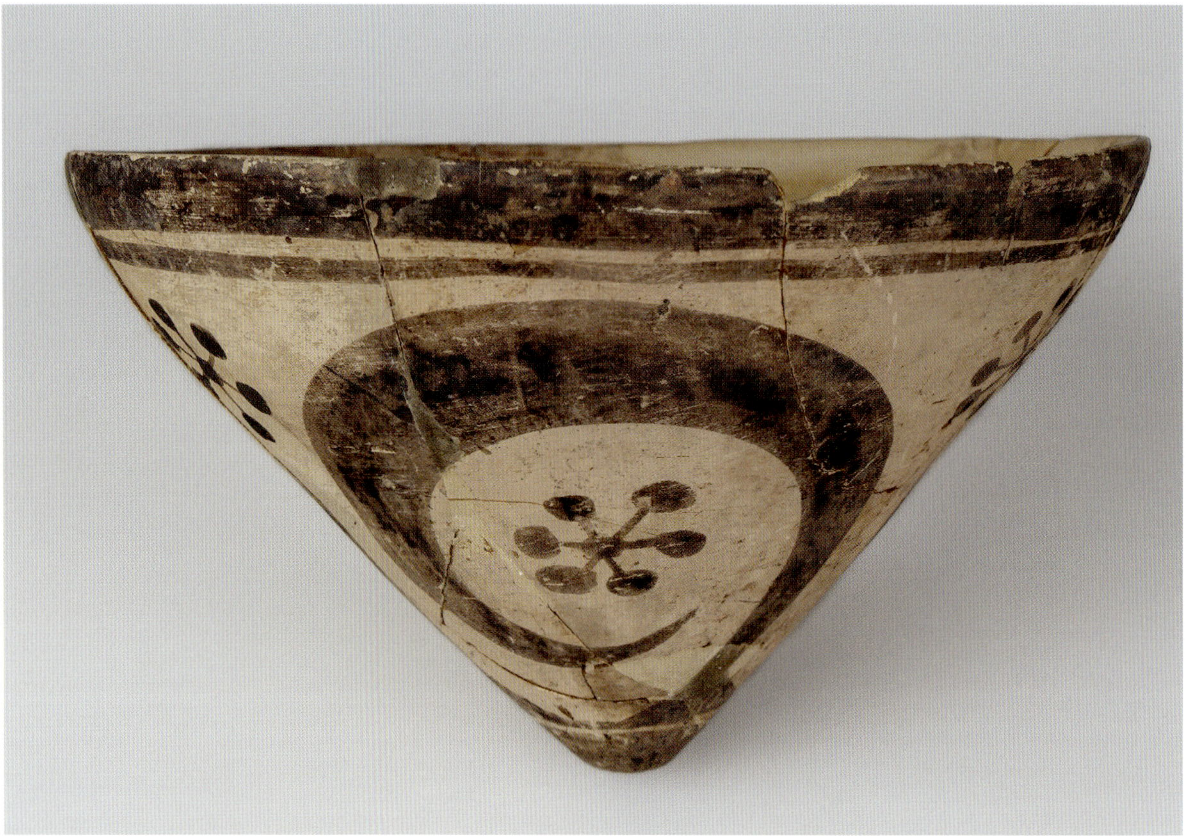

28. Conical Cup

Baked clay, paint
Iran, Tall-e Bakun A
Bakun A period (ca. 4400–4000 BCE)
Excavated in 1932–1934
ISACM A20117

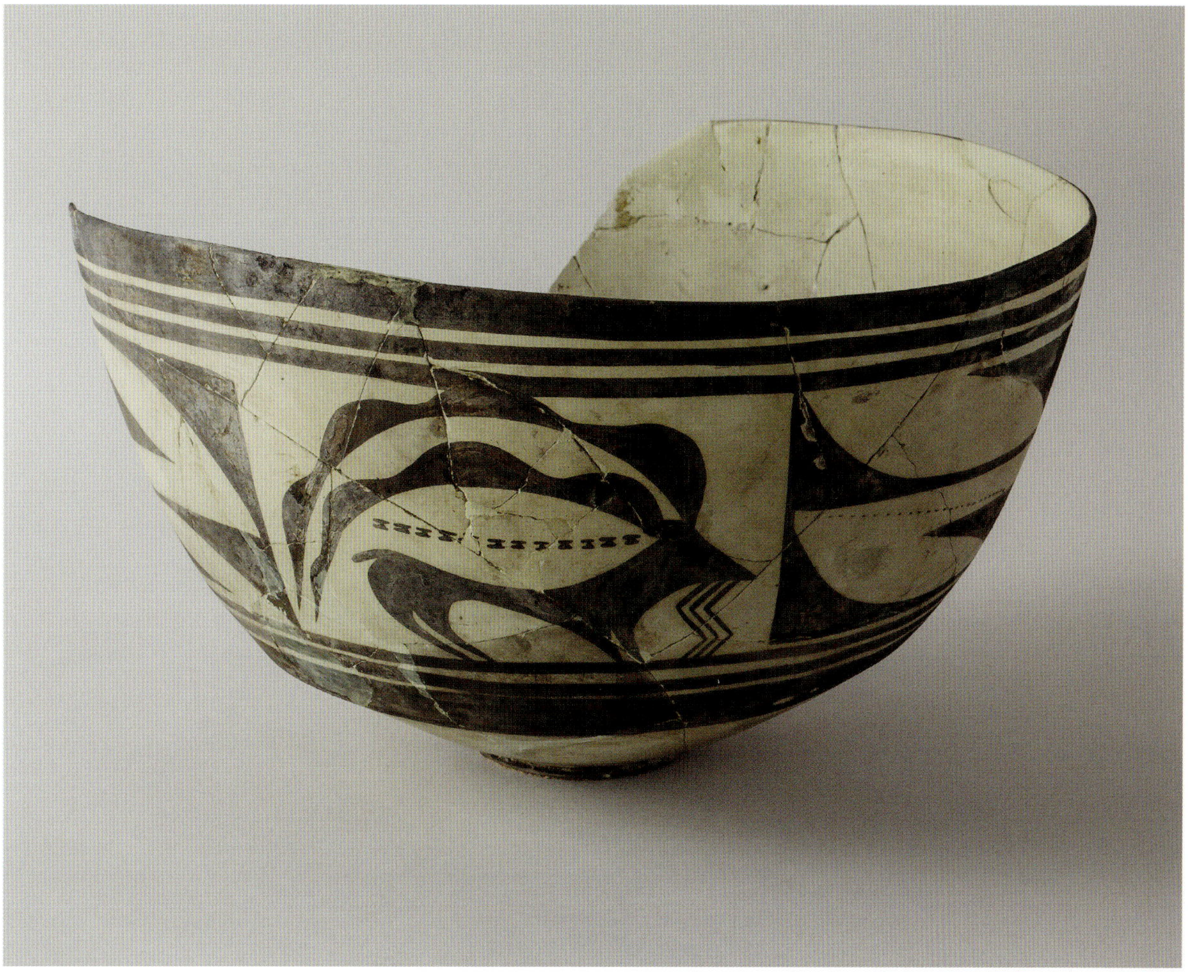

29. Fragmentary Bowl

Baked clay, paint

Iran, Tall-e Bakun A

Bakun A period (ca. 4400–4000 BCE)

Excavated in 1932–1934

ISACM A20217

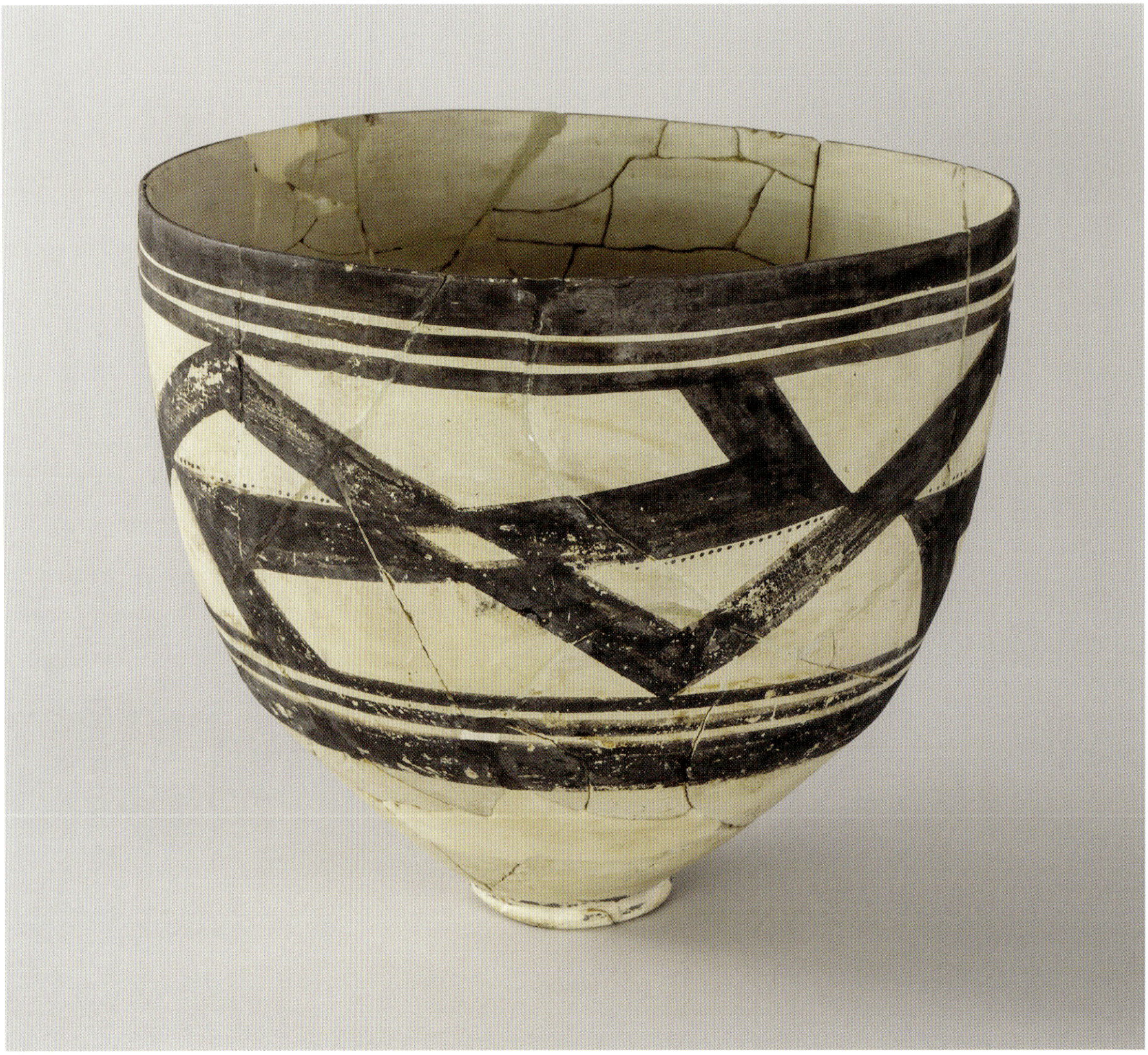

30. Bowl

Baked clay, paint

Iran, Tall-e Bakun A

Bakun A period (ca. 4400–4000 BCE)

Excavated in 1932–1934

ISACM A20218

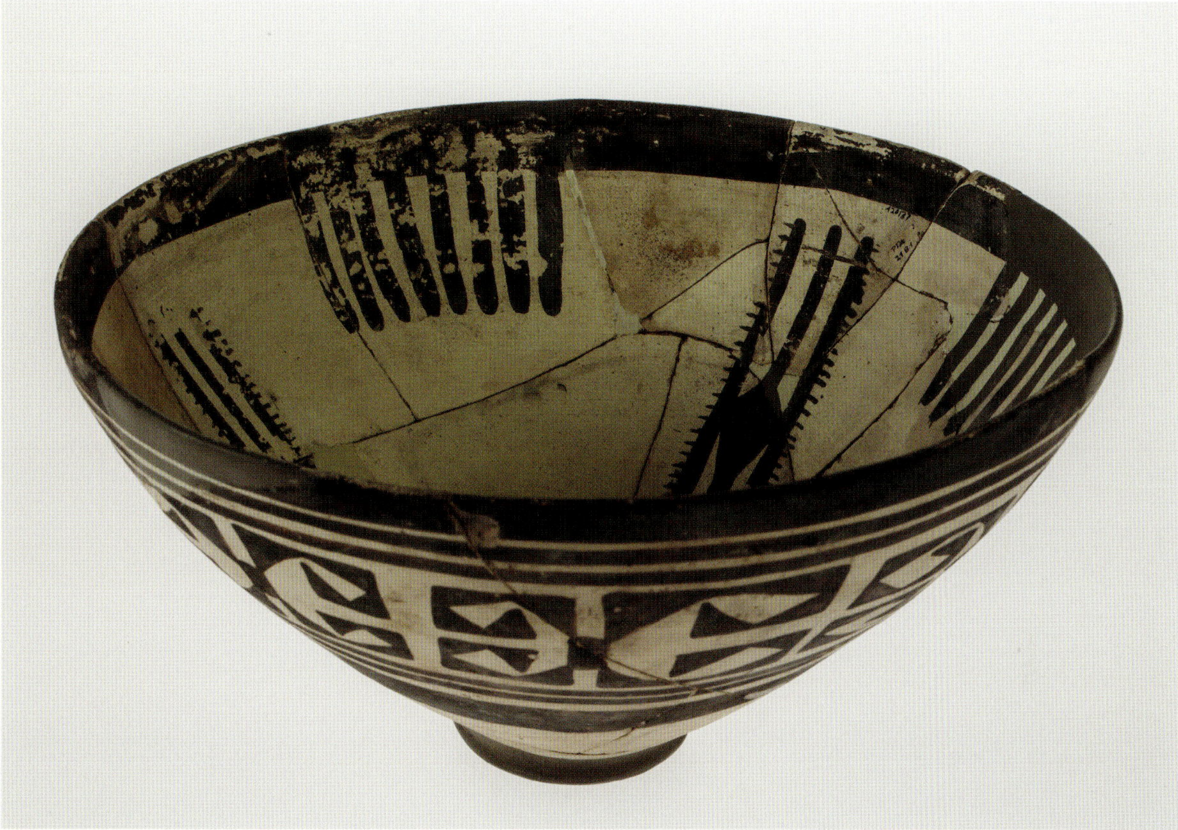

31. Bowl

Baked clay, paint
Iran, Tall-e Bakun A
Bakun A period (ca. 4400–4000 BCE)
Excavated in 1932–1934
ISACM A20137

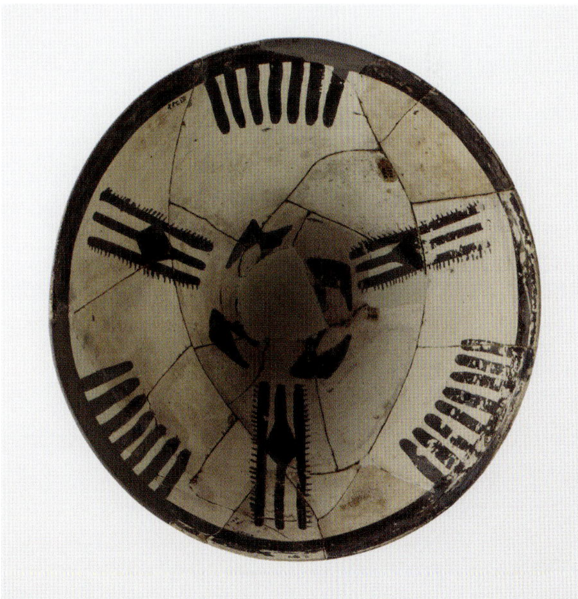

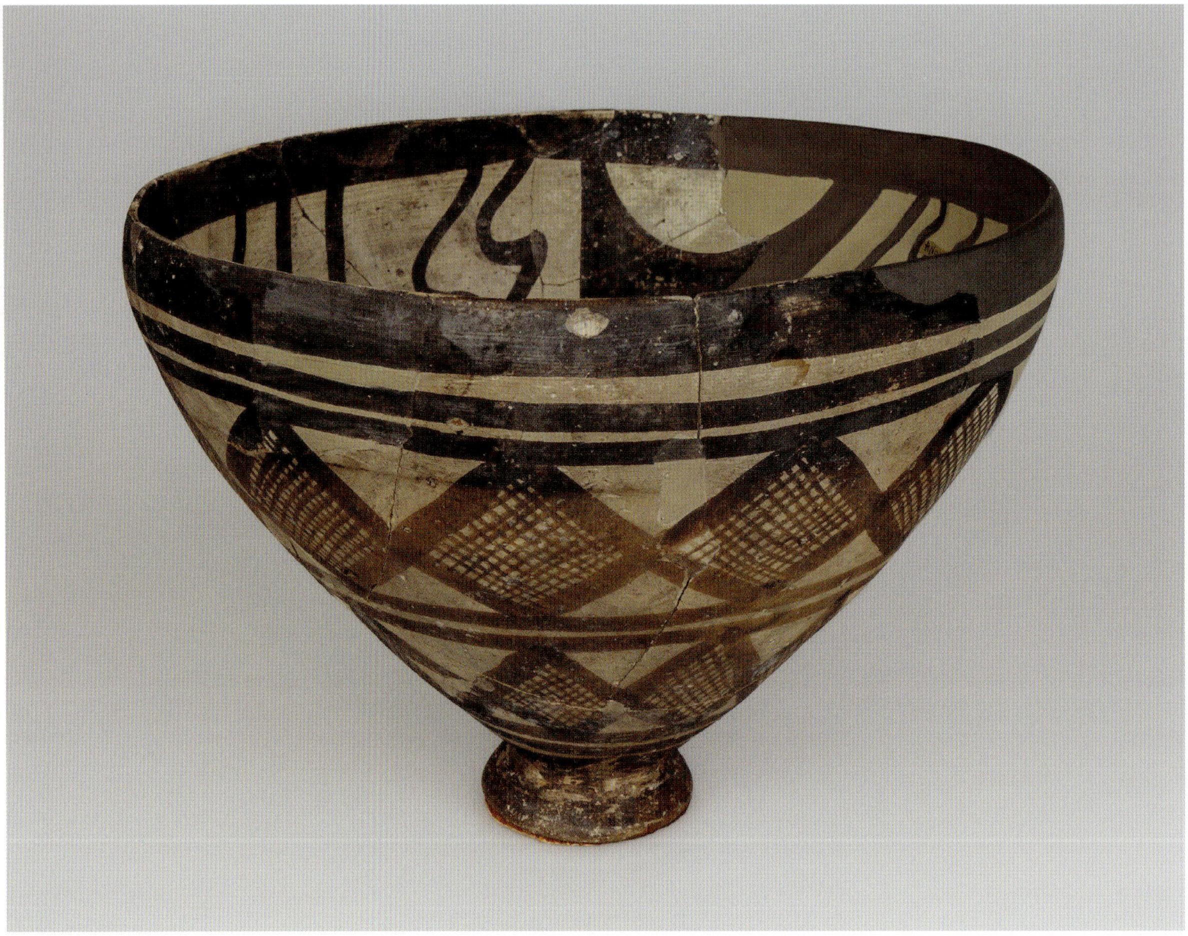

32. Bowl

Baked clay, paint
Iran, Tall-e Bakun A
Bakun A period (ca. 4400–4000 BCE)
Excavated in 1932–1934
ISACM A20114

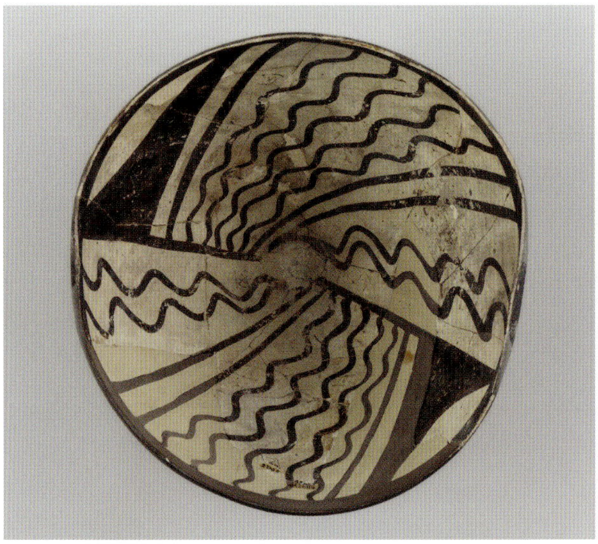

Human Figurines

Figurines appeared at the settlement of Tall-e Bakun A some two hundred years after the initial occupation of the site. The variety of human figurines, primarily female, is remarkable. Most of them are made of baked clay, and almost all of them are decorated with black and dark-brown paint (**cat. nos. 33–36**). The painted patterns on the bodies and faces most likely indicate tattoos, locks of hair, personal ornaments, and pubic hair. The point of breakage in some examples suggests that arms and legs were made separately. The body is primarily cylindrical, with wing-like projections serving as arms; in many cases, legs are simplified to a tapering cylinder with a flat base, as in the examples shown here. In a few cases, such as **cat. no. 35**, the legs are articulated but joined at the ankle to form the flat base. This technical feature suggests that such figurines were meant to be viewed standing on their feet.

Most of the figurines have elongated heads with coffee bean–shaped eyes, as shown in the line drawings of **cat. no. 33**. Although such figurines are also common in southern Mesopotamia, Tall-e Bakun A is the only site in Iran where these figurines have been found. In almost all the extant examples, the heads or legs—or both—are broken, perhaps ritualistically.

The front of **cat. no. 36**, an elaborately decorated figurine, is embellished with abstract sun circles, wavy lines, and a row of chevrons. The back shows three flowing locks of hair and two sets of superimposed "hills."

The type of orange-reddish female clay figurine represented by **cat. no. 37** has an hourglass-shaped body that merges into a stick-like head without a neck. The nose is indicated by a small ridge, and what seem to be the eyes extend outward from each side of the nose. Pubic hair is indicated by a triangular area with punctations.

Cat. nos. 38 and **39** are extraordinary examples of naturalistically modeled figurines unique in prehistoric Southwest Asia. One represents a male, the other a female. The heads are missing. Both specimens are well proportioned, and anatomical details are clearly and naturalistically rendered. Although they were found in different areas of the site, their similar size, material, decoration, and modeling suggest that they originally formed a pair, perhaps representing a high-status couple, ancestors, or deities.

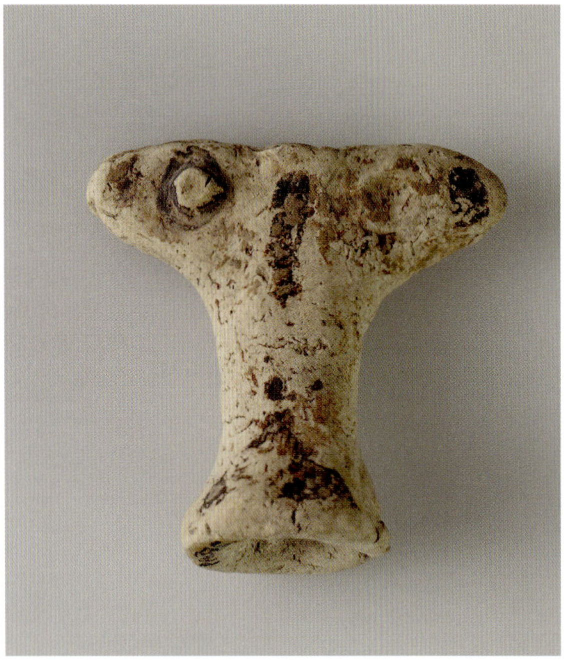

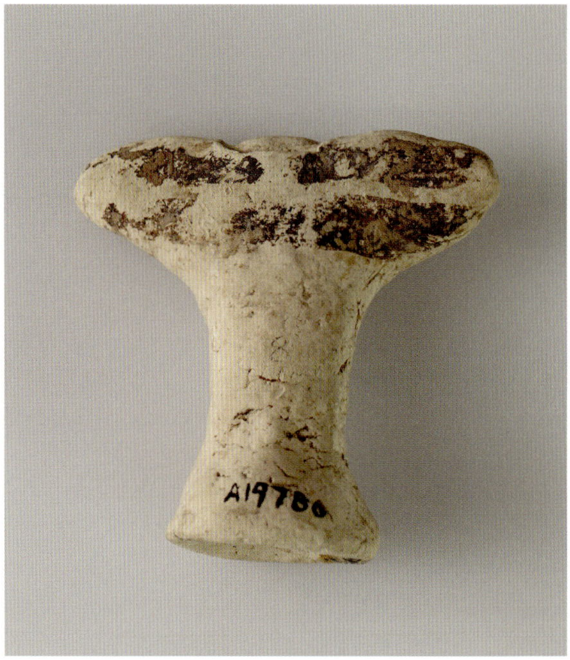

33. Human Figurine

Baked clay

Iran, Tall-e Bakun A

Bakun A period (ca. 4400–4000 BCE)

Excavated in 1932–1934

ISACM A19780

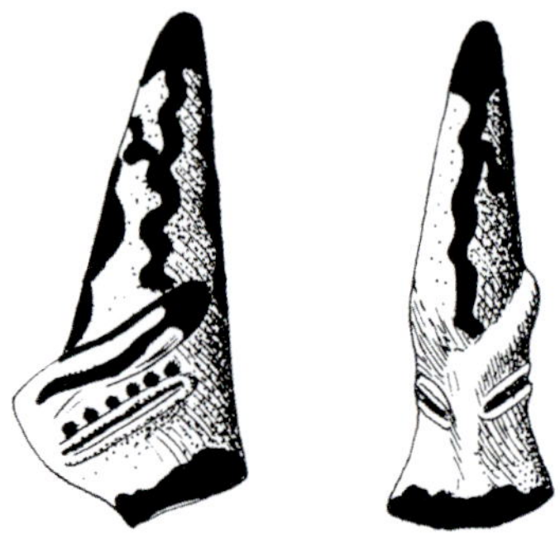

Reconstructed head of human figurine. Drawings by A. Alizadeh.

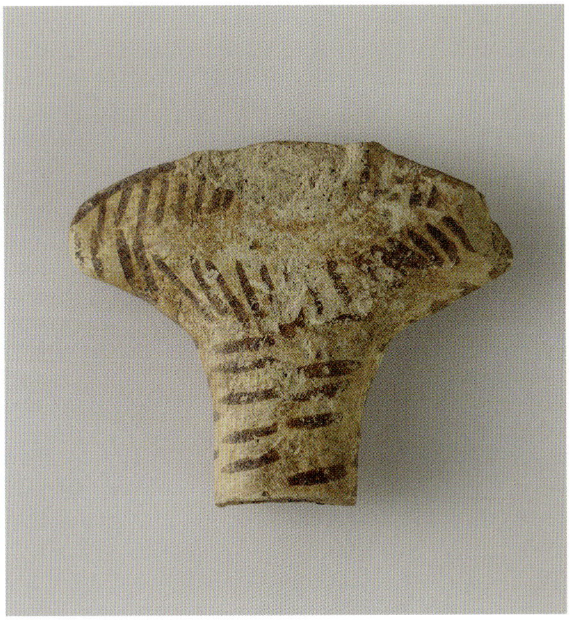

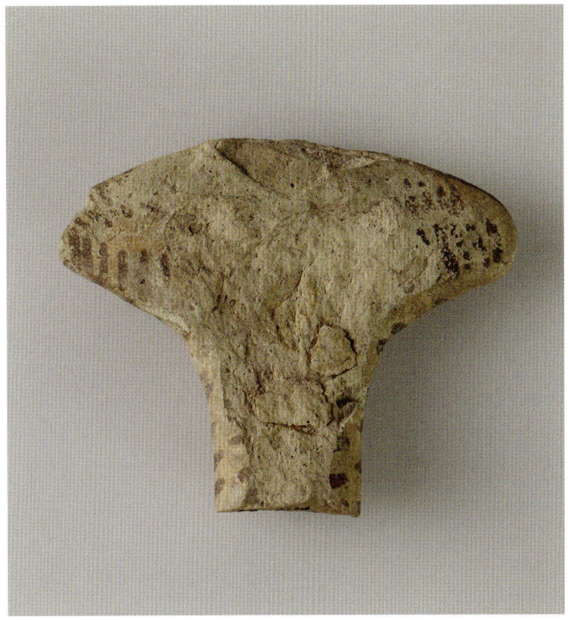

34. Human Figurine

Baked clay

Iran, Tall-e Bakun A

Bakun A period (ca. 4400–4000 BCE)

Excavated in 1932–1934

ISACM A19781

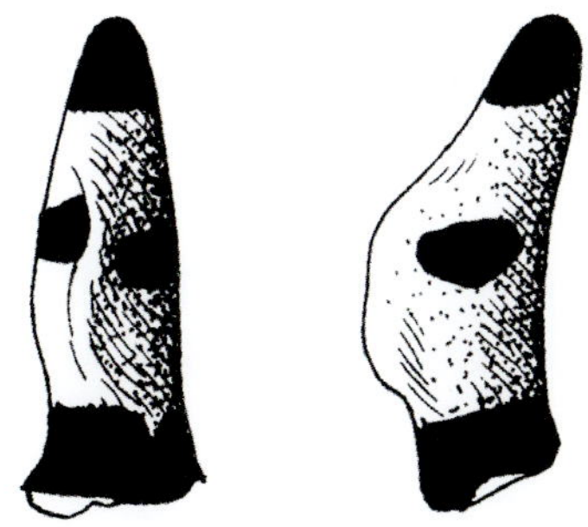

Reconstructed head of human figurine. Drawings by A. Alizadeh.

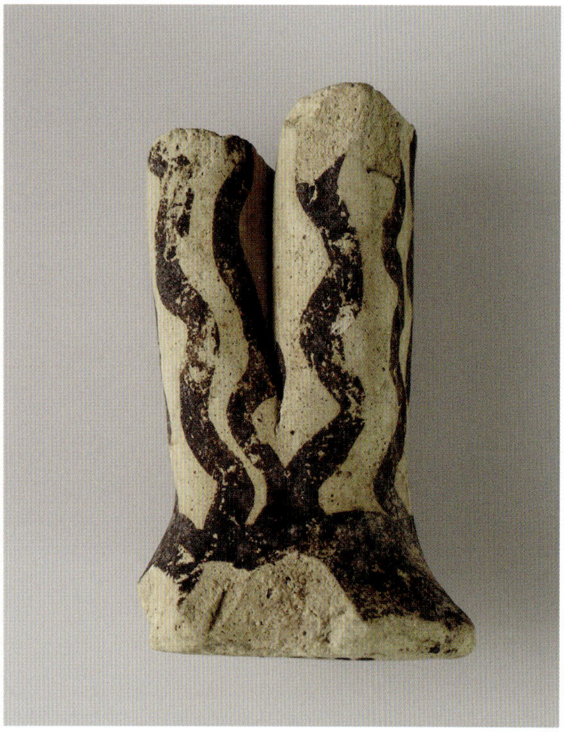

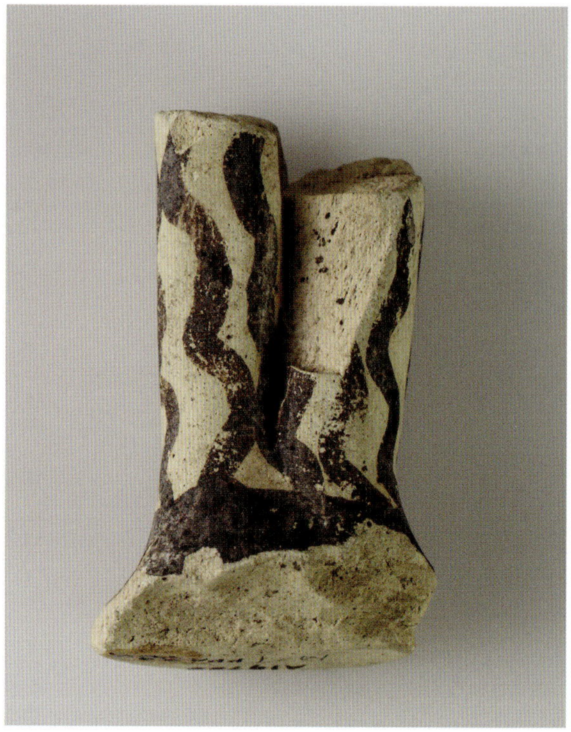

35. Human Figurine

Baked clay

Iran, Tall-e Bakun A

Bakun A period (ca. 4400–4000 BCE)

Excavated in 1932–1934

ISACM A19783

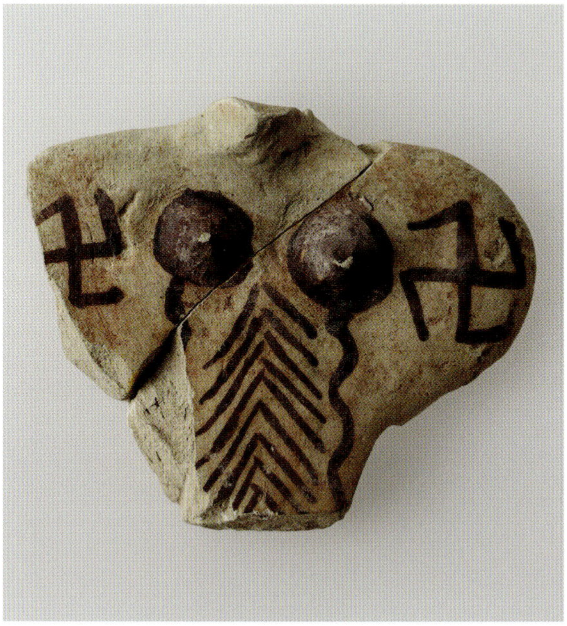

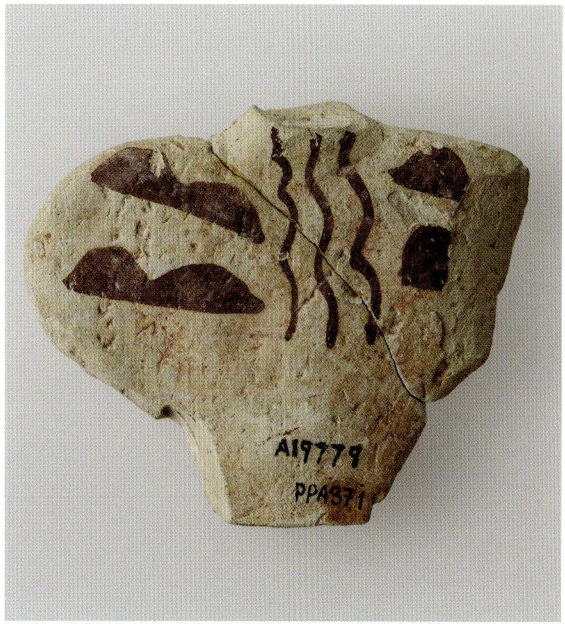

36. Human Figurine

Baked clay

Iran, Tall-e Bakun A

Bakun A period (ca. 4400–4000 BCE)

Excavated in 1932–1934

ISACM A19779

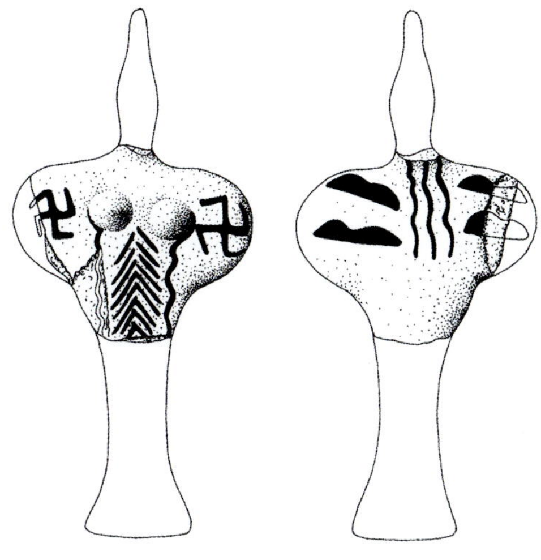

Drawings of ISACM A19779 by A. Alizadeh.

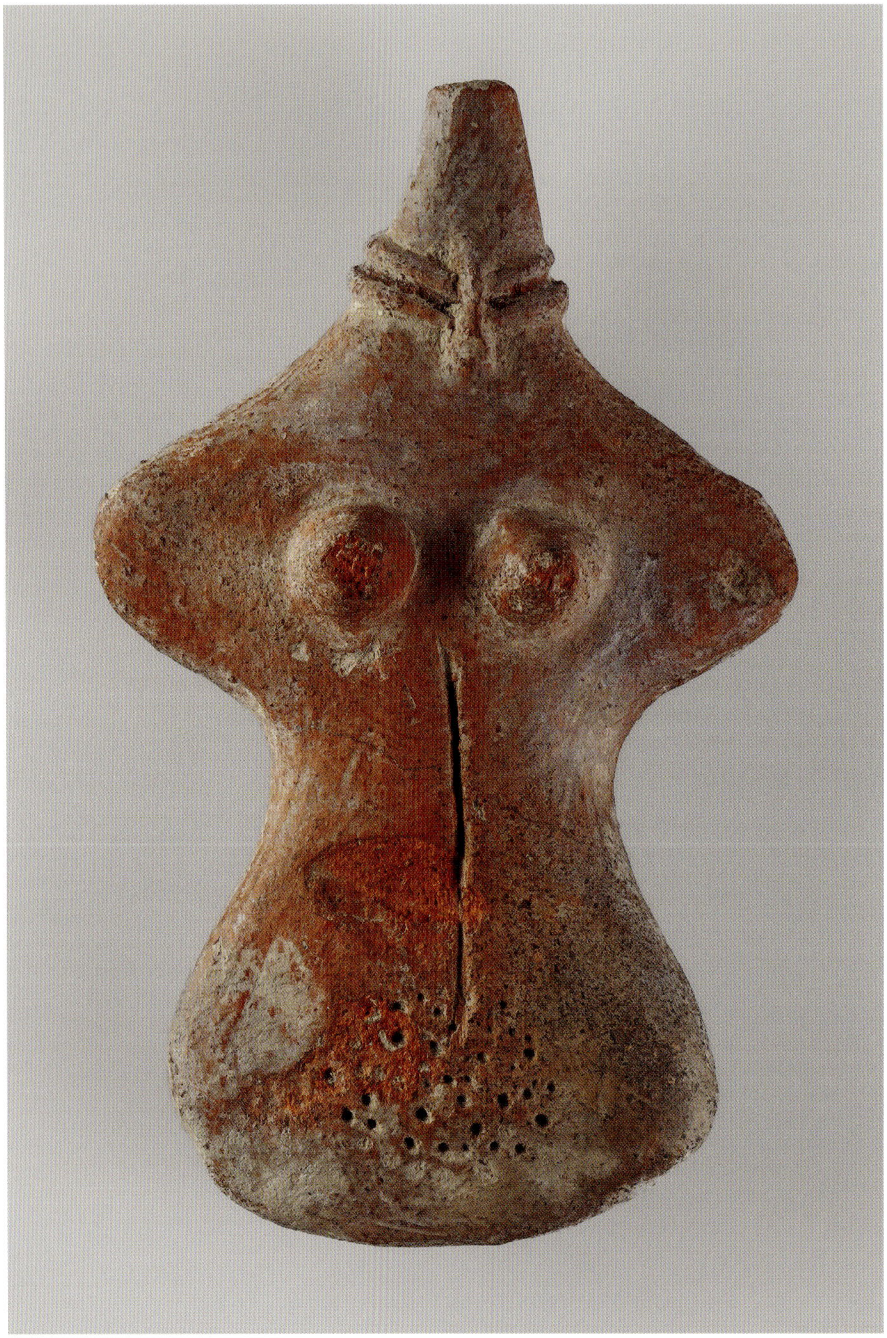

37. Human Figurine

Baked clay

Iran, Tall-e Bakun A

Bakun A period (ca. 4400–4000 BCE)

Excavated in 1932–1934

ISACM A19786

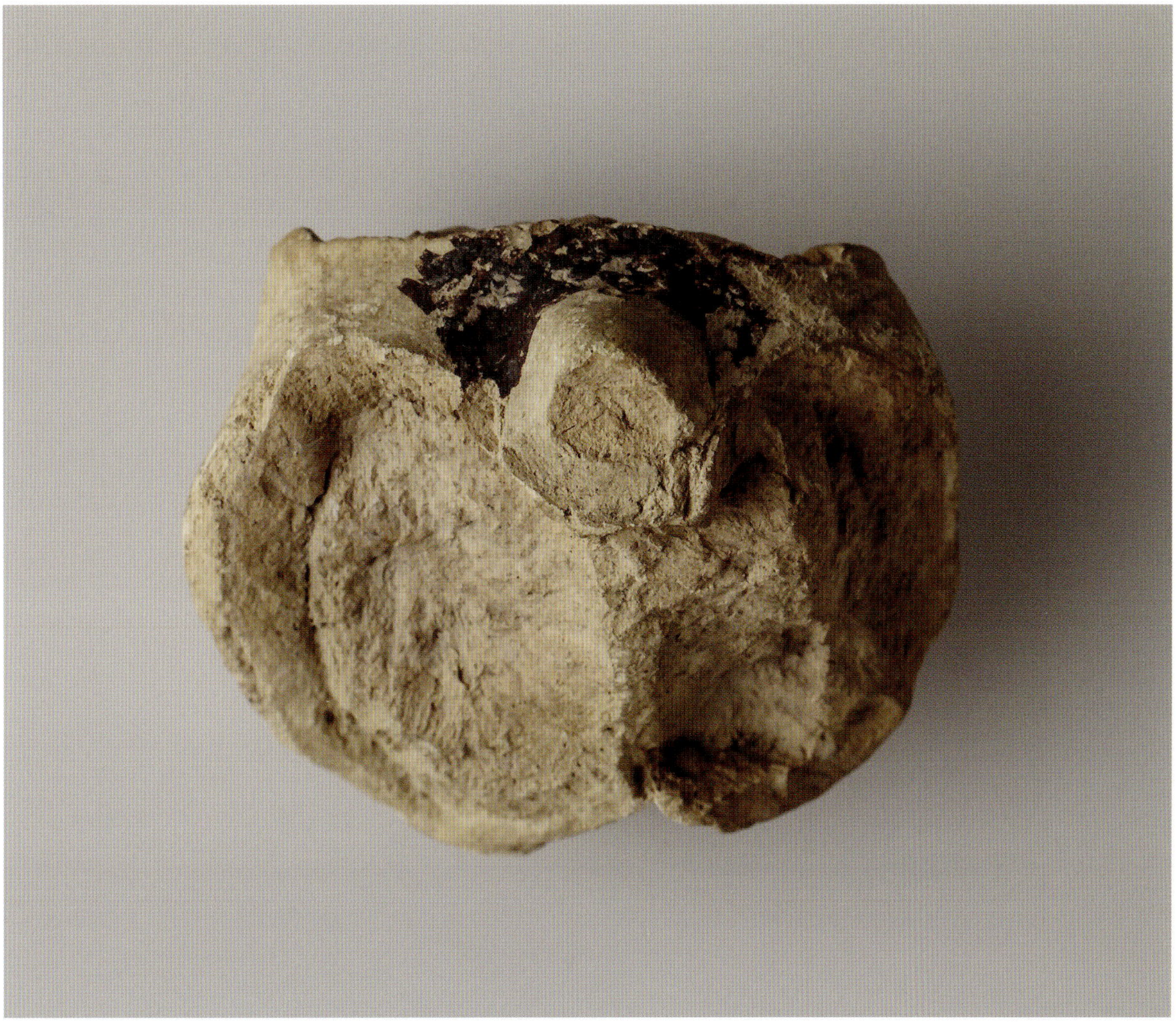

38. Seated Human Figurine

Baked clay
Iran, Tall-e Bakun A
Bakun A period (ca. 4400–4000 BCE)
Excavated in 1932–1934
ISACM A19784

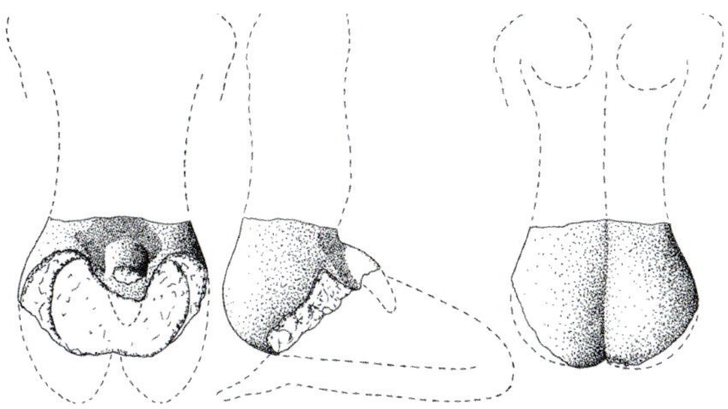

Reconstructed figurine. Drawings by A. Alizadeh.

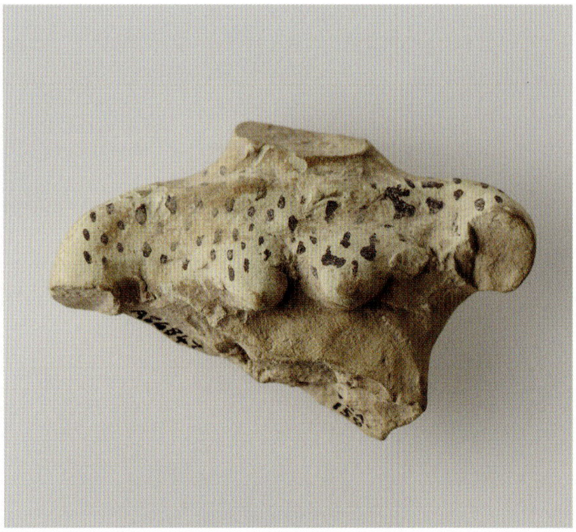

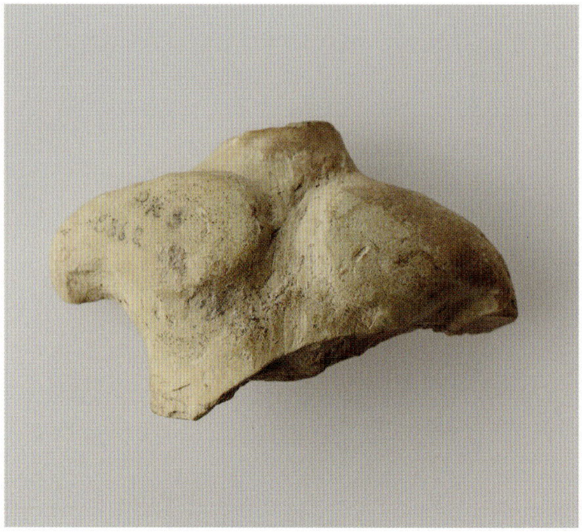

39. Seated Human Figurine

Baked clay

Iran, Tall-e Bakun A

Bakun A period (ca. 4400–4000 BCE)

Excavated in 1937

ISACM A24847

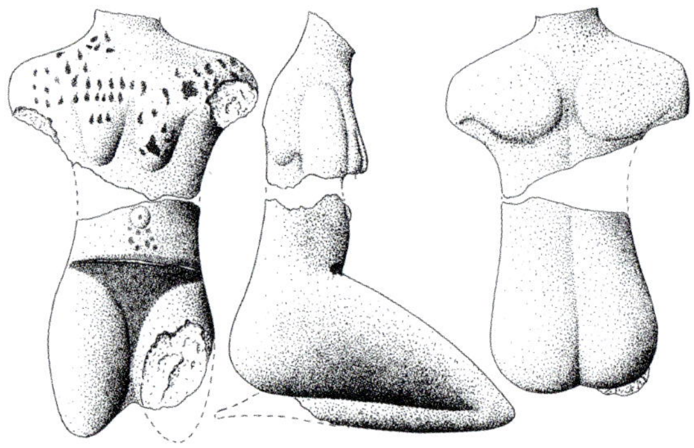

Reconstructed figurine. Drawings by A. Alizadeh.

Metallurgy

Small copper objects such as needles, rings, and pins formed by cold hammering appear, though rarely, in some early Neolithic villages in Iran, including Bakun. But cast-copper objects do not appear in the archaeological record until the late fifth and early fourth millennia BCE.

Many pins, chisels, blades, needles, and hooks were manufactured in the early stages of the settlement at Bakun (fig. 4.5). But **cat. nos. 40** and **41**—a large copper dagger and a complex copper stamp seal—are unique for late prehistoric times, since it was not until the early third millennium BCE that such daggers and objects—made primarily of bronze—were manufactured. The dagger (**cat. no. 40**) is furnished with a low ridge that runs its entire length. Such an impressive object must have belonged to an important and wealthy member of Bakun society.

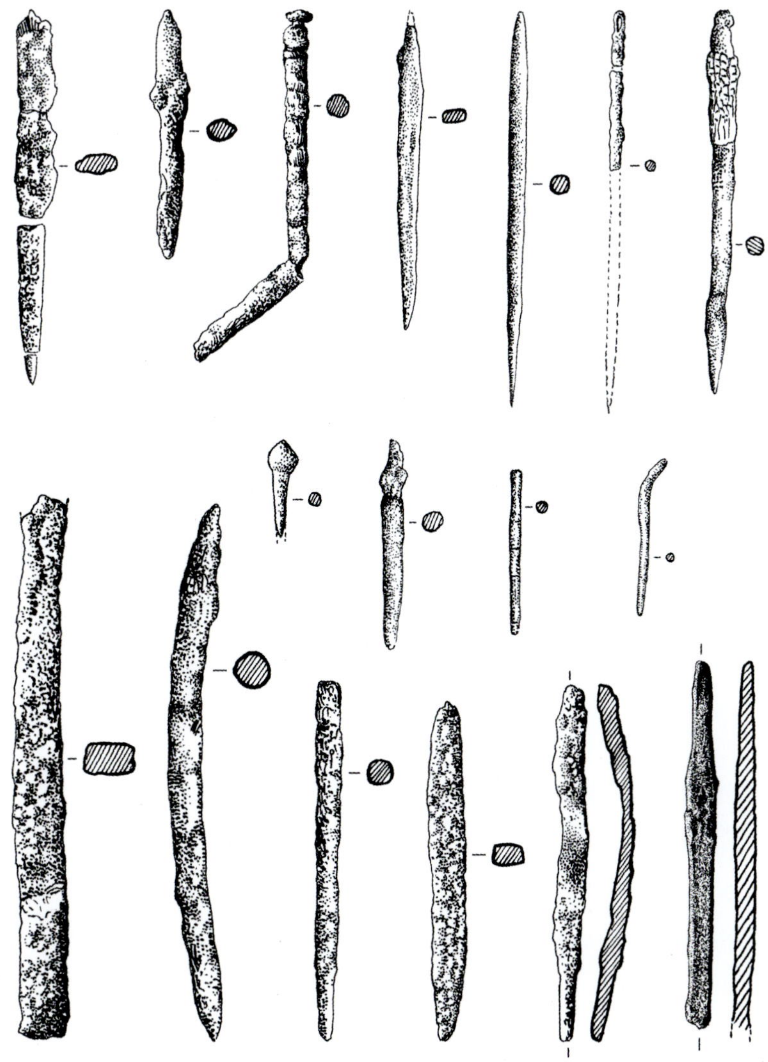

Figure 4.5. Various copper tools from Tall-e Bakun A. Drawings by A. Alizadeh.

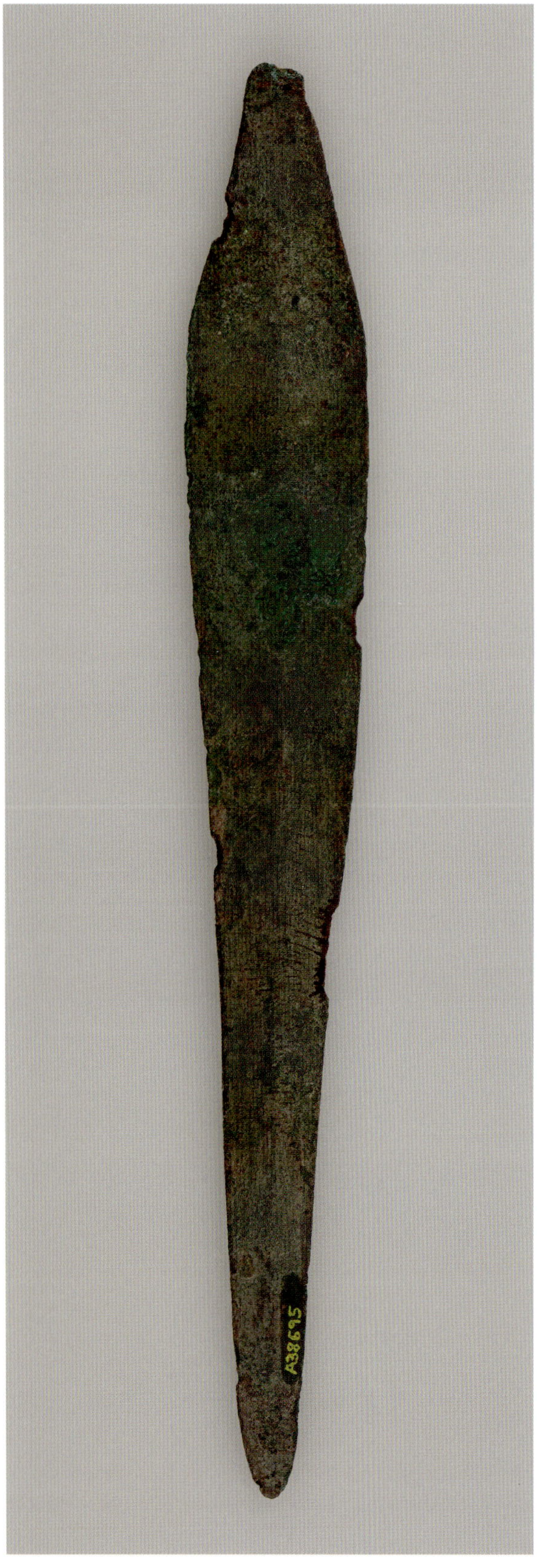

40. Dagger

Copper alloy

Iran, Tall-e Bakun A

Bakun A period (ca. 4400–4000 BCE)

Excavated in 1932–1934

ISACM A38695

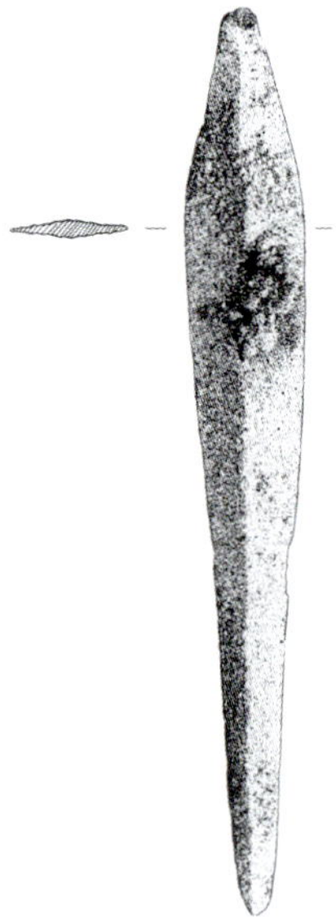

Drawing after Schmidt 1939, fig. 92.

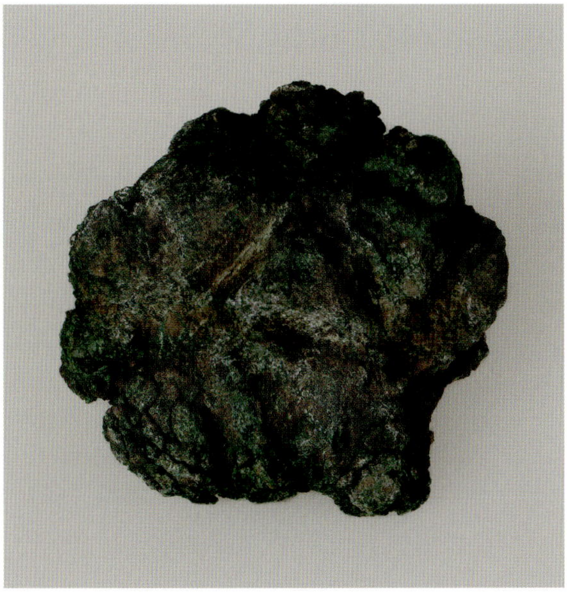

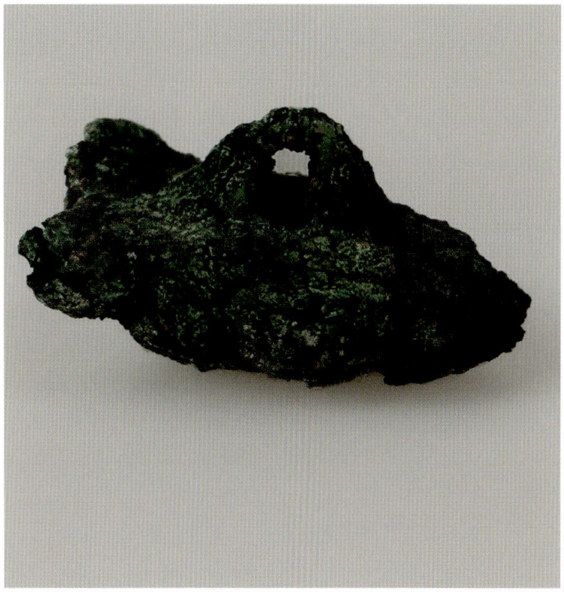

41. Copper Stamp Seal

Copper alloy

Iran, Tall-e Bakun A

Bakun A period (ca. 4400–4000 BCE)

Excavated in 1932–1934

ISACM A38694

Administrative Technology: Door Sealings

The earliest examples of door sealings discovered to date come from Tall-e Bakun A (**cat. no. 42**). Door sealings are conically shaped lumps of clay impressed with a stamp or cylinder seal; these cone-shaped clay lumps have a flattish base and originally covered a string that was attached to the door of a warehouse and wrapped around a wooden peg located next to the door (fig. 4.6). When the door was opened, the sealing was broken. This feature of administrative technology was invented at Bakun, spread throughout the ancient Near East, and remained in use well past the Neo-Assyrian and Achaemenid periods.

Only authorized persons could break the sealing and enter the warehouse to withdraw or deposit goods. Since each seal represented an individual or an office, the broken sealings were kept as a record of who entered the warehouse and resealed the door.

The use of door sealings is perhaps the most important clue to the level of socioeconomic complexity in a given prehistoric society. The practice goes beyond a mere means of control over personal property and storage, since a lump of clay is obviously no deterrent against unauthorized entry; rather, it is the attending political sanction that underlies its administrative importance. Door sealings, therefore, may be taken as the earliest tangible evidence of a socioeconomically hierarchical society.

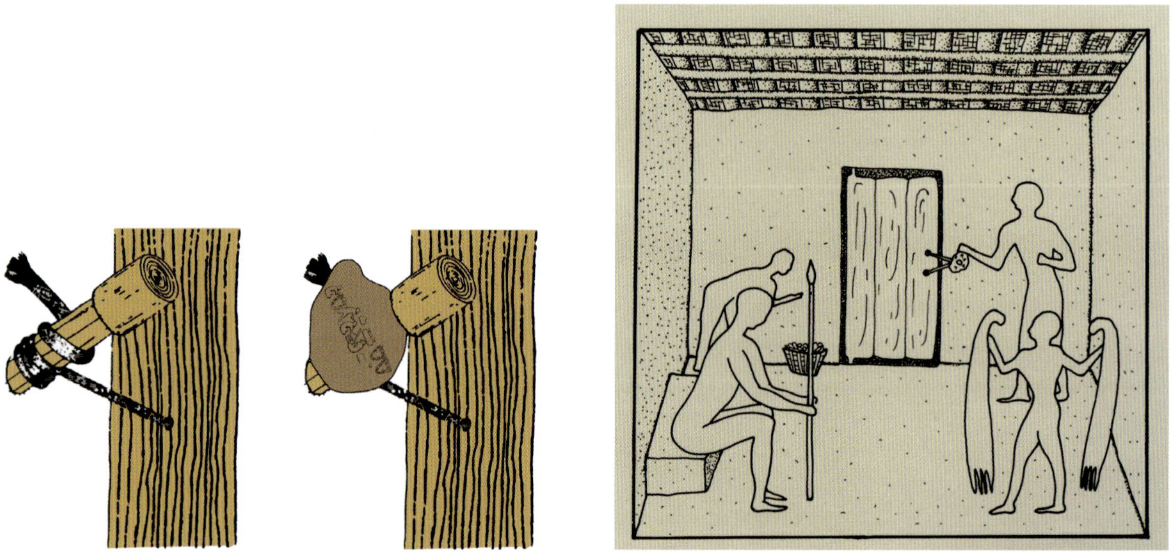

Figure 4.6. Left: Reconstruction of a door sealing. Right: The process of sealing a warehouse door, based on later historical examples. Drawings by A. Alizadeh.

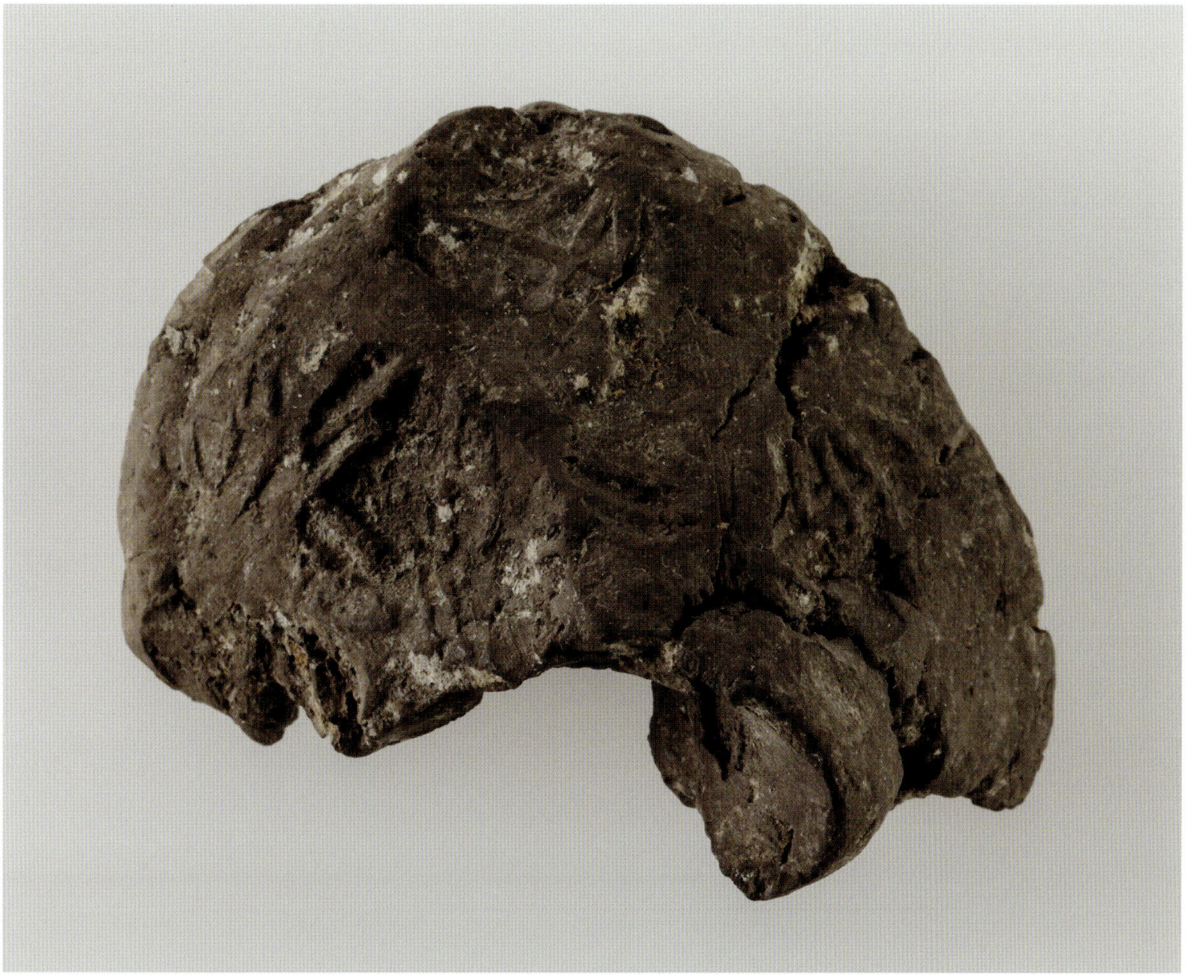

42. Door Sealing

Clay

Iran, Tall-e Bakun A

Bakun A period (ca. 4400–4000 BCE)

Excavated in 1932–1934

ISACM A20242

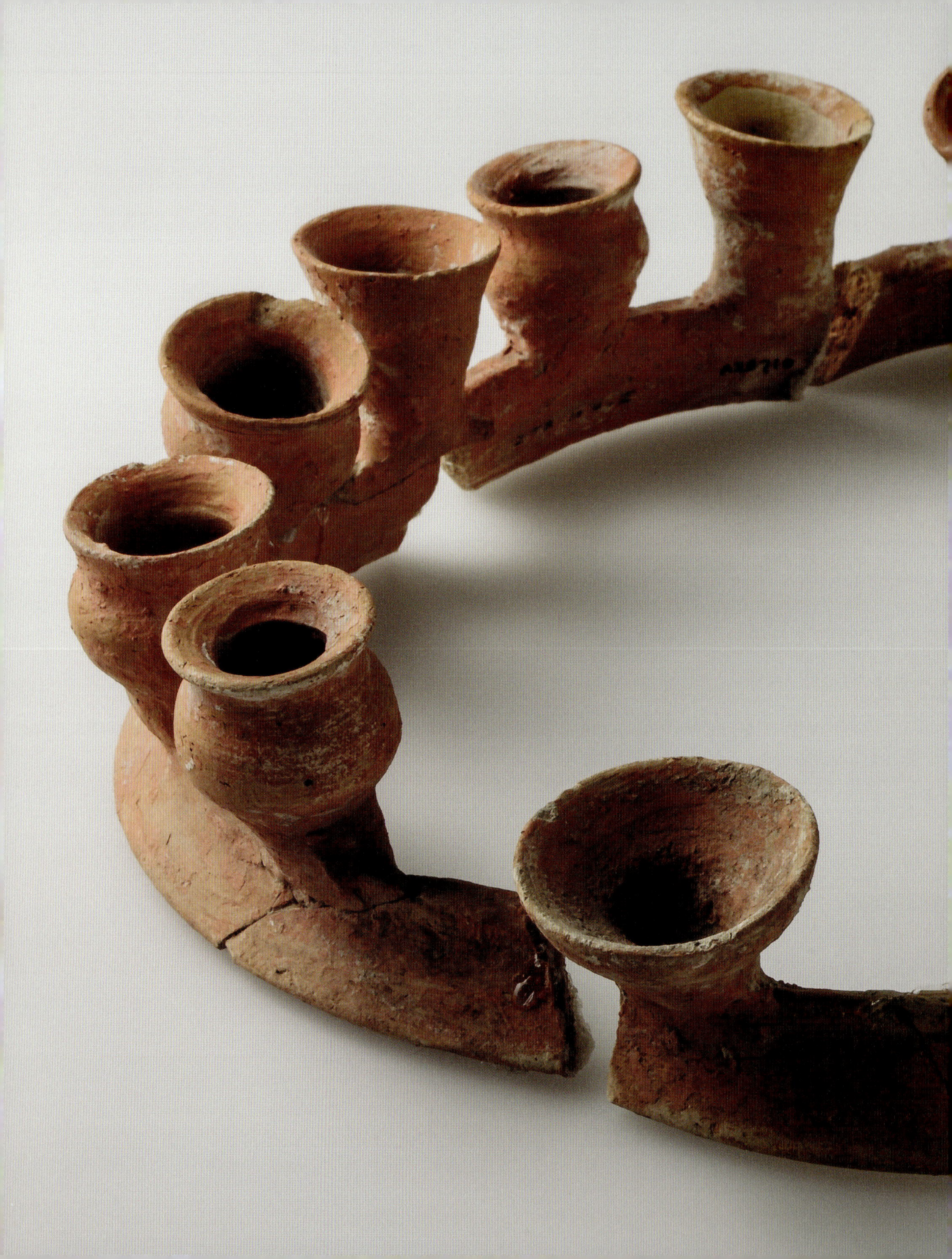

5 Tall-e Geser

Tall-e Geser (formerly Ghazir) is a major settlement in the Ram Hormuz plain in southeastern Khuzestan, ancient Susiana (fig. 5.1). Excavated by ISAC in 1949 and 1950, the site was occupied in about 4500 BCE and, apart from some short periods of abandonment, remained occupied for several millennia. Of all the periods attested at the site, the Proto-Elamite period, extending from about 3100 to 2600 BCE, proved the most interesting. This period is best known at Susa in lowland Susiana and at Malyan (ancient Anshan) in Fars. These two major Elamite centers served as a lowland–highland dual center of power that endured throughout much of Elamite history.

In the past three decades, numerous excavations, discoveries, and analyses have helped produce a sharper image of the culture and civilization we now know as Proto-Elamite. Today we can define Proto-Elamite as a period of high artistic creativity in sculpture and glyptic art, as well as a period of economic and social interaction between spheres that shared a material culture which included an outstanding class of mono- and polychrome painted pottery; sculptures; stone vessels; numerical, pictographic, and logographic administrative tablets; specific glyptic styles; architectural plans; and building techniques.

Sometime early in the third millennium, perhaps around 2800 BCE, the vast Proto-Elamite sphere of interaction collapsed, the colonies and nodes of interregional communication were abandoned, and Susiana itself came under the cultural and perhaps political influence of southern Mesopotamia.

Baked-clay kernos ring from Tall-e Geser, Iran. **Cat. no. 48**.

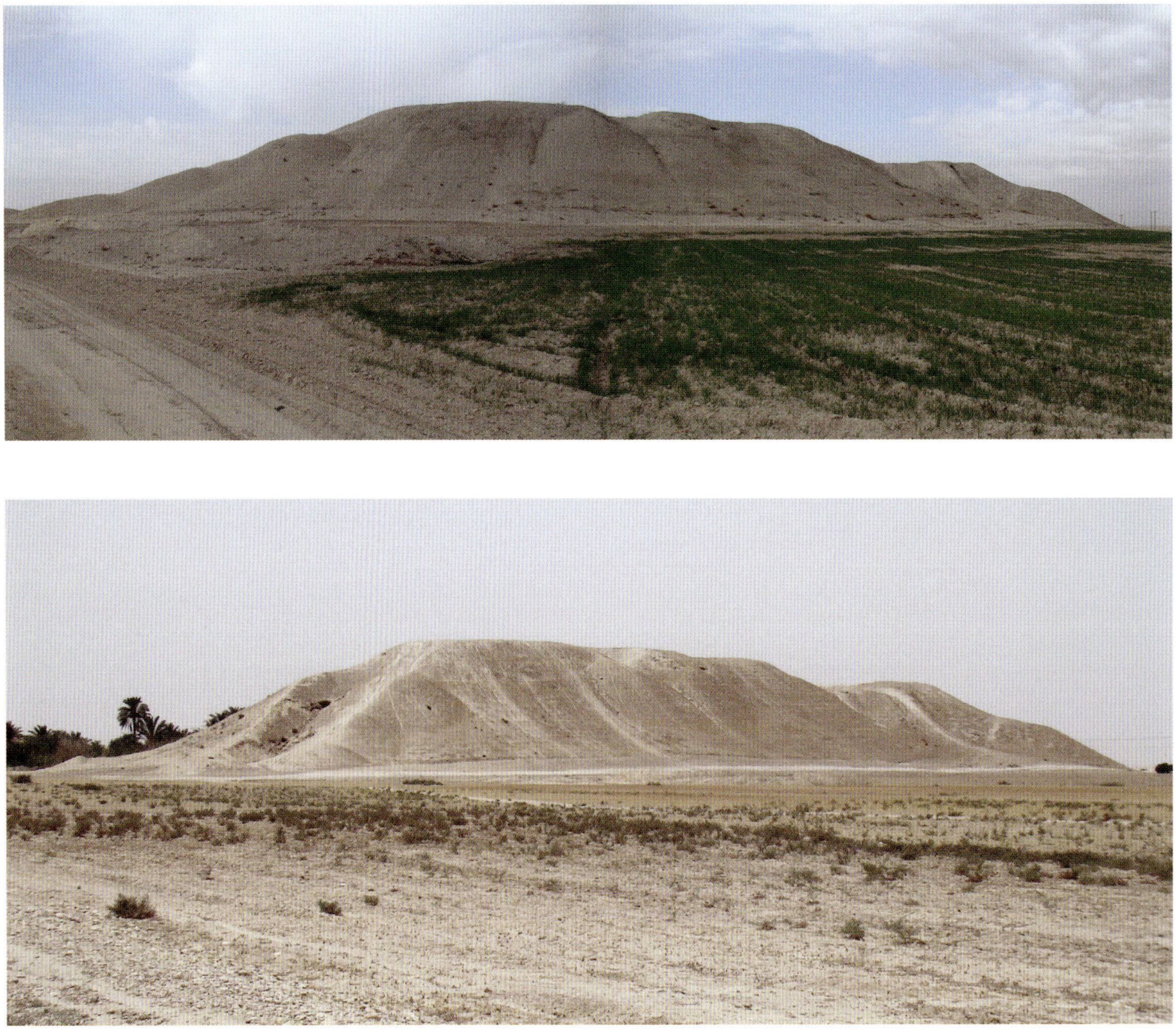

Figure 5.1. Two views of Tall-e Geser. Photos by A. Alizadeh.

Stone Weights

Some archaeologists refer to objects similar to **cat. no. 43** as *mace-heads* or *loom weights*. Clearly, however, such objects did not serve as part of a mace, because their flat bases make it impossible to mount them effectively on a handle. And loom weights are usually found in large numbers in archaeological contexts and lack definite shapes. A piece of rock or a lump of clay could serve quite adequately as a loom weight, so no one would have invested effort in carving specific shapes and sizes for such a mundane use. It is likelier that these objects served as weights for a scale (fig. 5.2).

In Iran, such stone weights have been found at Susa, Chogha Mish, Abu Fanduweh, and Tall-e Geser. Outside Iran, they have been reported from Uruk and Jemdet Nasr in Iraq, Habuba Kabira in Syria, and Hacinebi in Anatolia. All published examples show two distinct sizes: the widest diameter of one group ranges from 7.8 to 8.3 centimeters and that of the other group from 9.7 to more than 10 centimeters. Since the objects are handcrafted, slight variations in size and weight within each group are to be expected. **Cat. no. 43** weighs 906 grams (about 2 pounds). Considering that such weights have been found at sites with strong connections to Susiana and Uruk and that they are identical in shape, we may conclude that weights were standardized to facilitate economic interactions.

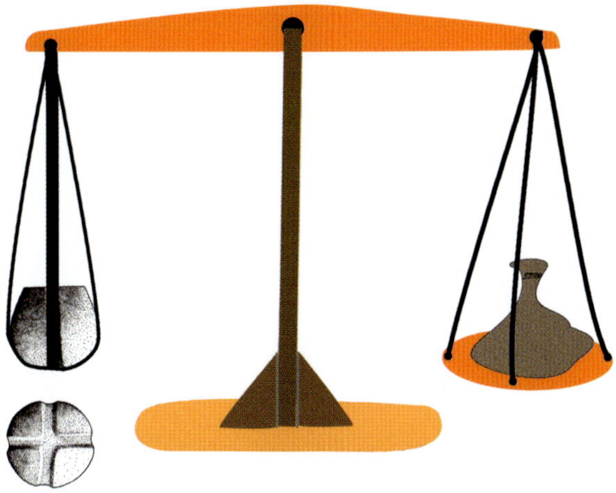

Figure 5.2. Hypothetical reconstruction of an ancient scale. Drawing by A. Alizadeh and L. Ahmadzadeh.

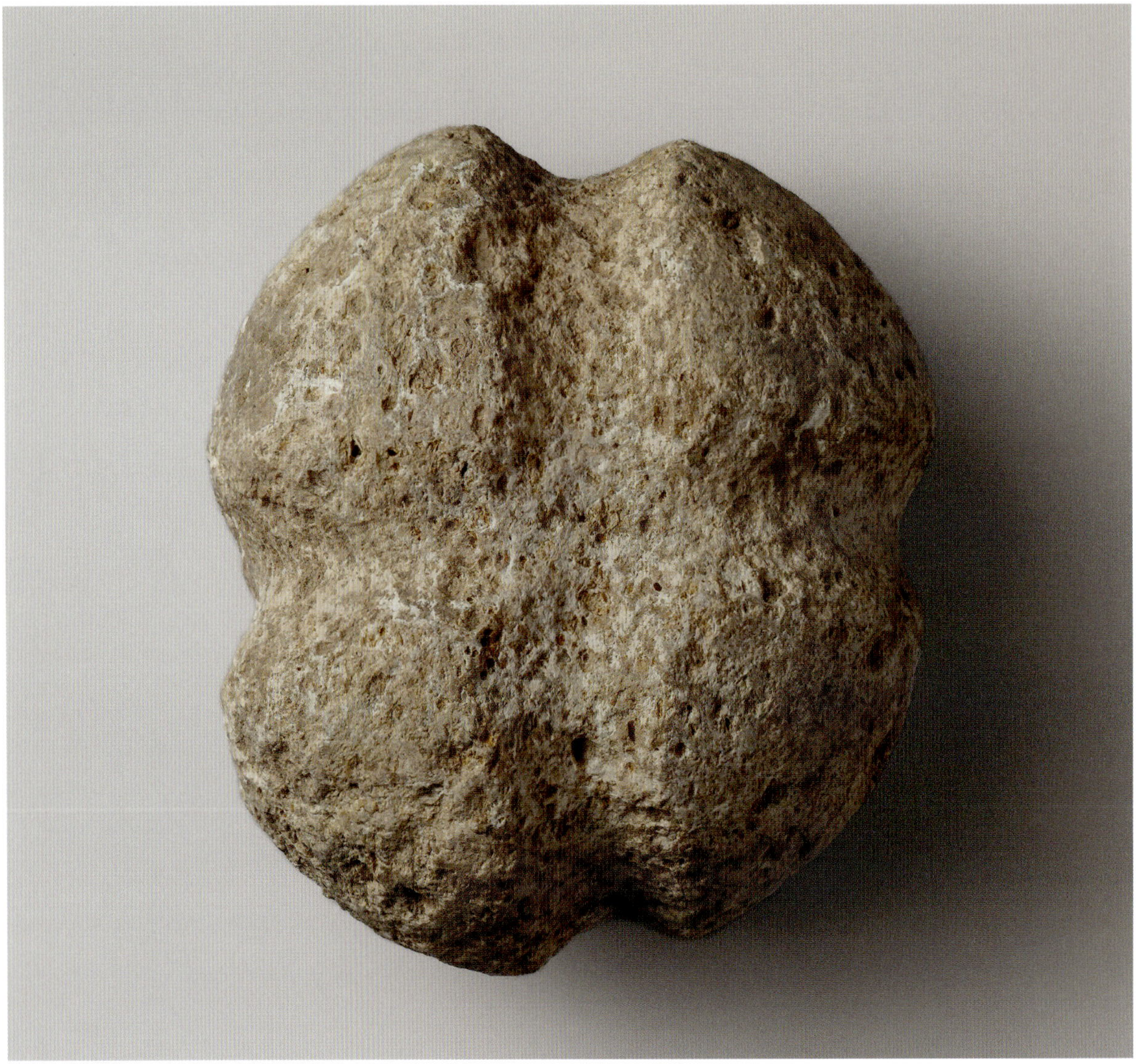

43. Stone Weight

Stone

Iran, Tall-e Geser

Proto-Elamite period (ca. 3100–2600 BCE)

Excavated in 1947–1948

ISACM A27931

Ceramics

The most characteristic feature of the Proto-Elamite ceramic phase is its surface treatment. The pottery is wheel made and, in many cases, tempered with fine chaff. Prominent forms include four-lugged jars, usually with sharp carination and one or two ridges on the shoulder (**cat. nos. 44** and **45**); spouted vessels; cylindrical and bottle forms with or without nose lugs; low- and high-pedestaled goblets; bell-shaped or flaring carinated bowls; both standard and tall, slender, beveled-rim bowls; and shallow trays. Proto-Elamite potters commonly applied at least two colors of wash to the exterior of the vessel; open forms received wash on both the interior and exterior surfaces. The washes range in color from bright red to maroon to light brown, dark brown, and sometimes even gray-brown (**cat. no. 45**). The wash was applied unevenly, and the vessel's surface often appears streaky. Apart from the colorful washes applied to the surface of the pottery, both open- and closed-vessel forms are frequently decorated with broad white, brown, maroon, or red bands or a combination of such bands with painted geometric shapes. No human, animal, or floral designs occur.

Glazed objects first appeared in the Middle Elamite period, around 1300 BCE. But glazed pottery vessels seem to have appeared during the Neo-Elamite period (ca. 1000–550 BCE). **Cat. no. 46** is a handled flask made of buff clay with an overall light greenish-gray glaze. The decorative continuous double zigzag was made by using a thicker glaze of the same color. **Cat. no. 47** is a cylindrical jar that originally had a flat lid, which would have been secured to the container through the pierced lugs. It is covered both inside and outside with a light greenish-gray glaze.

Kernos (pl. *kernoi*) is a Greek term for a pottery object with a round base with several small cups attached for holding offerings such as seeds, candles, cereals, oil, and the like. In ancient Greece, the kernos was used primarily in the cults of Demeter and Persephone. Unlike most known kernoi, which have a hollow, tubular base, the kernoi of Proto-Elamite Geser have a solid, circular, low band base (**cat. no. 48**). The ware and decoration are typical of Proto-Elamite pottery: pinkish buff ware with chaff inclusions and a thick, matte, flaky reddish-brown wash.

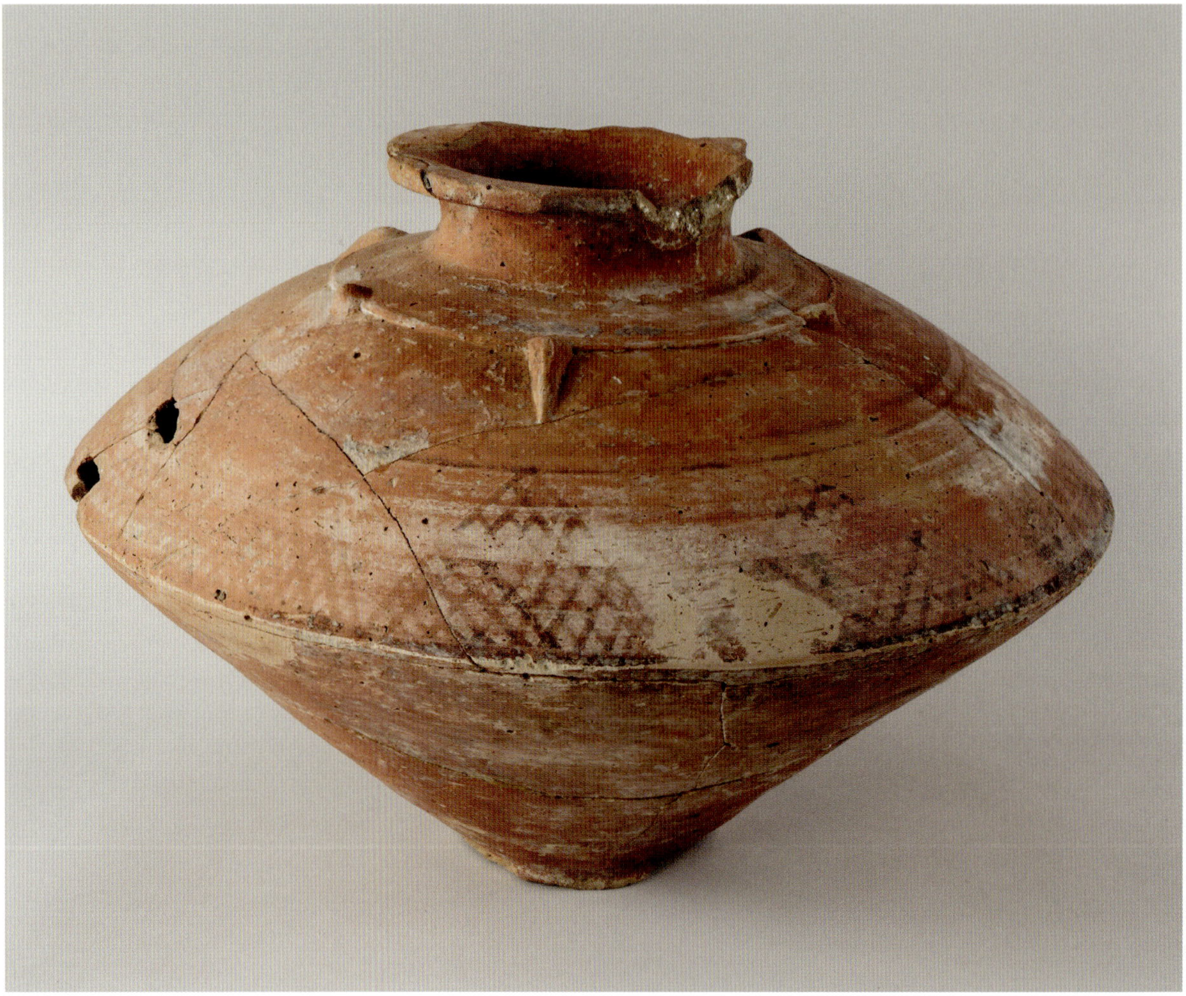

44. Jar

Baked clay

Iran, Tall-e Geser

Proto-Elamite period (ca. 3100–2600 BCE)

Excavated in 1949

ISACM A28726

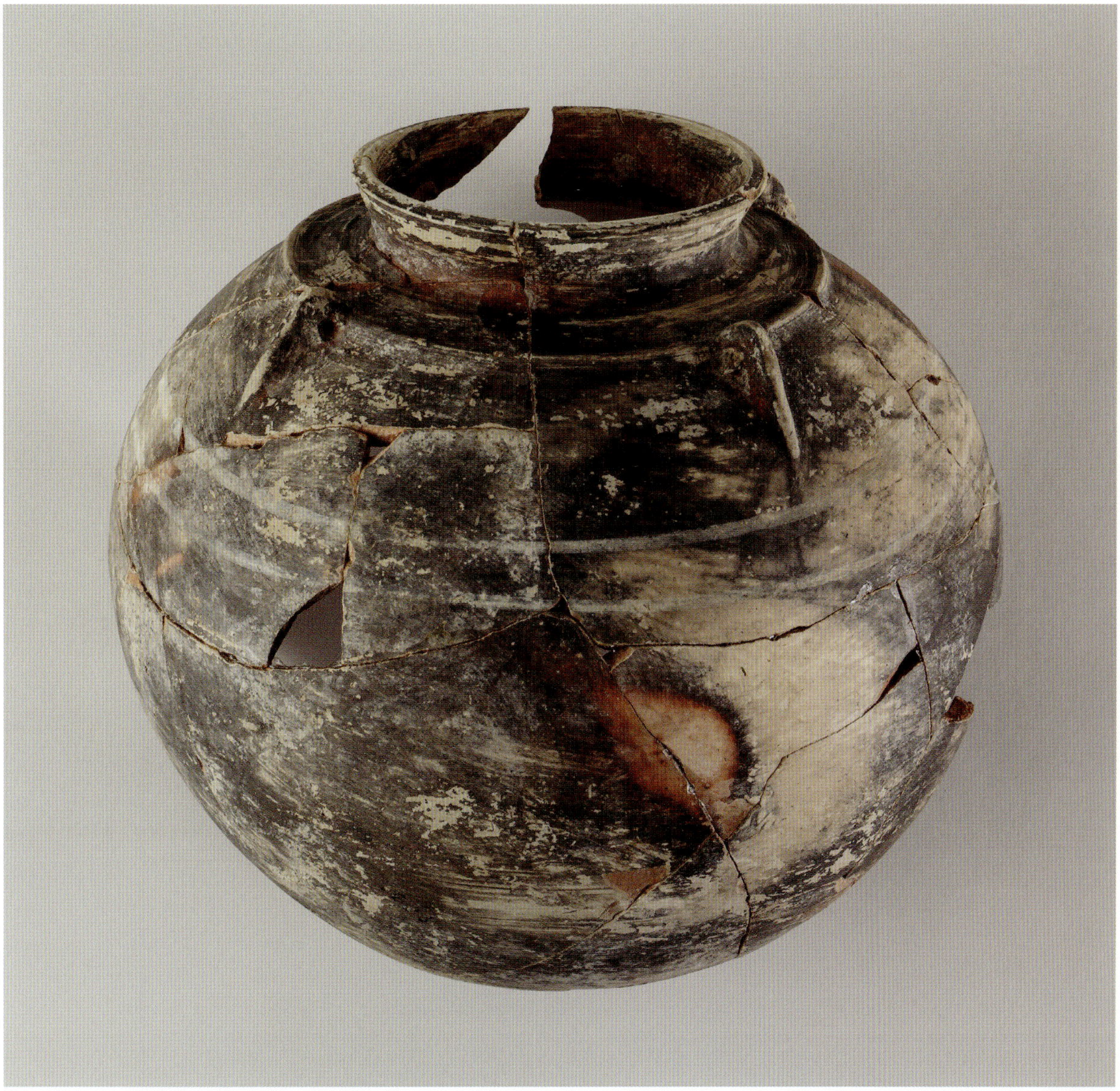

45. Jar

Baked clay

Iran, Tall-e Geser

Proto-Elamite period (ca. 3100–2600 BCE)

Excavated in 1949

ISACM A28731

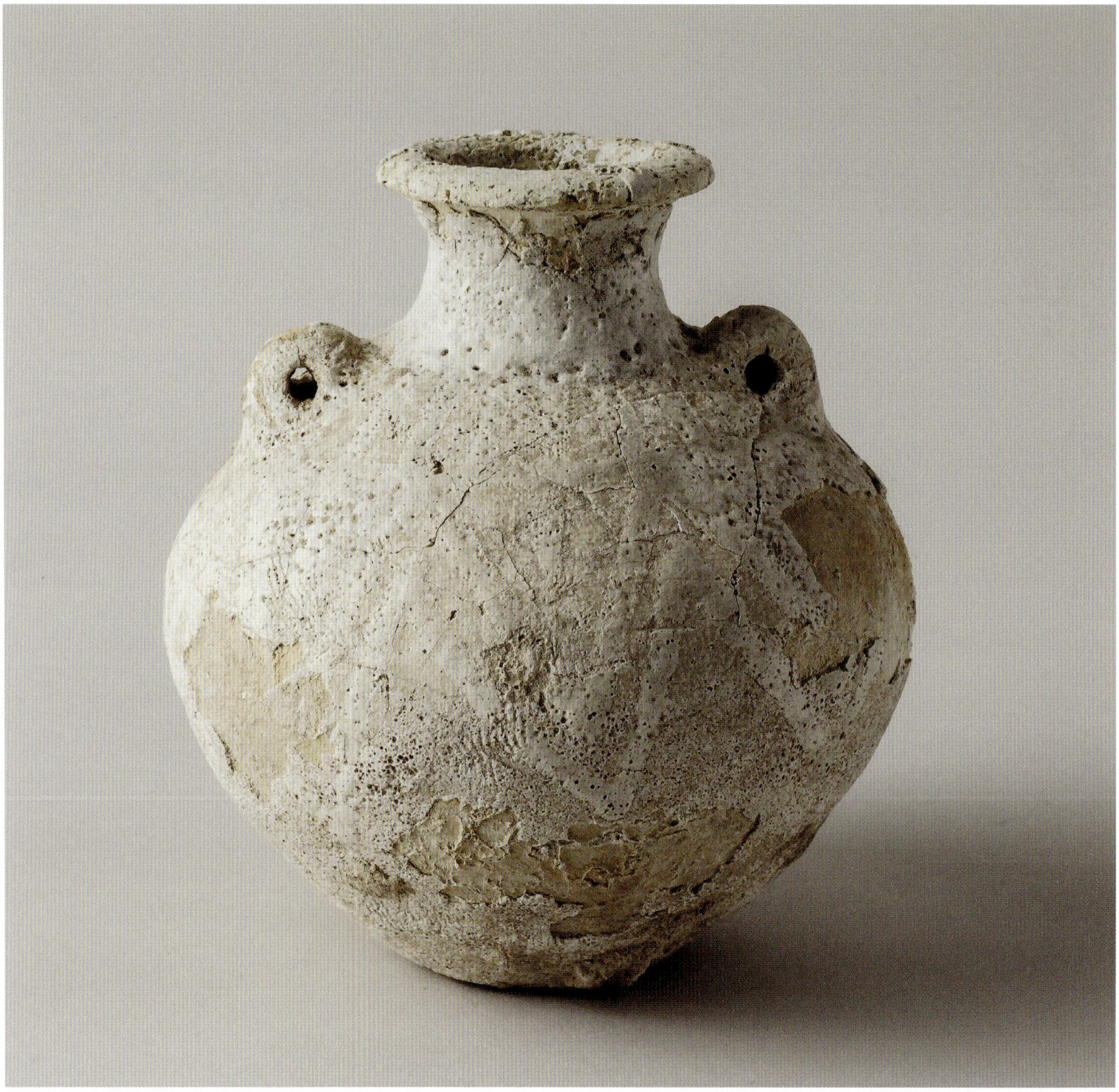

46. Glazed Pottery Flask

Baked clay

Iran, Tall-e Geser

Neo-Elamite period (ca. 650 BCE)

Excavated in 1947–1948

ISACM A27939

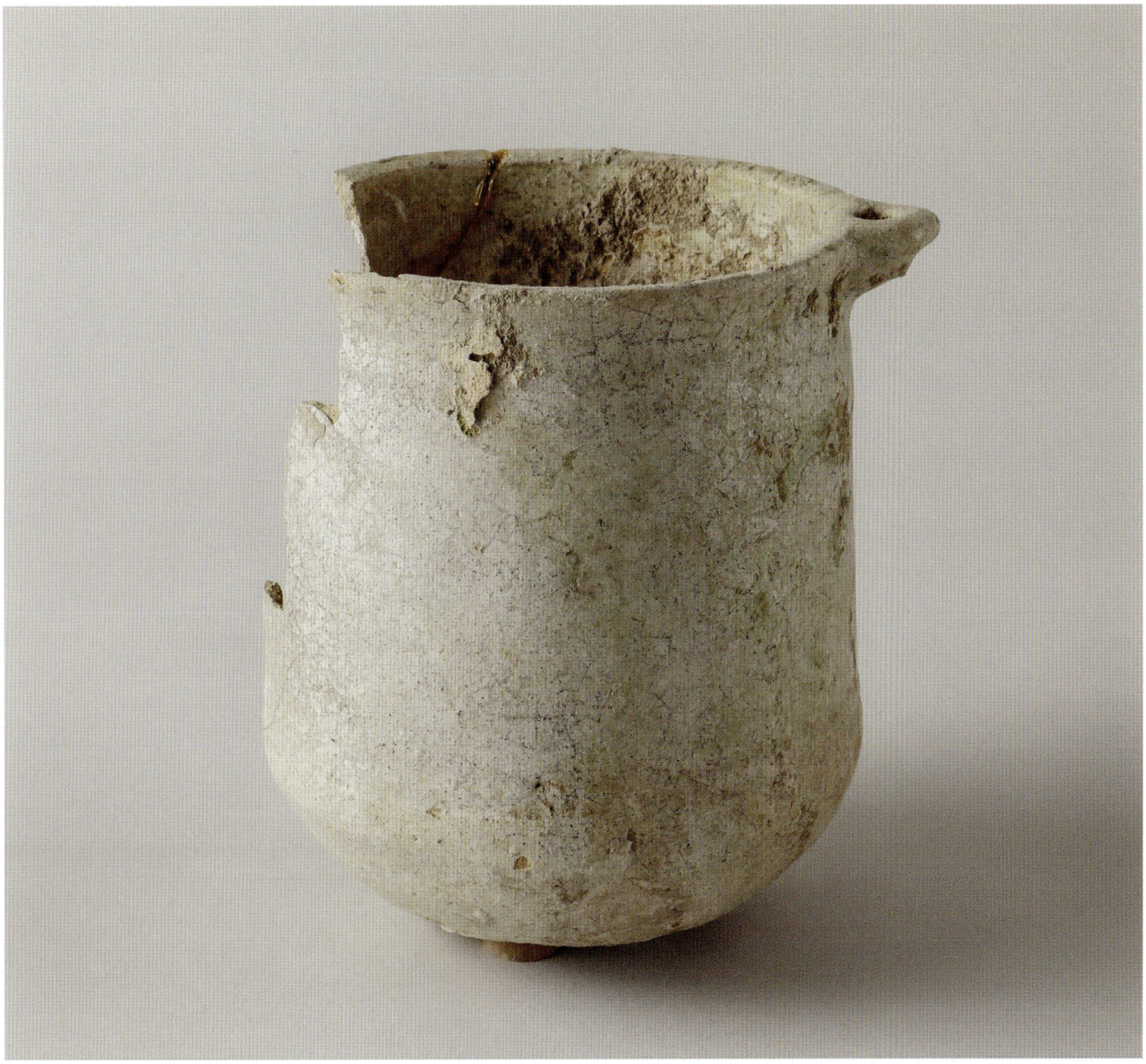

47. Glazed Pottery Jar

Baked clay

Iran, Tall-e Geser

Neo-Elamite period (ca. 650 BCE)

Excavated in 1947–1948

ISACM A27940

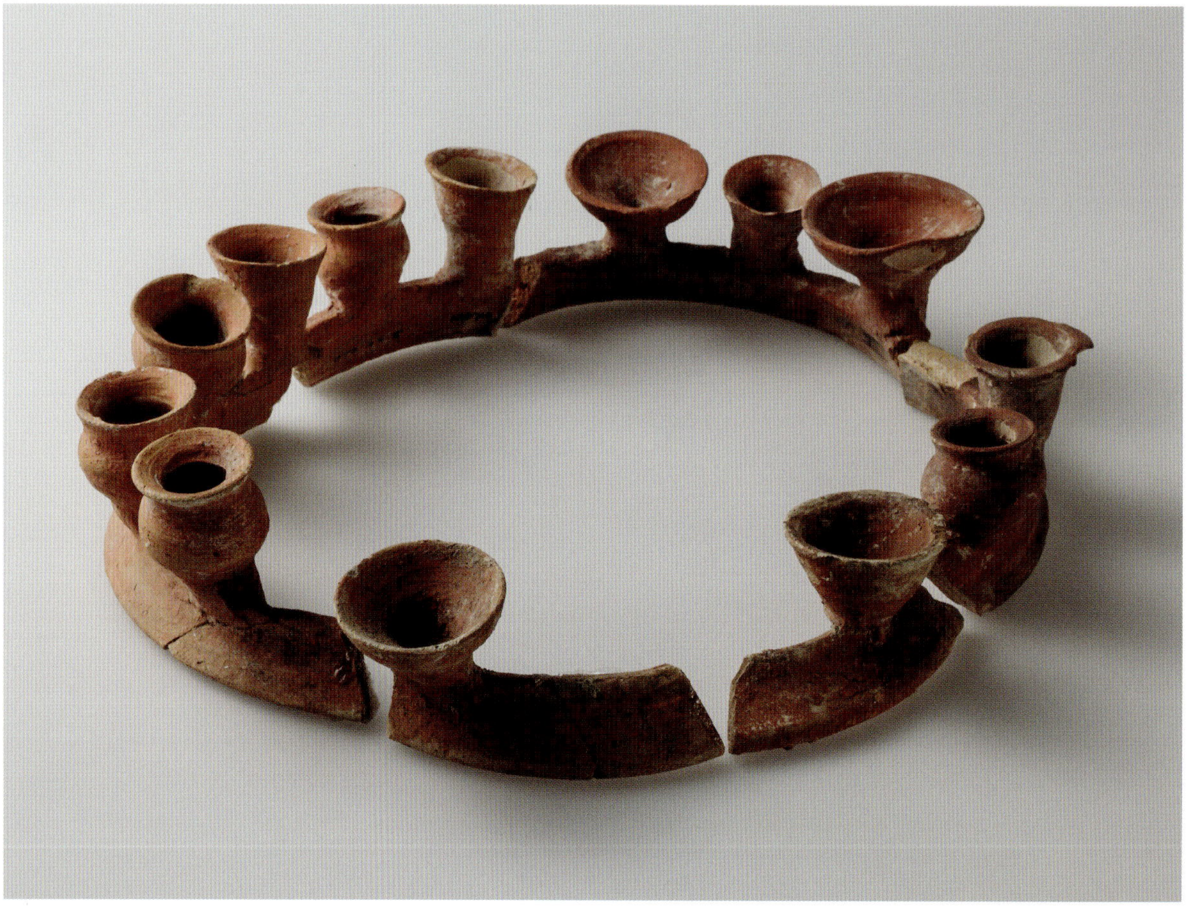

48. Kernos

Baked clay

Iran, Tall-e Geser

Proto-Elamite period (ca. 3100–2600 BCE)

Excavated in 1949

ISACM A28709–28712

Sculpture

Cat. no. 49 is a rare example of sculpture from the Proto-Elamite period. The animal, shown seated and probably a bear, is covering its mouth with its hands. The body is decorated with carved parallel zigzags and was painted red.

Miniature vases in the shape of animals and birds have been discovered at some Near Eastern archaeological sites dating to the late fourth and early third millennia BCE. **Cat. no. 50** represents a bird, likely a duck; the legs, now missing, served as the base. Because such miniature vessels are rare and not found in common archaeological contexts, we may conclude that they were most likely used in rituals.

Cat. nos. 51 and **52** constitute the only examples of Sukkalmah (Old Elamite) figurines in the ISAC Museum. Such female figurines with flattened backs were made in baked-clay molds (fig. 5.3). They are either images of goddesses or votive objects representing individuals appealing to deities for fertility, good health, and the like.

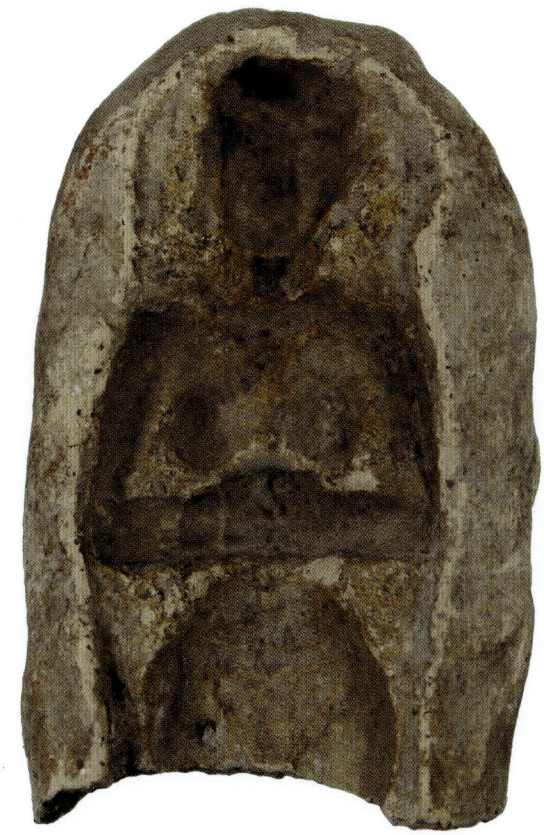

Figure 5.3. Figurine mold made of baked clay, National Museum of Iran, Tehran. Photo by A. Alizadeh.

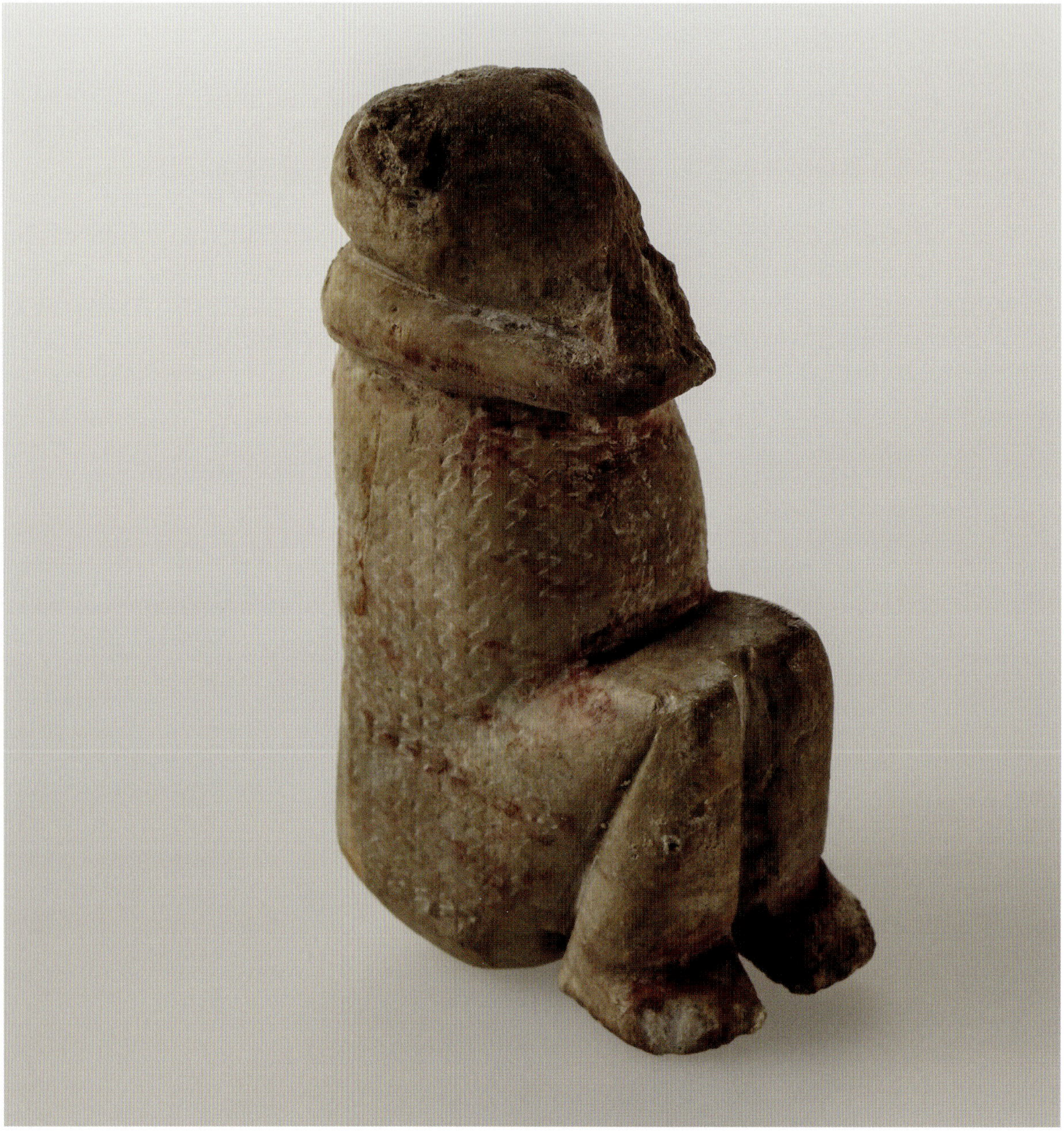

49. Seated Bear

Stone, paint

Iran, Tall-e Geser

Proto-Elamite period (ca. 3100–2600 BCE)

Excavated in 1947–1948

ISACM A27919

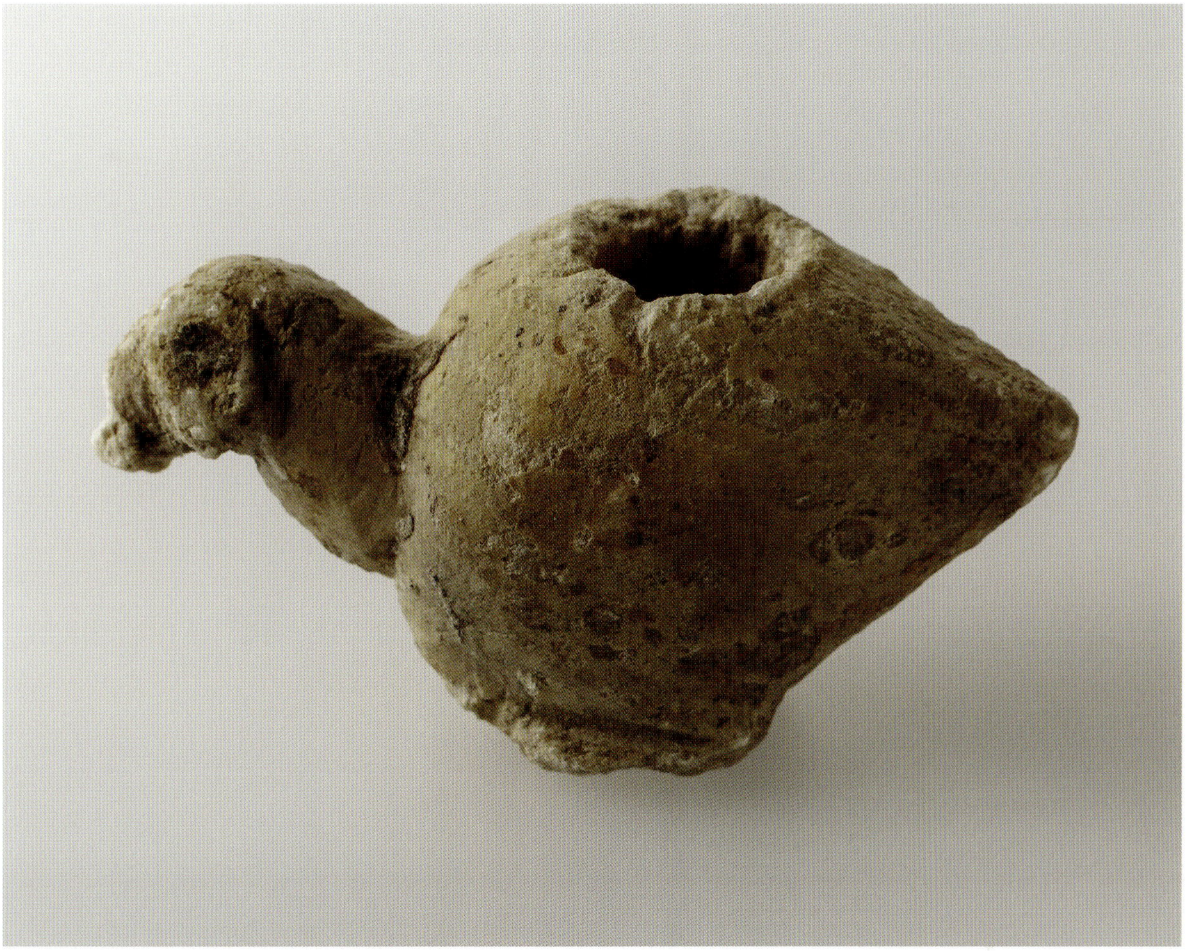

50. Miniature Bird Vessel

Stone

Iran, Tall-e Geser

Proto-Elamite period (ca. 3100–2600 BCE)

Excavated in 1949

ISACM A28675

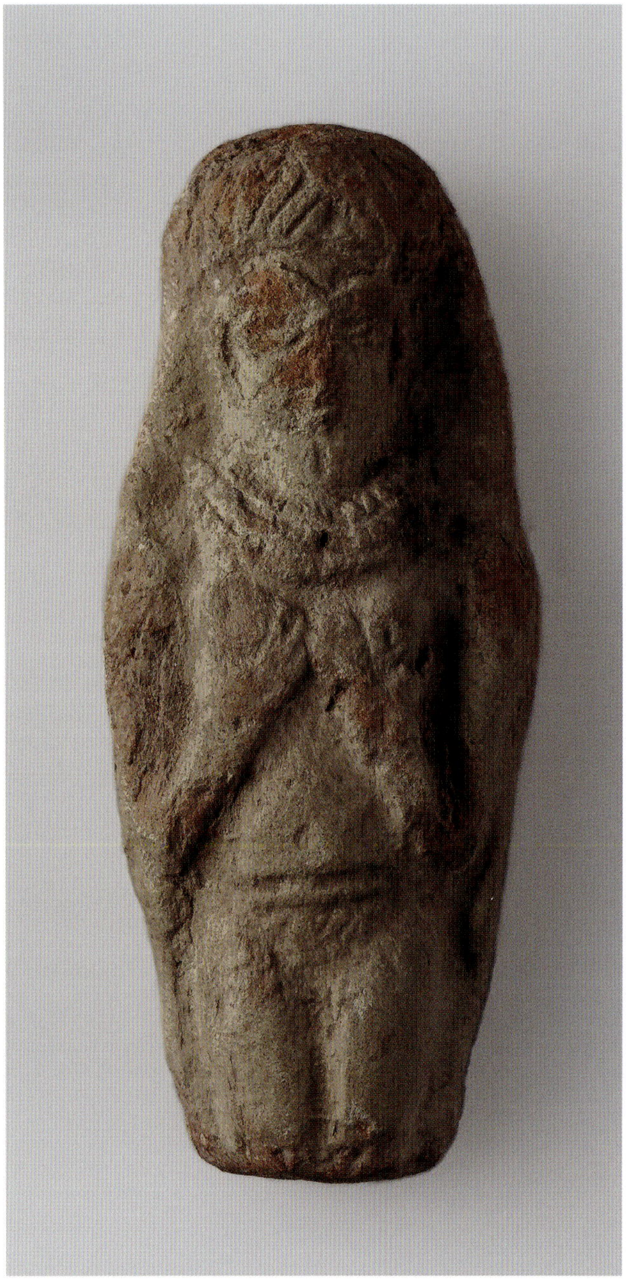

51. Molded Female Figurine

Baked clay
Iran, Tall-e Geser
Sukkalmah period (ca. 1800 BCE)
Excavated in 1947–1949
ISACM A27967

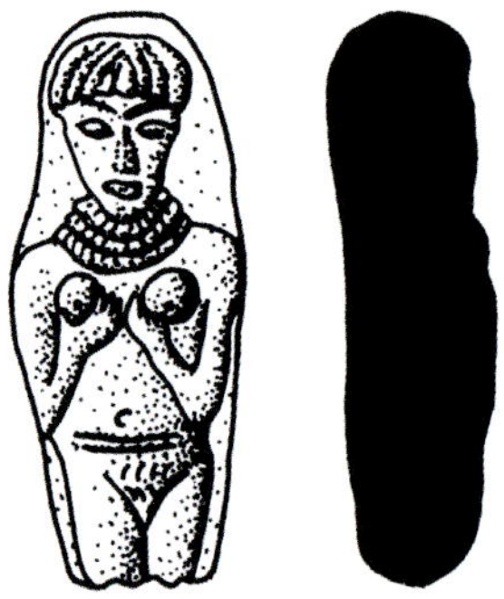

Drawings by A. Alizadeh.

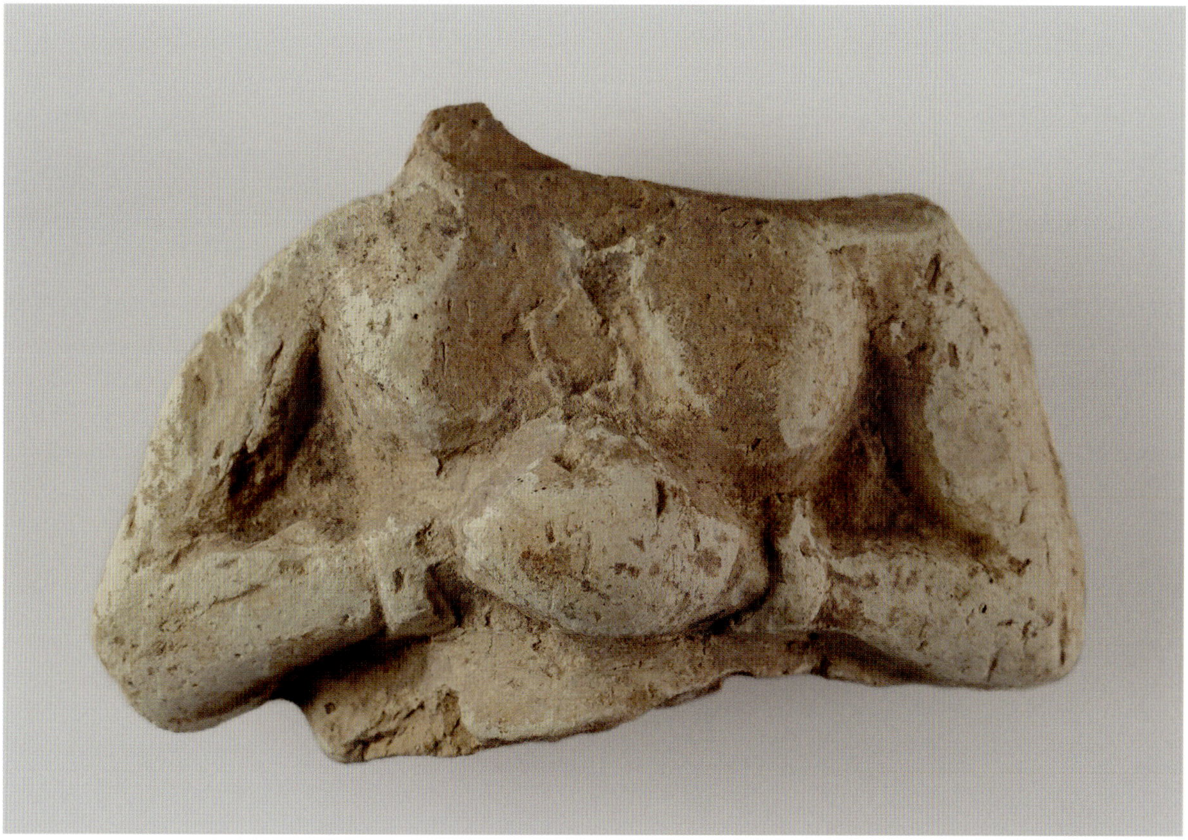

52. Molded Female Figurine

Baked clay

Iran, Tall-e Geser

Sukkalmah period (ca. 1800 BCE)

Excavated in 1947–1948

ISACM A163150

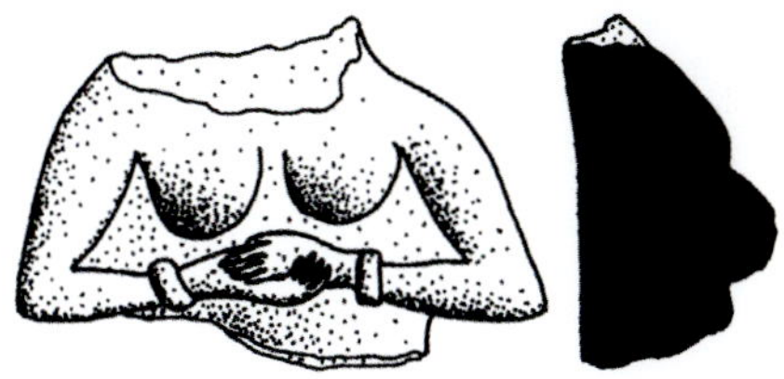

Drawings by A. Alizadeh.

Administrative Tablets

The most ancient writing systems in the world were developed around the turn of the third millennium BCE in Egypt (hieroglyphs), southern Mesopotamia (proto-cuneiform), and Iran (Proto-Elamite). While the first two systems could be deciphered thanks to their continuity, the Proto-Elamite script remains undeciphered because of a break in scribal tradition in about 2800 BCE. Proto-Elamite appeared around 3100 BCE and was used widely in Iran, from the central plateau to Kerman, Fars, and Khuzestan; most examples of the script come from Susa, however, where it may have originated. Although it has not been deciphered, Proto-Elamite shares many numerical systems with the known proto-cuneiform systems of southern Mesopotamia. Thus its numerical values are understood rather well, allowing philologists to ascertain the contents of many texts, though not their meanings.

Cat. no. 53, a fragmentary Proto-Elamite tablet from Tall-e Geser, most probably recorded a grain transaction. The impressed signs on the tablet are identified with numbers with the prefixes M and N. The M stands for the last name of philologist Piero Meriggi, who compiled a list of nonnumerical Proto-Elamite signs and assigned each of them a number. The N stands for "numerical sign." According to François Desset, of the Laboratoire Archéorient—Maison de l'Orient et de la Méditerranée in Lyon, France, the tablet bears on its obverse the identification sign M351 plus one numerical value, N14. Next to these marks are five cone-shaped impressions, representing five measures of some unknown commodity. On the reverse, three N01 numerical signs and three fingernail impressions (probably representing values of one-fifth) are impressed. While we know that in the ancient numerical systems the cone-shaped impressions represent ones or tens (depending on the context), the notch impressed on the edge of the tablet is of unknown value. The types of impressed signs and the lack of pictographic signs on the tablet suggest that it dates to the very beginning of the Proto-Elamite period, about 3100 BCE.

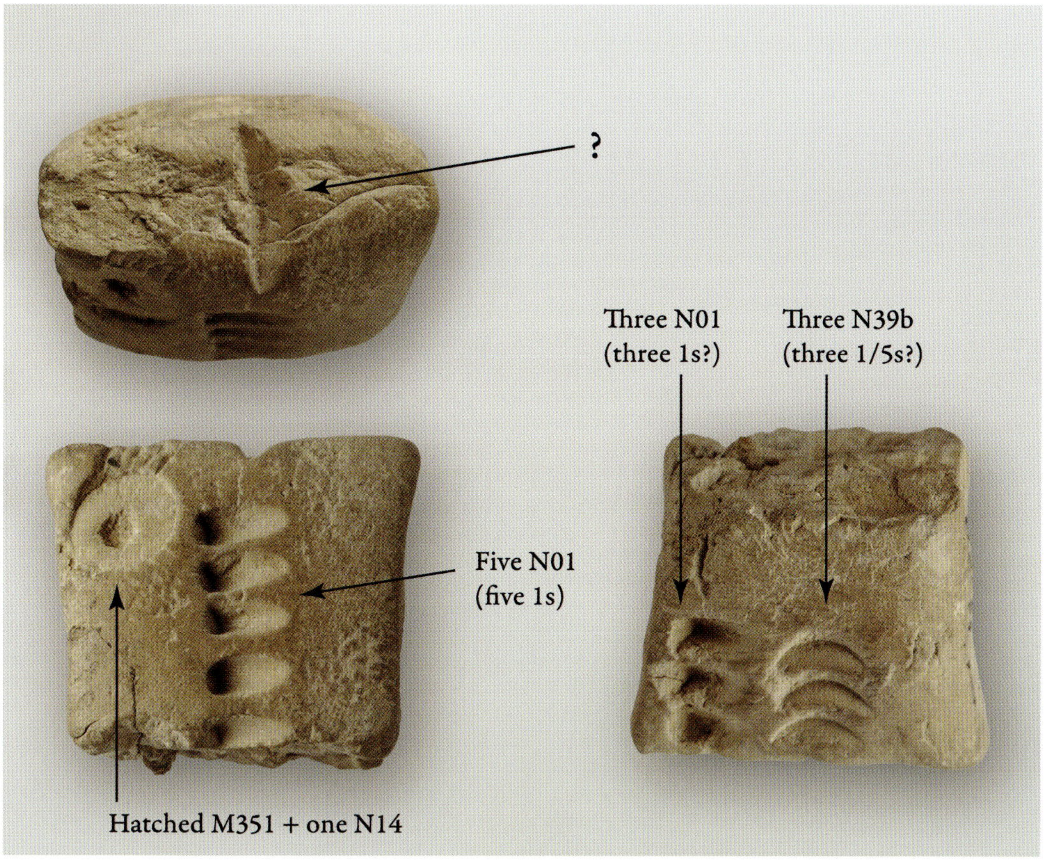

53. Proto-Elamite Tablet Fragment

Baked clay

Iran, Tall-e Geser

Proto-Elamite period (ca. 3100–2600 BCE)

Excavated in 1947–1948

ISACM A27921

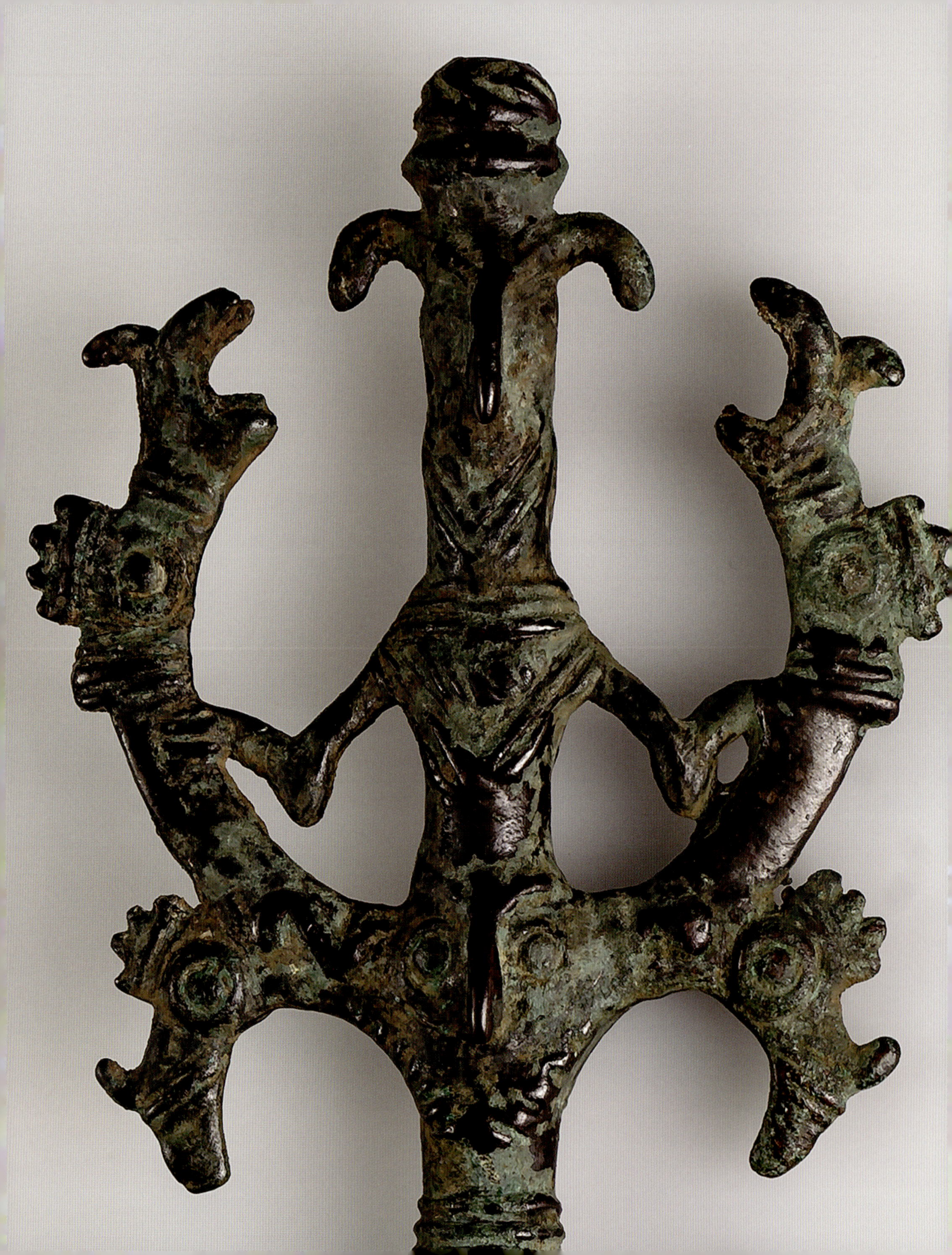

6 Surkh Dum-i-Luri and Luristan Bronzes

The site of Surkh Dum-i-Luri ("Red Slope of the Lurs") lies on the side of a rocky mountain bordering the Kuhdasht Valley in eastern Luristan. In 1938, ISAC's Erich Schmidt excavated what appears to have been the main building on the site—a sanctuary dating to the first half of the first millennium BCE (ca. 800–650 BCE). The interpretation of the building as a sanctuary is based on the ground plan, which shows features characteristic of contemporaneous temples at other sites in Iran, as well as nearly two thousand votive objects deposited, in groups, on and below the building's floor and in its walls (fig. 6.1). The more than 1,800 artifacts consisted primarily of pins made of bronze, iron, and bone but also included beads, rings, shells, spindle whorls, and stamp and cylinder seals.

Surkh Dum-i-Luri lies on one of the main routes followed by mobile pastoralists in both ancient and modern times on their biannual treks between summer pastures in the highlands and winter grazing grounds on the lower plain. It has been suggested that the sanctuary was dedicated to the "mistress of the mountain," who was believed to have power over wild animals and to whom hunters would offer token animals and other trinkets when praying for success in the chase or giving thanks for a successful hunt. The scarcity of weapons and the profusion of pins and other ornaments deposited in the sanctuary have been taken as strong indications that the deity (or deities) honored there was (or were) female.

Ethnographic data may suggest a possible explanation for the abundance of pins from Surkh Dum-i-Luri. In many cultures, nails, pins, or needles are used as tangible evidence of contracts of a legally binding nature, such as marriages. So it is possible that nomads stopped at Surkh Dum-i-Luri on their biannual trips between summer and winter pastures not only to pray for a successful hunting season but also to record or seal legal contracts.

Except for the bronze objects found by Erich Schmidt at the nomadic sanctuary of Surkh Dum-i-Luri, all Luristan bronzes on display in the ISAC Museum's Persian Gallery were purchased and come from unidentified locations in western

Copper-alloy standard finial with a "master of animals" from Luristan, Iran. **Cat. no. 57**.

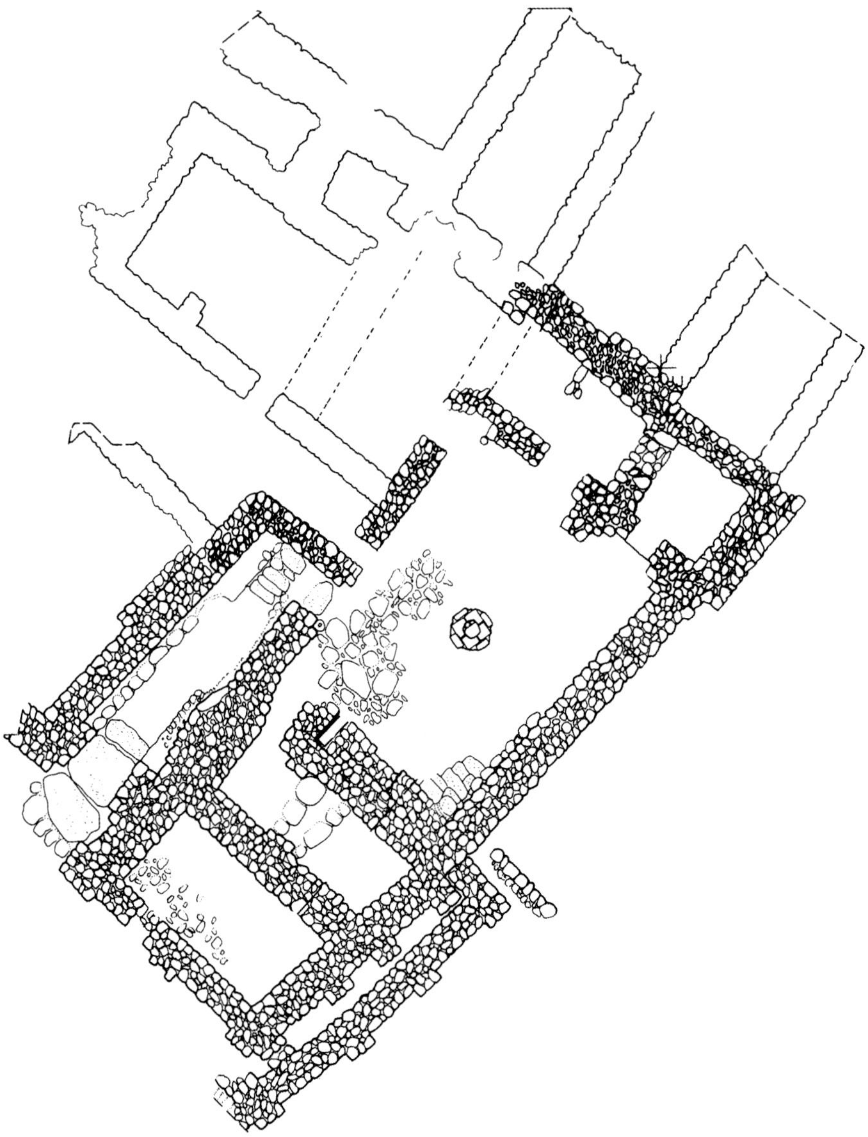

Figure 6.1. Plan of the Surkh Dum-i-Luri sanctuary. After Schmidt, van Loon, and Curvers 1989, pl. 51.

Iran. Luristan bronzes include a great variety of objects, including vessels, pins, standard finials, mirrors, and weapons. Among these items, many pins, finials, and votive plaques exhibit remarkable modernity in their abstract and highly stylized anthropomorphic and zoomorphic representations. These objects must have been created by craftsmen with great artistic imagination and vigor. Such bronzes are commonly called "Luristan bronzes" because they are found almost exclusively in the Luristan province of the central Zagros region or are reported to have come from there. Throughout its known history, this region was inhabited by tribespeople who deposited bronze utilitarian and votive objects in their ancient cemeteries and isolated shrines.

The metallurgical mastery and sophisticated imagery exhibited by the Luristan bronzes suggest that their producers may have been itinerant craftsmen who came primarily from the heart of the Elamite civilization in Khuzestan, ancient Susiana, for it is difficult to imagine that nomads could have mastered the complex art of metalworking. Even though some classes of Luristan bronzes, such as the standard finials and zoomorphic pins, have not been found outside Luristan, a few examples of glazed-pottery vessels from Susa depicting similar master-of-animals and fantastic-creature motifs may point to Susiana as the origin of such objects. Other classes of Luristan bronzes, especially weapons, are indistinguishable from their parallels in Mesopotamia and Elam.

Most Luristan bronzes were produced using the lost-wax technique, a process that allows great versatility in shaping complex forms (fig. 6.2). In this technique, the object was first shaped in wax, sometimes over a clay core, then covered with clay; heated over a fire, the wax melted out through vents, leaving a clay mold that could be filled with molten bronze.

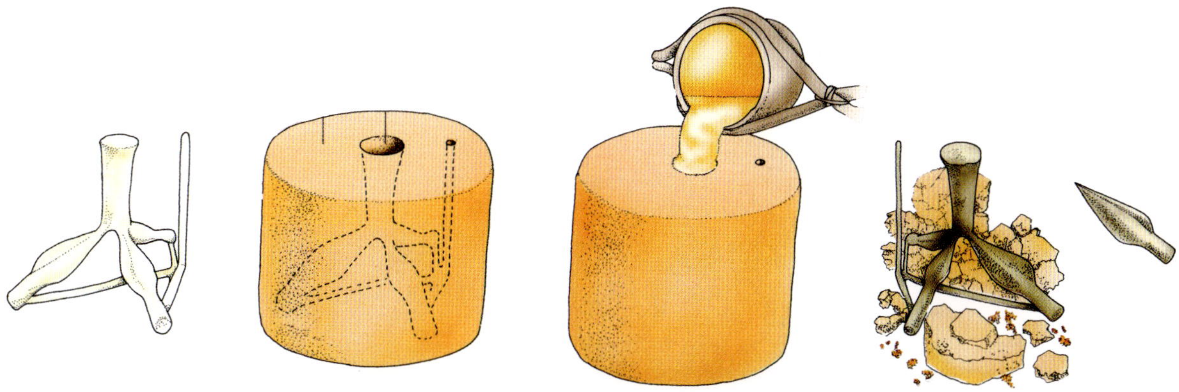

Figure 6.2. Schematic drawing of the production process in the lost-wax technique. After Roaf 1990.

Decorative and Votive Pins and Plaques

Prior to the modern period, metal objects were expensive. They were even more expensive in ancient times and, as such, served as status symbols. So what could demonstrate the devotion of a worshipper more than a votive offering made of metal? Disk-headed bronze pins are just one type among the numerous kinds of metal objects deposited at the Surkh Dum-i-Luri sanctuary.

Most disk-headed pins bear embossed or engraved decoration. **Cat. no. 54** has an eight-petaled rosette in the middle and a schematic human or lion face delicately engraved right above the thin shaft. In other cases, the center of such pins stands out in relief as a plain boss, rosette, lion's mask, or human face, such as in figure 6.3.

Cat. no. 55 is a flat, openwork, circular-headed pin consisting of a central standing female figure flanked by two rampant feline creatures. The central figure is shown with crescentic horns and curling sidelocks and wears a necklace and kilt or tunic decorated with a herringbone design. The figure holds the paws of the two feline creatures. The two ten-petaled rosettes between the mouths of the creatures and the figure's headdress may be part of her elaborate crown. Even though such objects are commonly referred to as "pinheads," they were probably used as icons and votive objects rather than as garment fasteners.

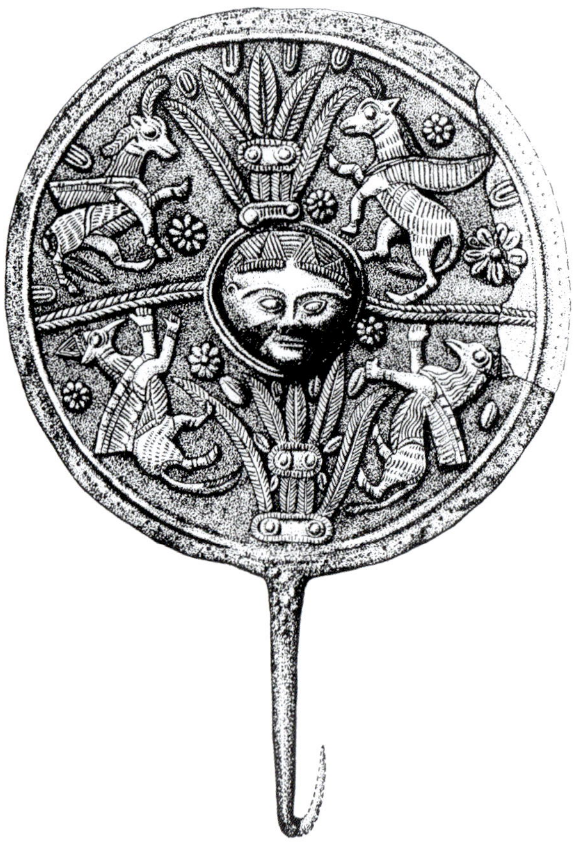

Figure 6.3. Drawing of a copper-alloy votive pin with hammered and embossed designs, of the Iron Age (ca. 800–650 BCE), Museum of Fine Arts, Boston (41.342). After Schmidt, van Loon, and Curvers 1989, pl. 265c.

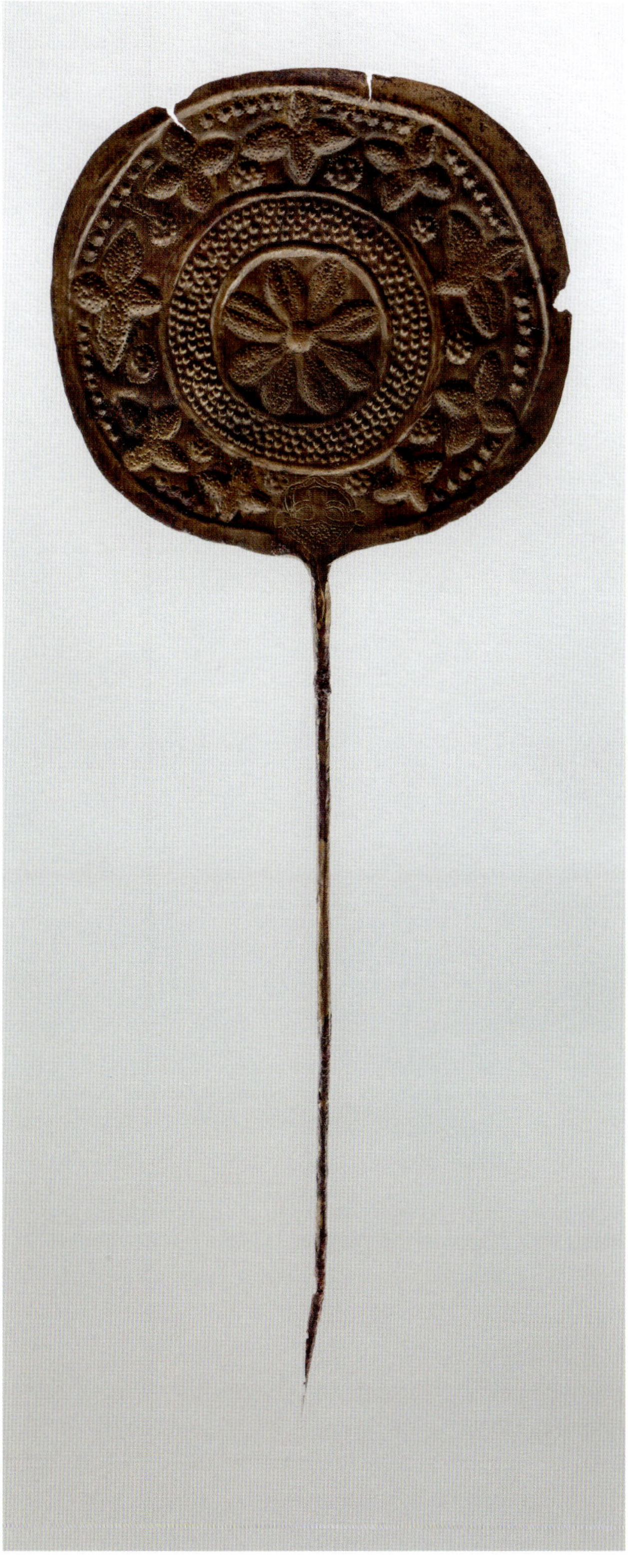

54. Disk-Headed Pin

Copper alloy

Iran, Surkh Dum-i-Luri sanctuary

Iron Age (ca. 800–650 BCE)

Excavated in 1938

ISACM A25293

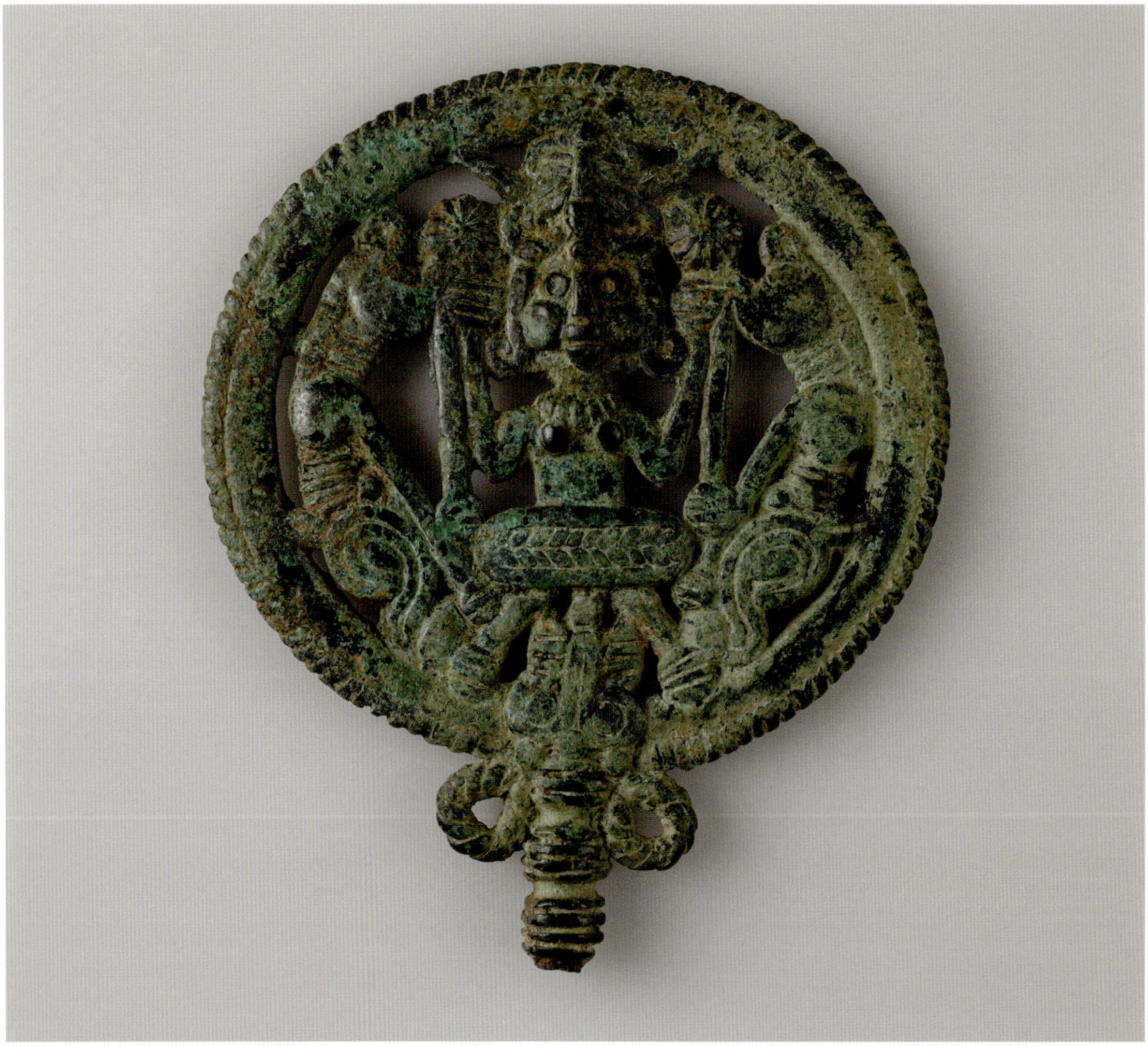

55. Openwork Pinhead with a "Mistress of Animals"

Copper alloy

Iran, Luristan

Iron Age (ca. 800–650 BCE)

Purchased in Tehran, 1939

ISACM A24177

Cylinder Seals

Many cylinder seals made of stone, faience, or iron were found at the Surkh Dum-i-Luri sanctuary (fig. 6.4). Most of them predate the building of the sanctuary and thus were heirlooms deposited in the sanctuary as votive objects.

Cat. no. 56—one of the 287 seals found at Surkh Dum-i-Luri—is also much older than the context in which it was deposited, as the seal dates to about 1000 BCE. The carving is primitive and coarse, but the scene is interesting. It shows two dancing humans and a striding boar; each figure has one hand raised and holds one folded leg with the other. The cross above the boar probably represents the rising sun, greeted by two simian creatures, as often portrayed in Egyptian art. Above the dancers flies an eagle, and just below the eagle is what appears to be an egg.

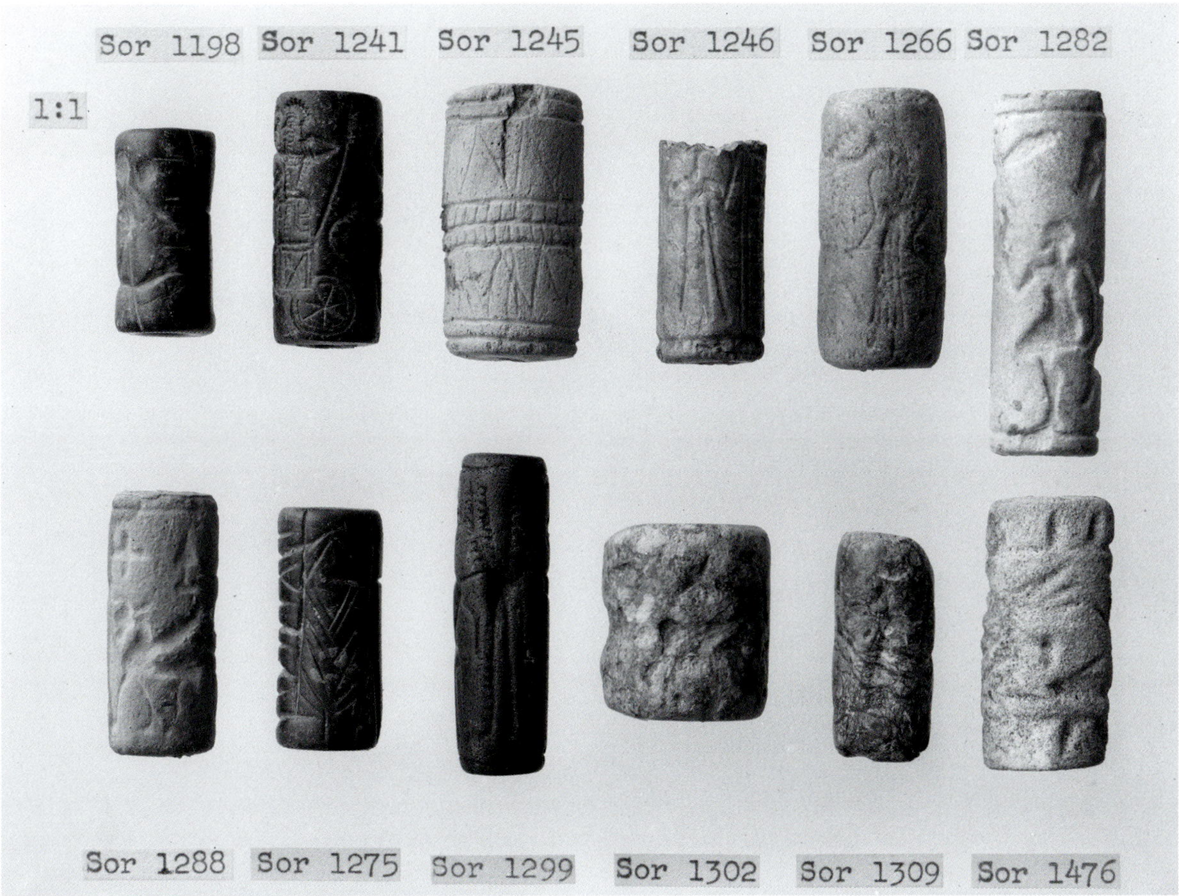

Figure 6.4. Archival photograph showing a selection of the cylinder seals uncovered by Erich Schmidt's excavations at Surkh Dum-i-Luri. ISACM Luristan LII-330.

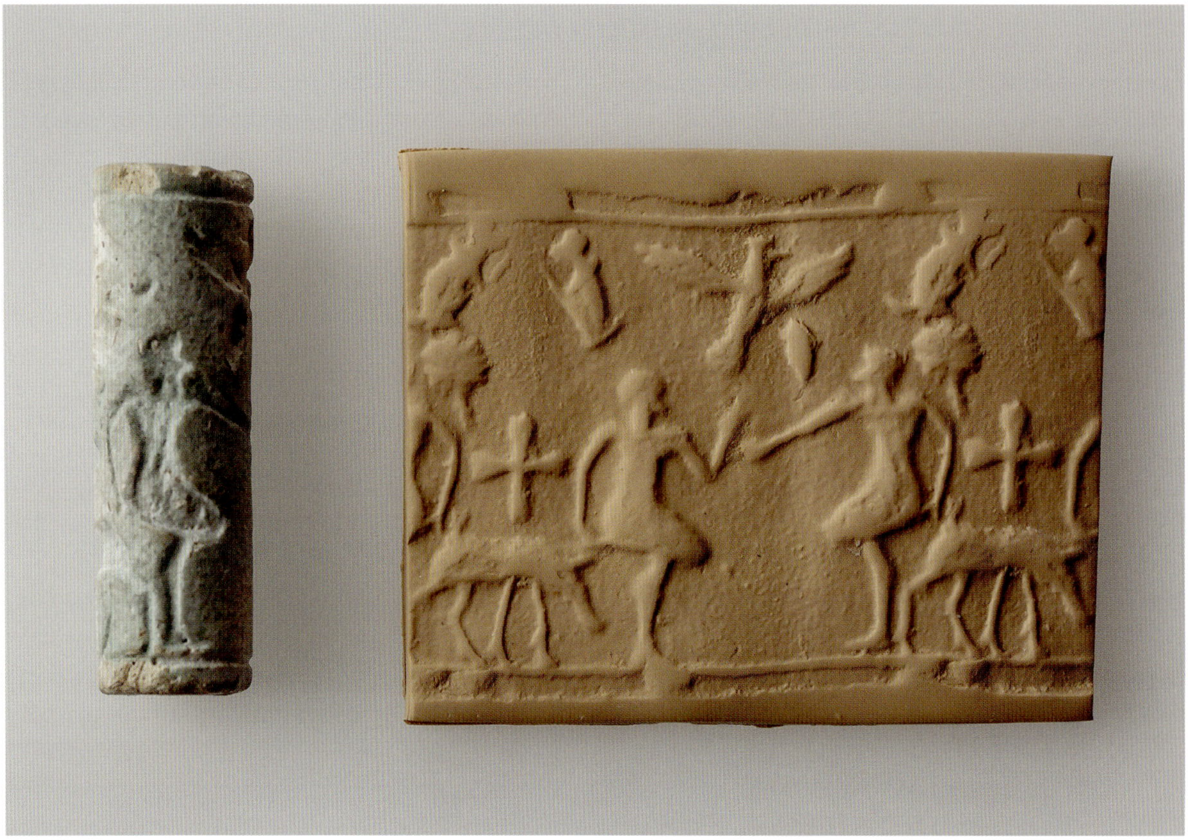

56. Cylinder Seal and Modern Impression: Two Dancing Figures Accompanied by a Boar, Monkeys, a Bird, and a Cross

Faience

Iran, Surkh Dum-i-Luri sanctuary

Iron Age (ca. 800–650 BCE)

Excavated in 1938

ISACM A25231, C1573

Standard Finials

Among the large and widely varied Luristan bronzes, those representing "masters of animals" are the most distinctive and striking. The type consists of a central figure subduing various types of natural, stylized, or mythological creatures, with extra flanking necks and rooster heads. The central figure may be rendered as a demon or as half man, half beast. The central tube is hollow, thereby allowing the object to be mounted on a shaft of wood, bone, or metal. Such objects were probably set up on a bottle-shaped support, commonly found in Luristan. Except for examples where the central figure is holding her breasts, the sex of these figures is ambiguous. This ambiguity certainly rules out identifying the figures as representations of the Mesopotamian hero Gilgamesh, an identification that even in Mesopotamian art is by no means certain.

Cat. no. 57 depicts a horned figure atop a central face, two threatening felines with elongated necks, two rooster heads jutting out from the felines' necks, and the back-to-back bodies of mythological creatures at the base. The elongated upper figure wears a necklace and straps crossing the chest. The figure's lower legs form the base, which would have been mounted on a shaft.

Cat. no. 58 is a less complex example. It consists of a central shaft that terminates in the body of a male figure wearing a cap, holding the muzzles of two flanking felines, and standing on their merged necks. The joined midsections of the felines form the middle of the shaft.

Cat. no. 59, an elegantly sculpted standard finial, represents two highly stylized rampant, winged ibexes with notched horns; the bodies are thin and elongated, and the tails are twisted. The ears are rendered erect and the eyes bulging. The fore and hind feet of the creatures rest on a horizontal ring.

The ancient Near Eastern artistic composition depicting rampant goats or ibexes flanking a central tree, a composition commonly referred to as the "tree of life," dates to prehistoric times. Like many other motifs and compositions of the Luristan bronzes, this composition is inspired by Elamite art, with its center in southwestern Iran. The scene on a Surkh Dum-i-Luri cylinder seal in the ISAC Museum's collection shows a similar theme (ISACM A25137).

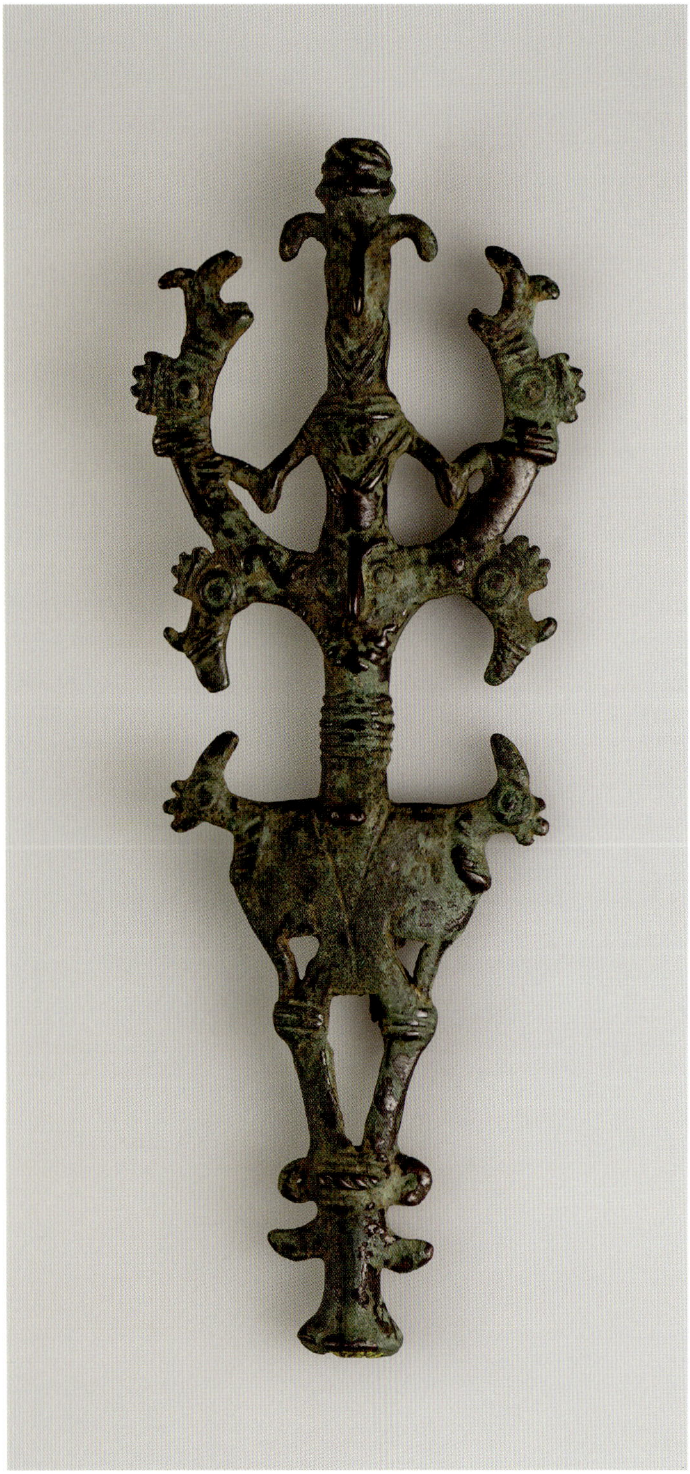

57. Standard Finial with a "Master of Animals"

Copper alloy

Iran, Luristan

Iron Age (ca. 800–650 BCE)

Purchased in New York, 1930

ISACM A7276

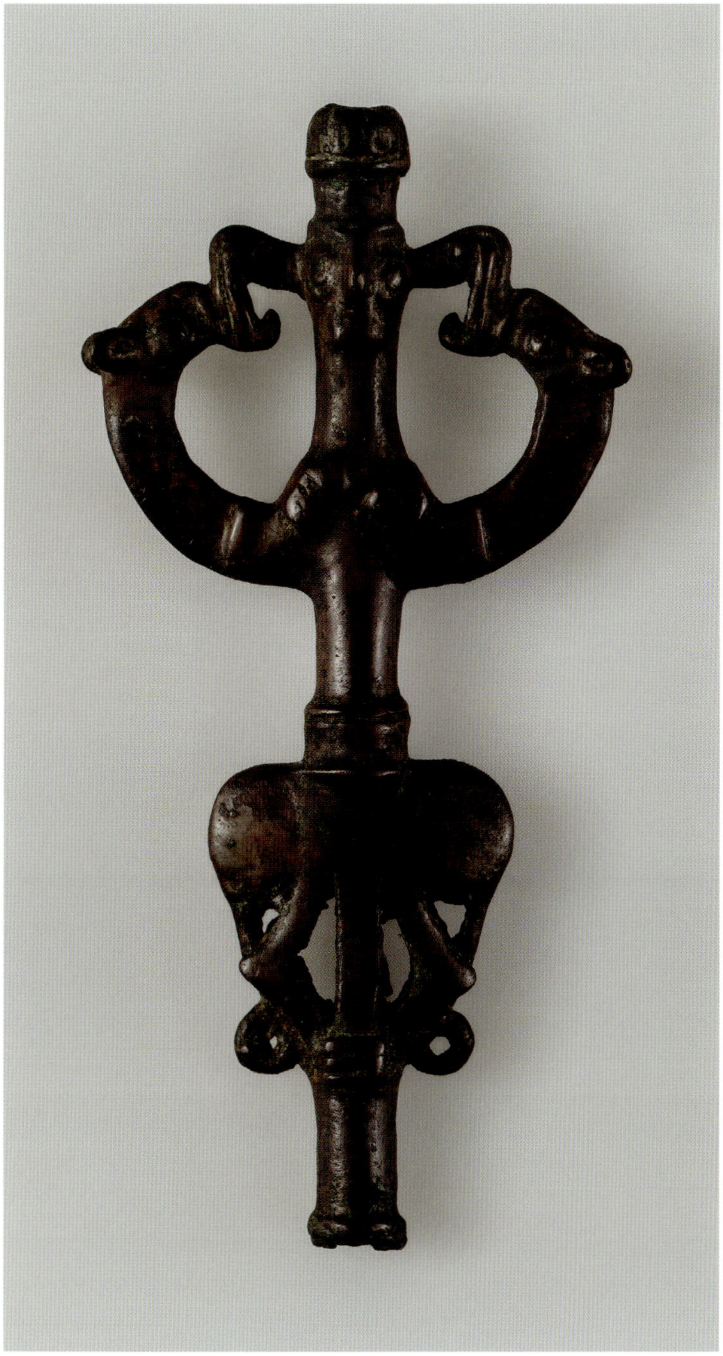

58. Standard Finial with a "Master of Animals"

Copper alloy

Iran, Luristan

Iron Age (ca. 800–650 BCE)

Purchased in Tehran, 1939

ISACM A24181

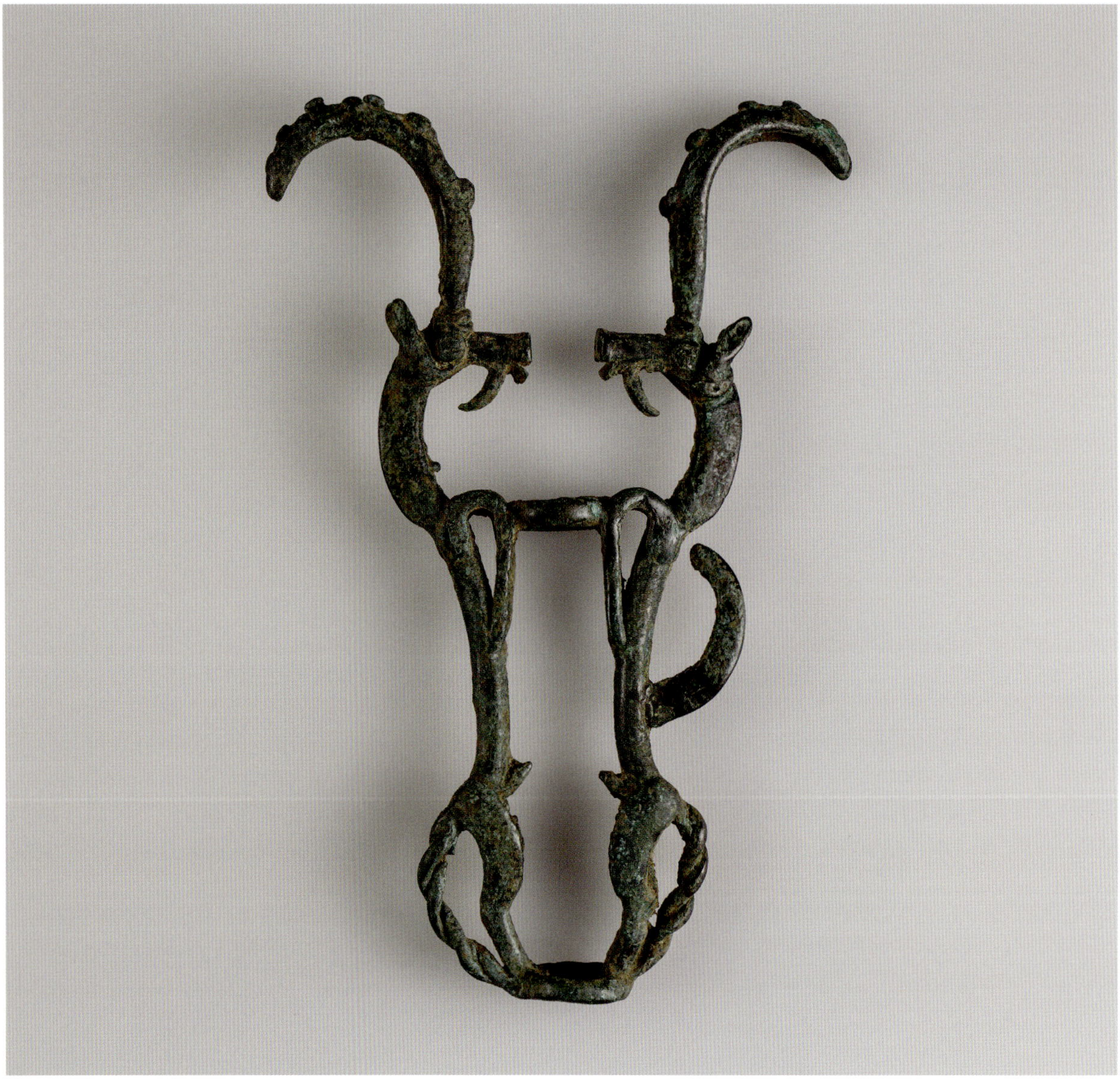

59. Standard Finial with Ibexes

Copper alloy

Iran, Luristan

Iron Age (ca. 800–650 BCE)

Purchased in New York, 1930

ISACM A7285

Decorative Pins, Horse Bits, Situlae, and Axes

Cat. no. 60 is a decorative votive pin consisting of a simple, tapering shaft and a head molded as an ibex attacked from behind by an extremely stylized and simplified feline. The attacking animal was probably molded separately, then attached. Such richly decorated pins with elaborate floral and zoomorphic images seem to be specific to western Iran, with no parallels elsewhere. Pins of this kind gradually disappeared with the introduction of bronze fibulae (safety pins) in the late Iron Age.

From Assyrian sources, we know that western Iran was renowned for its excellent horses. The earliest horse burial in Luristan (ca. 1500–1300 BCE) comes from Tappeh Godin in the central Zagros region. Horse bits in various shapes and sizes come from illicit excavations of isolated nomadic cemeteries in the region. Even though horse bits are also found in northern and northwestern Iran and Assyria, those from Luristan are much more ornate and have elaborate cheek pieces (**cat. nos. 61** and **62**). **Cat. no. 61** consists of two cheek pieces in the shape of winged mouflons set on a ground line, plus a mouthpiece with a square cross section. The curved shape of the mouflons' wings suggests a later date in the Iron Age closer to Achaemenid times, as curved wings are typical of Achaemenid iconography.

Bronze sheet-metal situlae with vertical sides and rosette-shaped bases were common in ancient western Iran and Mesopotamia. The upper registers of **cat. no. 63** are decorated with guilloche (an ornamentation resembling braided or interlaced ribbons) and hanging loops. The body is decorated with a very stylized form of the so-called tree of life with nine cones. Two winged, human-headed ibexes flank the tree.

The butt of **cat. no. 64**—a decorated axe head with a cylindrical shaft hole—is elongated into tipped spikes. The ridges that reinforce the spikes extend along the upper body of the blade and merge into a single, arrowhead-like point. The blade springs from the shaft in a sweeping downward curve. Axes with this type of curved blade do not seem practical as weapons and were probably made as votive objects.

Battle-axes with crescent-shaped blades were contemporary with spiked axes in Luristan. The hollow shaft of such axes is often decorated with a crouching feline (**cat. no. 65**). Unlike the spiked axes, crescentic axes were functional weapons.

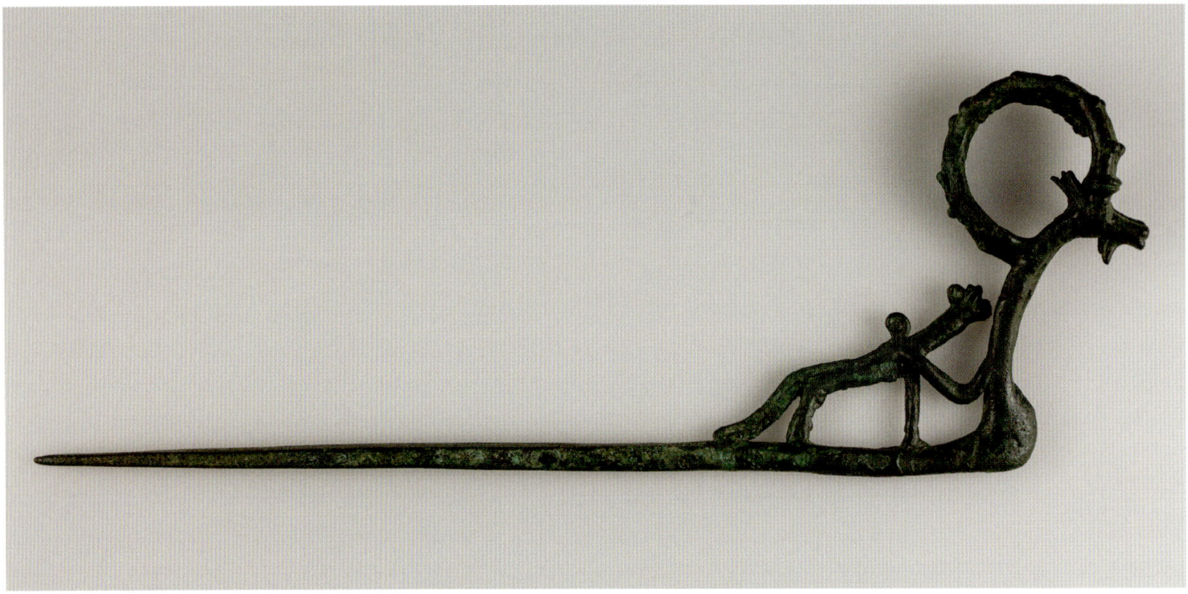

60. Pin with Decorative Head Showing a Feline Attacking an Ibex

Copper alloy

Iran, Luristan

Iron Age (ca. 800–650 BCE)

Purchased in Tehran, 1939

ISACM A24178

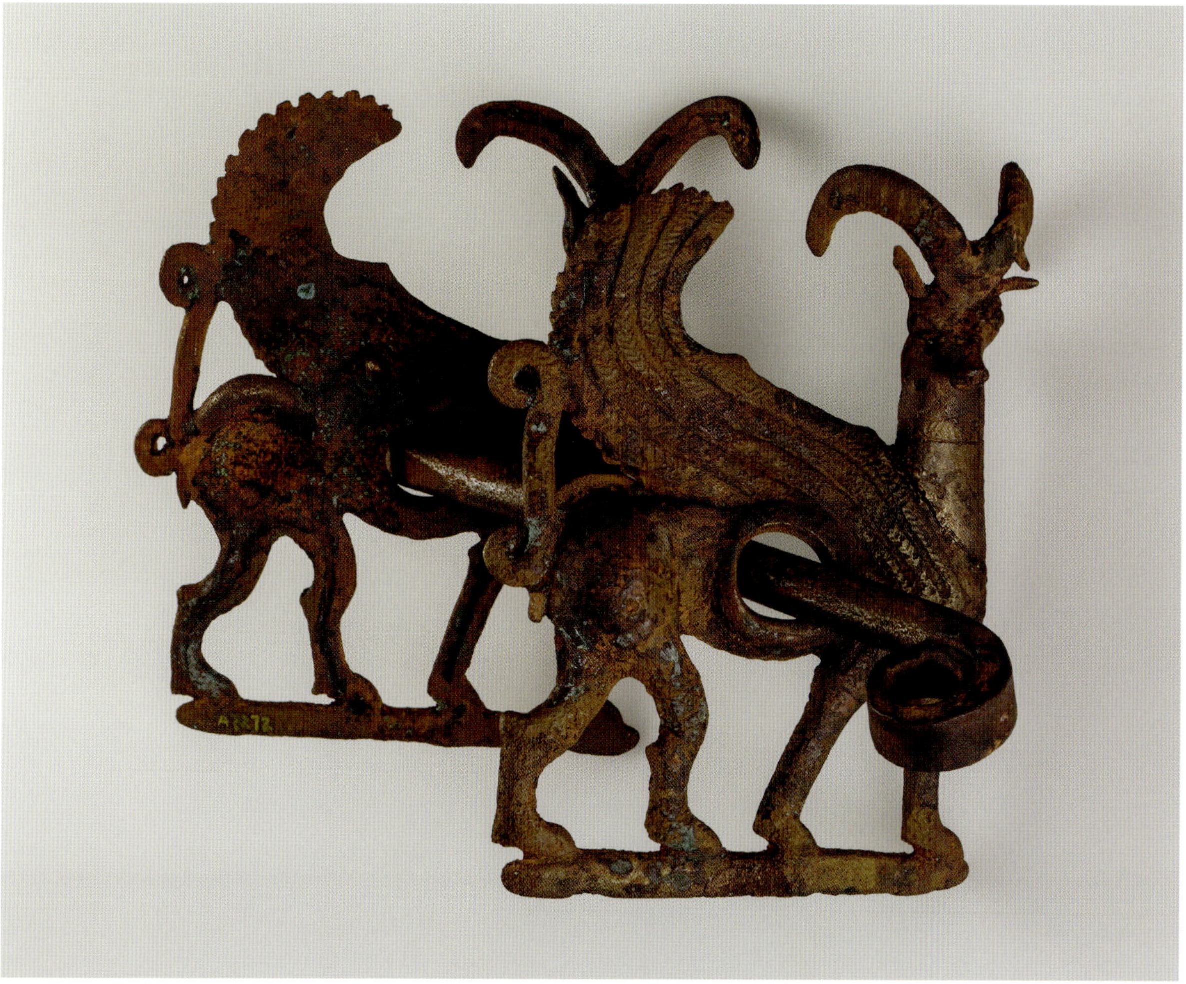

61. Horse Bit with Winged Mouflon Figures

Copper alloy

Iran, Luristan

Iron Age (ca. 800–650 BCE)

Purchased in New York, 1930

ISACM A7272

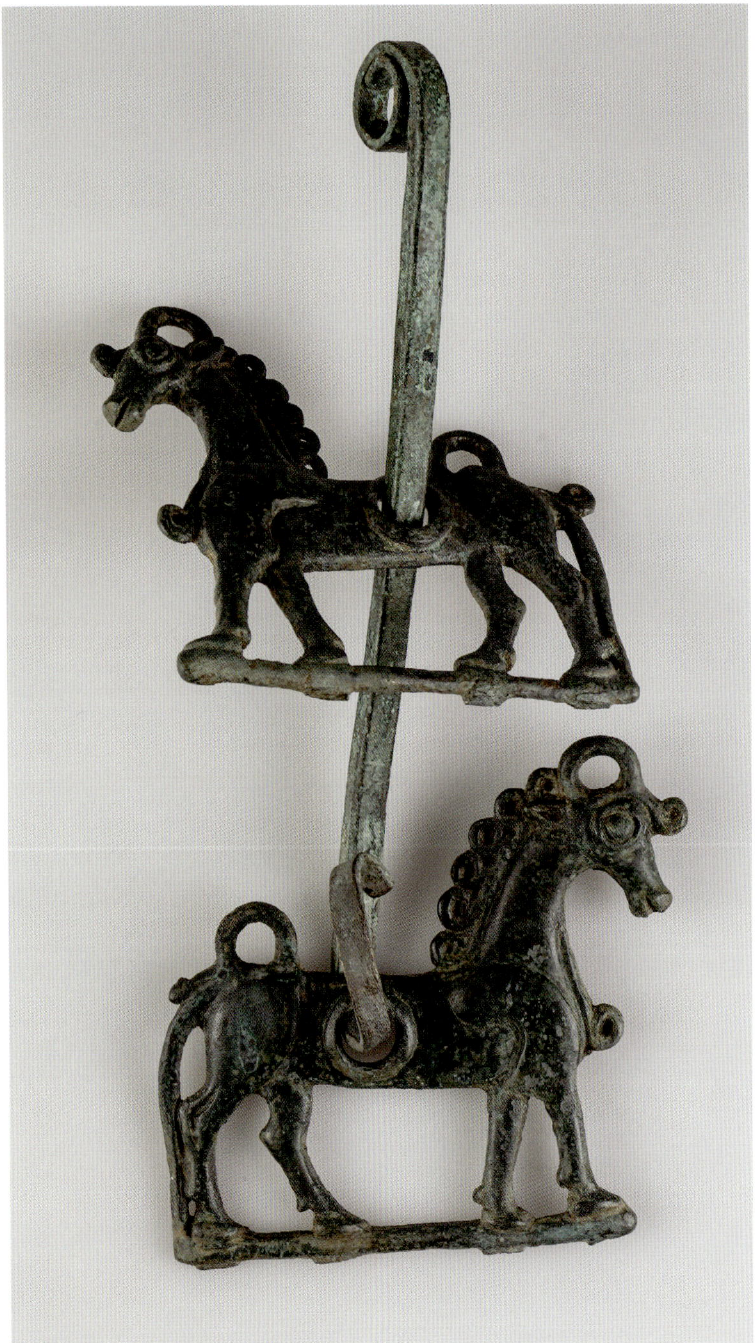

62. Horse Bit with Horse Figures

Copper alloy

Iran, Luristan

Iron Age (ca. 800–650 BCE)

Purchased in New York, 1930

ISACM A7278

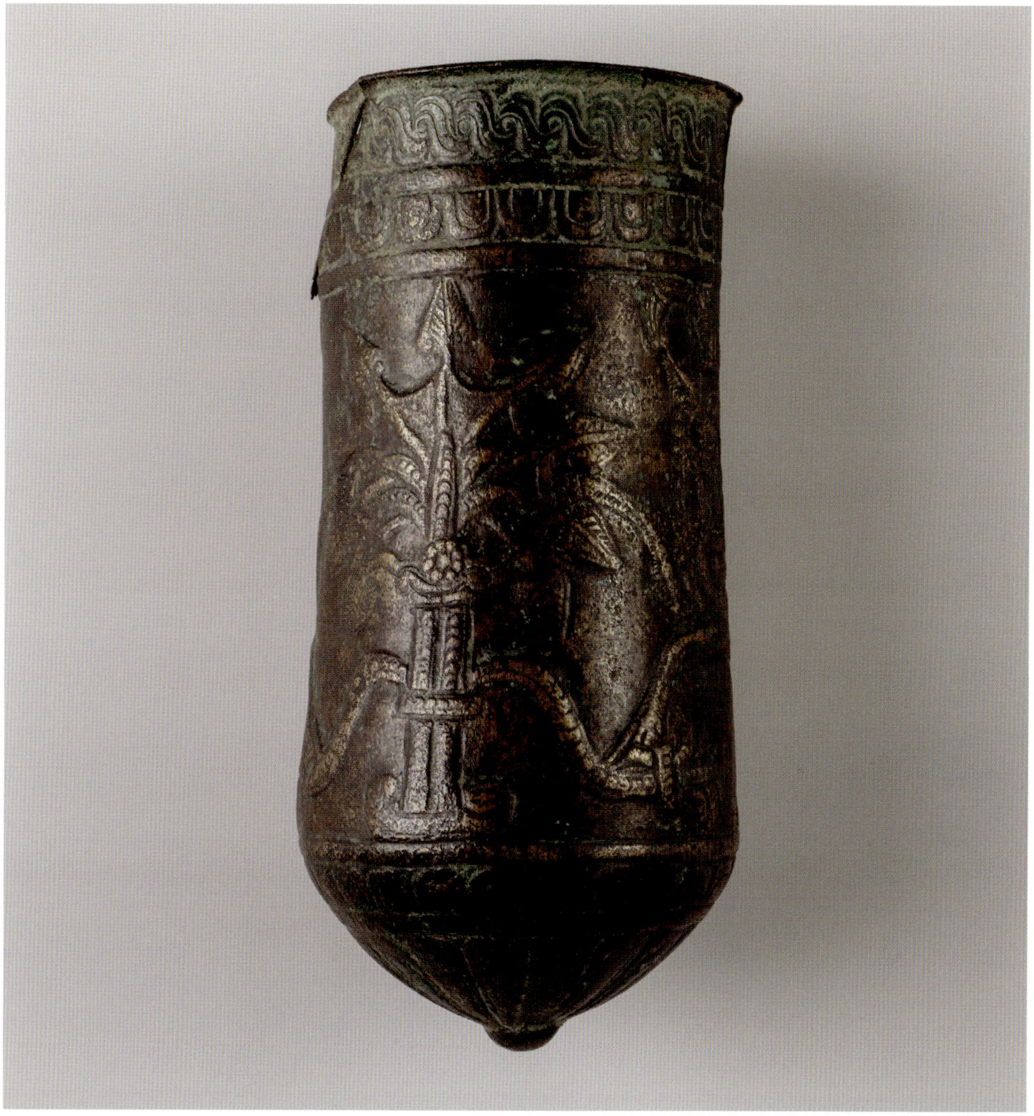

63. Situla with Human-Headed Winged Ibexes Flanking a Sacred Tree

Copper alloy

Iran, Luristan

Iron Age (ca. 800–650 BCE)

Purchased in Tehran, 1939

ISACM A24179

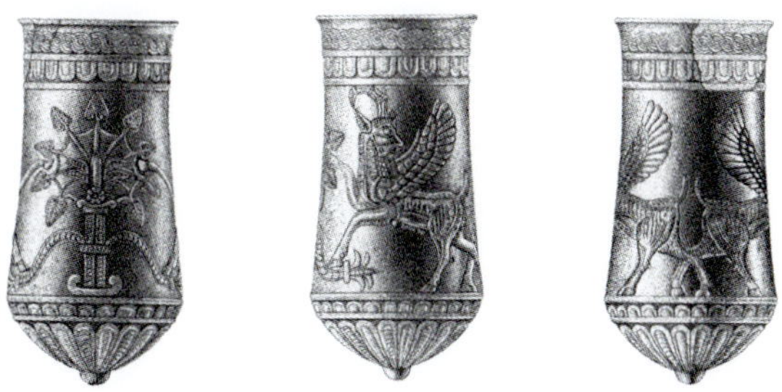

Drawing after Schmidt, van Loon, and Curvers 1989, pl. 264a.

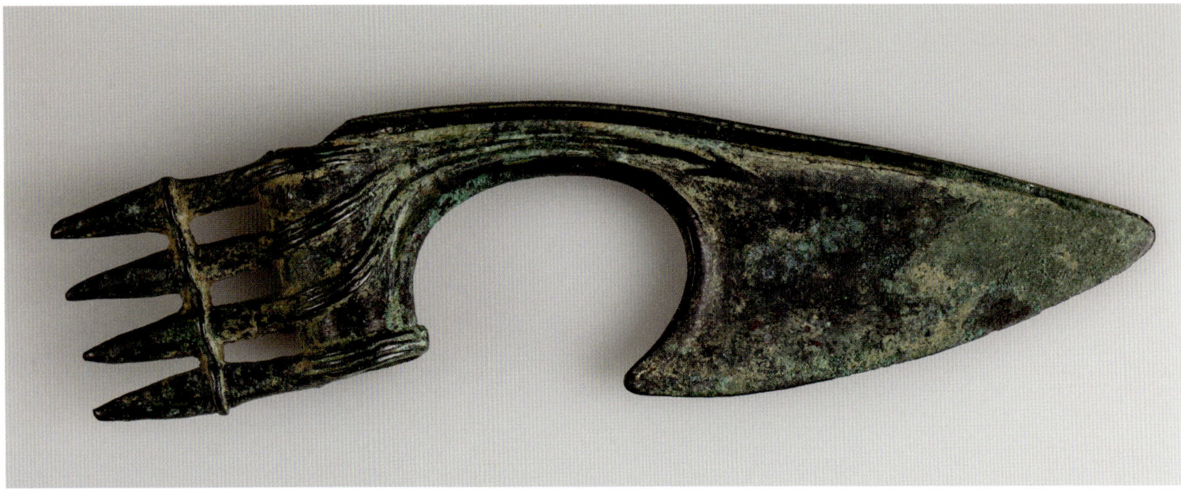

64. Spike-Butted Axe Head

Copper alloy

Iran, Luristan

Iron Age (1100–800 BCE)

Purchased in New York, 1930

ISACM A7275

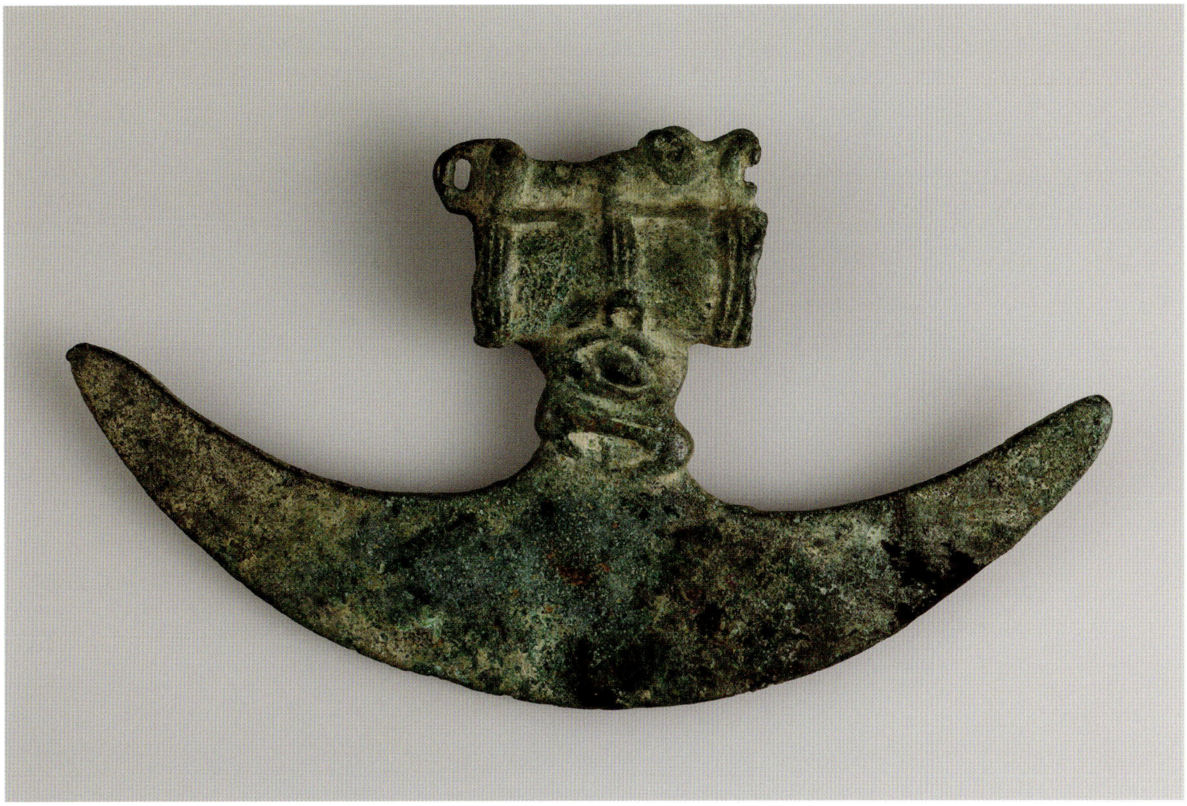

65. Crescent-Shaped Battle-Axe Head

Copper alloy

Iran, Luristan

Iron Age (1100–800 BCE)

Purchased in Nice, 1930

ISACM A7330

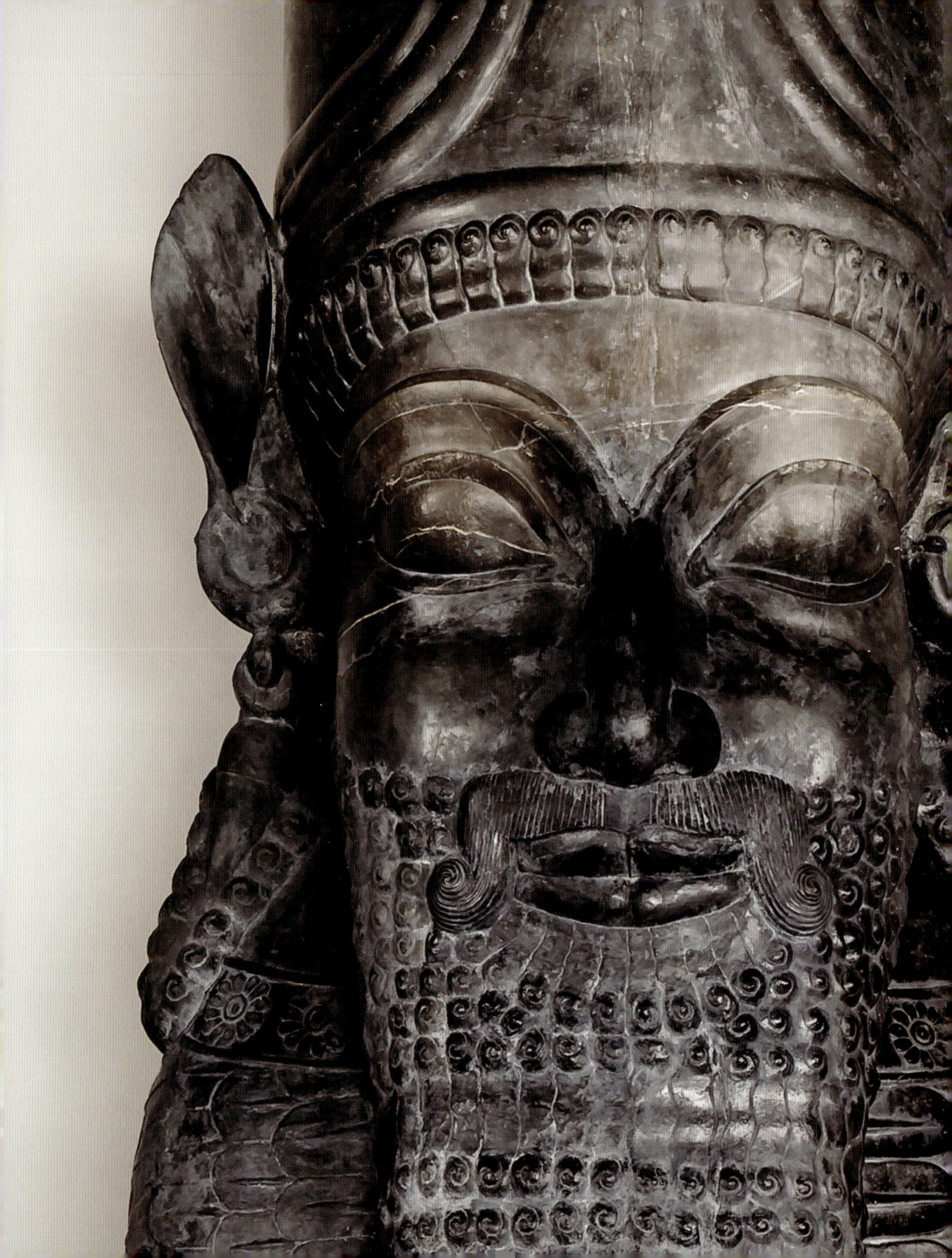

7 Persepolis and the Achaemenid Empire

After the initial expansion of Persian territory under Cyrus II and his son Cambyses II (550–522 BCE), the Achaemenid Persian Empire—named after Achaemenes, the ancestor of Cyrus II—reached its zenith under Darius I (522–486 BCE). Its borders extended from the Nile River to the Indus Valley and included the region of Thrace in northern Greece. Nothing like it had ever existed before, and its size and durability were not repeated until the Roman Empire in the second century CE.

Susa, Babylon, and possibly Hagmatana (modern-day Hamadan, or Greek Ecbatana, "The Place of Gathering") were the empire's major capital cities. Of them, Susa was the oldest, having been founded in prehistoric times (ca. 4500 BCE) and having served for millennia as the capital city of the Elamites. Babylon was younger; from the late third millennium BCE it existed as a town, then rose to prominence and prestige during the reign of Hammurabi in the early second millennium BCE. About Hagmatana we have only the reference of Herodotus, who mentions this city as the summer residence of the Achaemenid kings. Excavations at the site, however, have not revealed any archaeological remains earlier than the Parthian period (126 BCE–227 CE). Nevertheless, on the outskirts of Hamadan, at a site known locally as Ganj Nameh, "Treasure Epistle," two rock-cut inscriptions of Darius I and Xerxes I in Old Persian, Elamite, and Babylonian indicate the importance of the place for the Achaemenids.

Neither Herodotus nor any other Greek prior to Alexander III of Macedon (356–323 BCE, also known as Alexander the Great) mentions Persepolis. While ancient palaces were usually embedded in urban settings, Persepolis seems to have been an isolated complex of palaces and buildings without any urban structure in its vicinity (figs. 7.1 and 7.2). Persepolis may have been visited by Achaemenid kings on special occasions, such as celebrations of the new year, but it does not appear to have been the primary locus of the Achaemenid court. The discovery of thousands of administrative cuneiform tablets at the site, however, suggests that at least until the end of the reign of Xerxes I (486–465 BCE), Persepolis was the center of local administration.

Fragment of a limestone column capital from the Central Building at Persepolis, Iran. **Cat. no. 67**.

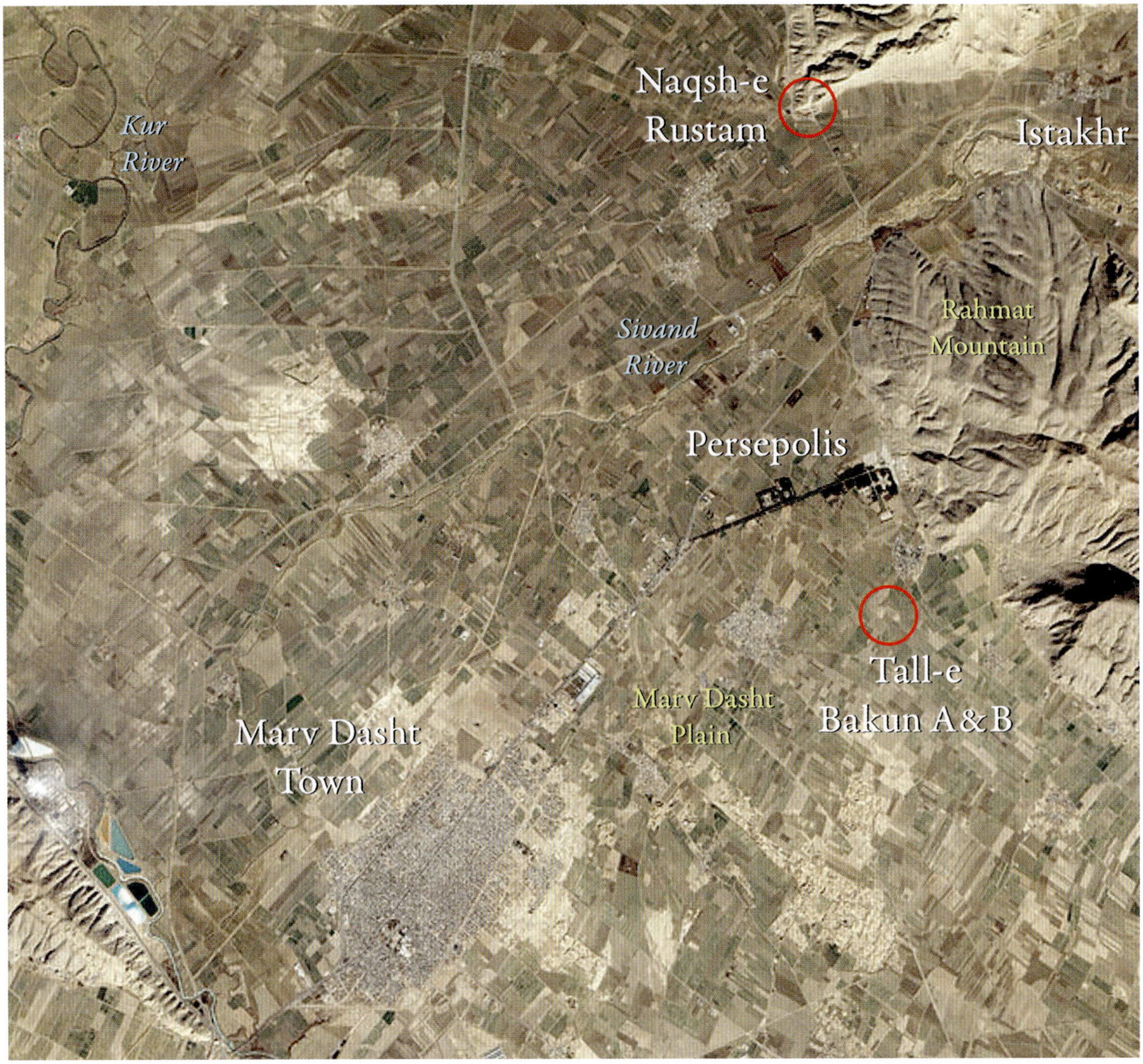

Figure 7.1. Satellite image of the Marv Dasht plain, showing the locations of Persepolis, Naqsh-e Rustam, Istakhr, and other ancient sites. Google Earth image with labels added by A. Alizadeh.

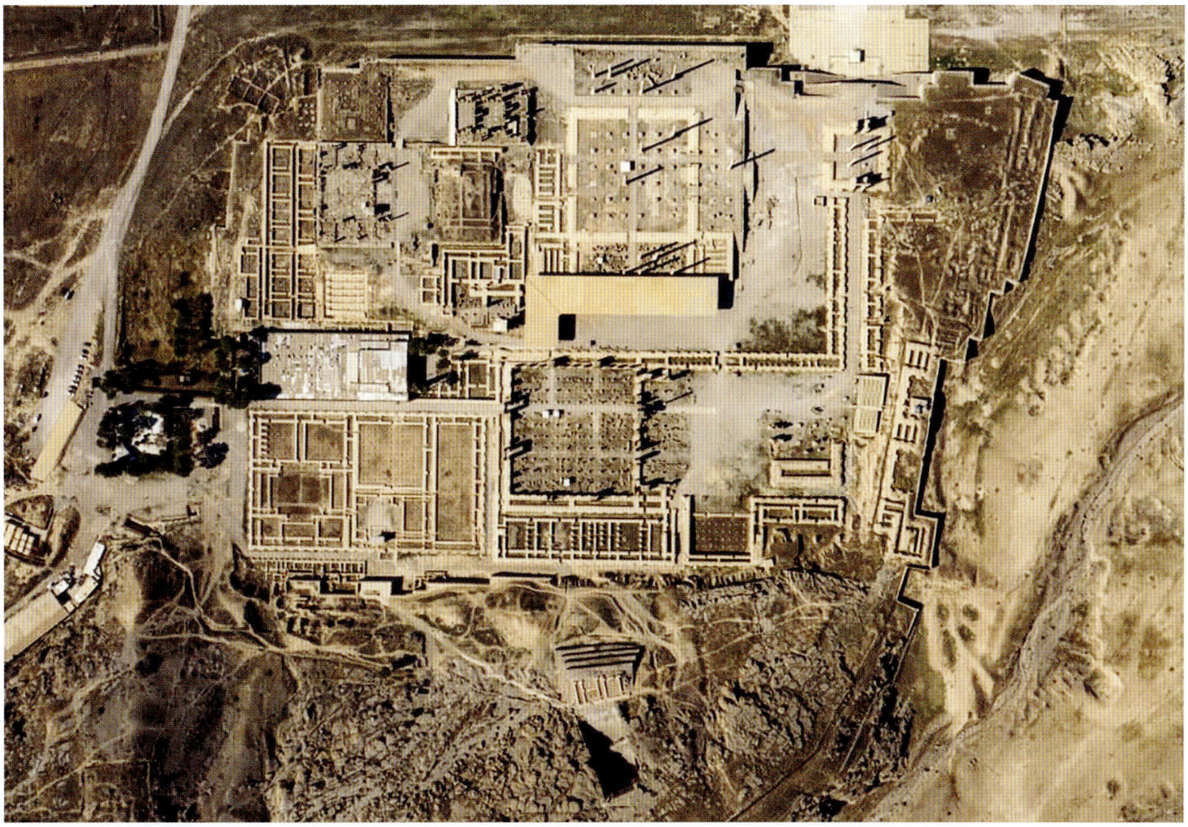

Figure 7.2. Aerial view of Persepolis. Image courtesy of M. Talibian.

Persepolis Terrace

Persepolis—known in Iran as Takht-e Jamshid, "Throne of Jamshid," after a legendary king—is the most iconic ancient site in Iran. It was excavated by ISAC under the direction of Ernst Herzfeld and Erich Schmidt from 1931 to 1939 and later by several Iranian archaeologists, including Mohammad-Taqi Mostafawi, Ali Sami, and Ali-Akbar Tajwidi. In 1979, UNESCO registered Persepolis as a World Cultural Heritage site.

The Achaemenids referred to Persepolis as Parsa, a Greek appellation meaning "City of Persians." The city was founded by Darius I between 520 and 510 BCE. Succeeding Achaemenid kings continued the construction until the city was destroyed by Alexander in 330 BCE. Even after its destruction, the standing ruins of Persepolis comprised one of the most imposing monuments of the ancient Near East and were described by European travelers as early as the fifteenth century CE. In the eighteenth century, travelers' copies of the various inscriptions at Persepolis served as the starting point for deciphering cuneiform scripts.

The buildings at Persepolis were erected on a terrace measuring roughly 455 meters wide and 300 meters deep and were constructed of colossal stone blocks and rubble fill over a low spur of Rahmat Mountain ("Mountain of Mercy"), which rises immediately to the east (figs. 7.3 and 7.4). The stone blocks were cut into polygonal shapes and joined, without mortar, by means of iron clamps. The floors, doorjambs, windows, and columns of the palaces were made of stone, while the surrounding walls were built of mudbrick. The column shafts of smaller buildings were made of timber.

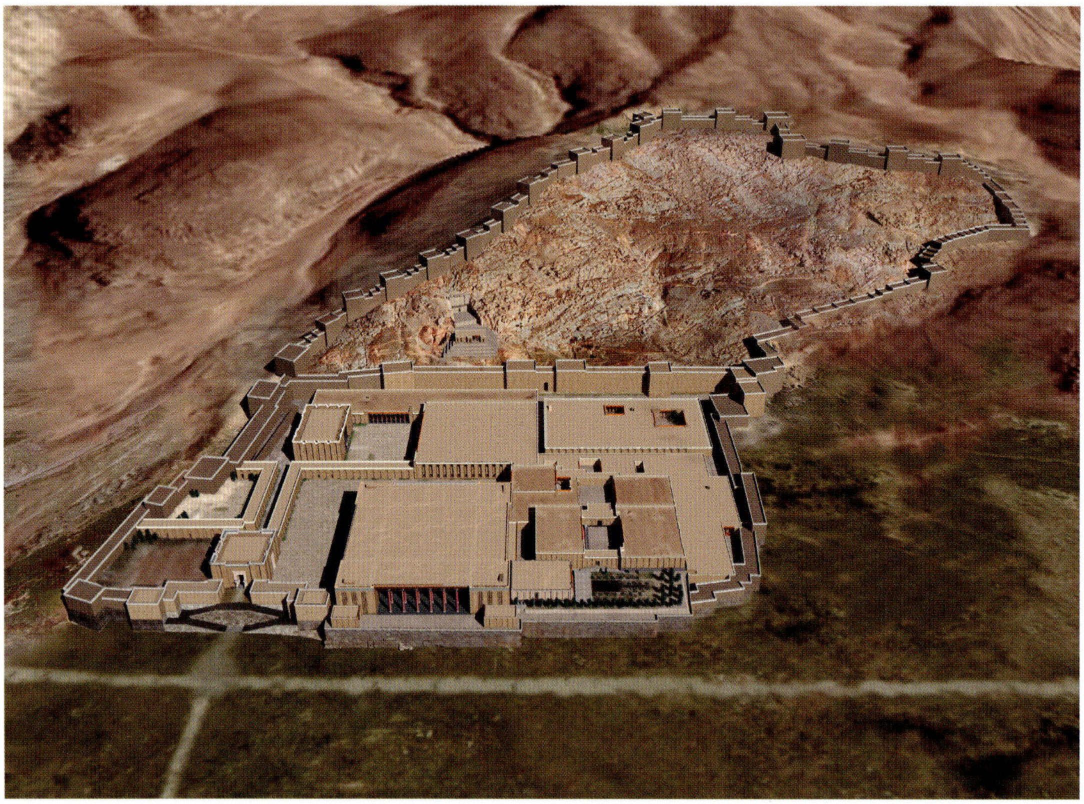

Figure 7.3. Digital reconstruction of Persepolis. Image courtesy of K. Afhami, Gambke Persepolis 3D.

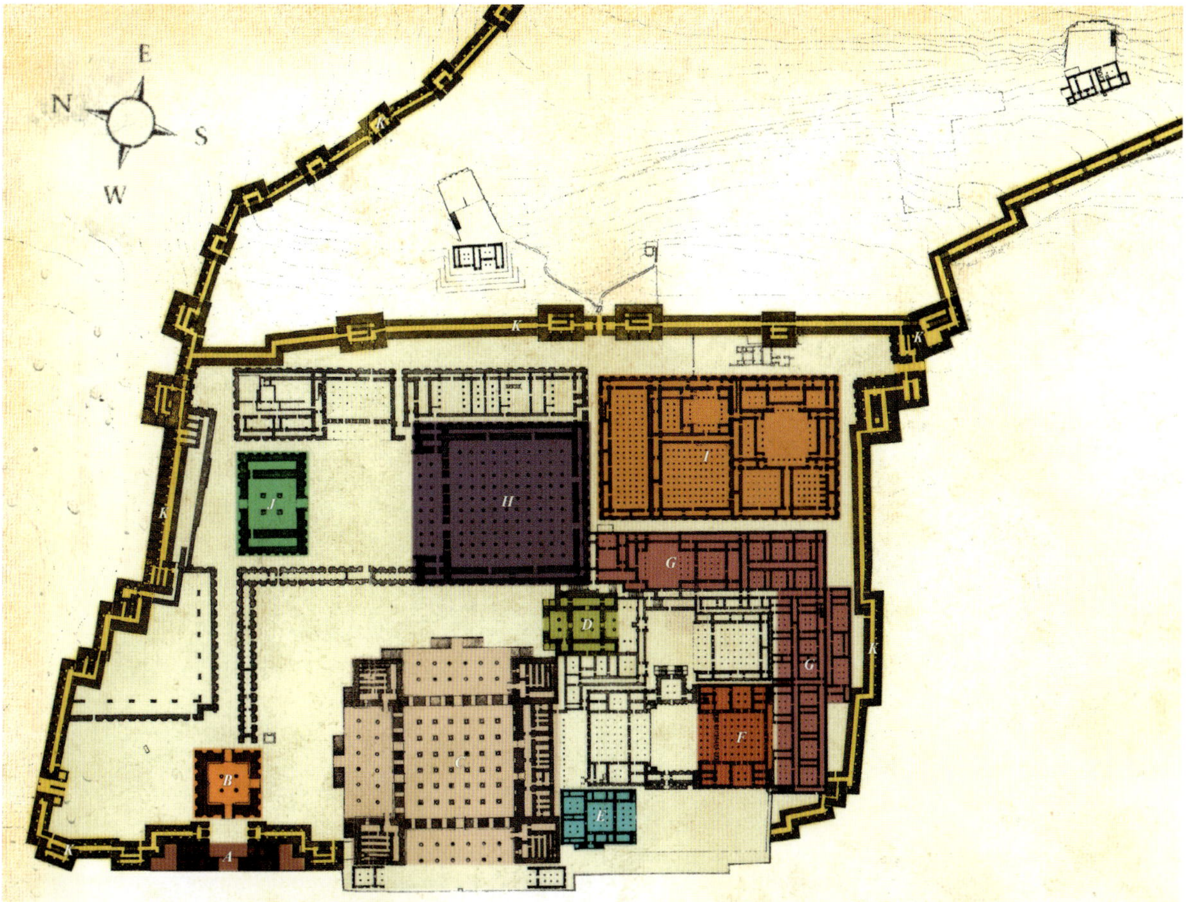

Figure 7.4. The high terrace of Persepolis with various buildings. *A*, entrance staircase; *B*, Gate of All Nations; *C*, Apadana; *D*, Tripylon; *E*, palace of Darius I; *F*, palace of Hadish; *G*, "Harem"; *H*, Hall of a Hundred Columns; *I*, Treasury; *J*, unfinished gate; *K*, fortifications. Image courtesy of F. Rezaeian.

Persepolis "Harem"

Erich Schmidt called a large, elongated building in the southwestern sector of the complex the "Harem." No textual or archaeological evidence attests this function for the building, and the appellation is probably rooted in the Western orientalist legacy, as exemplified by British painter Edwin Long's *Queen Esther* (fig. 7.5). The multichambered building was completely reconstructed by Friedrich Krefter, Ernst Herzfeld's superb architect, and from 1934 onward served as a museum, offices, and living quarters for various expeditions (fig. 7.6).

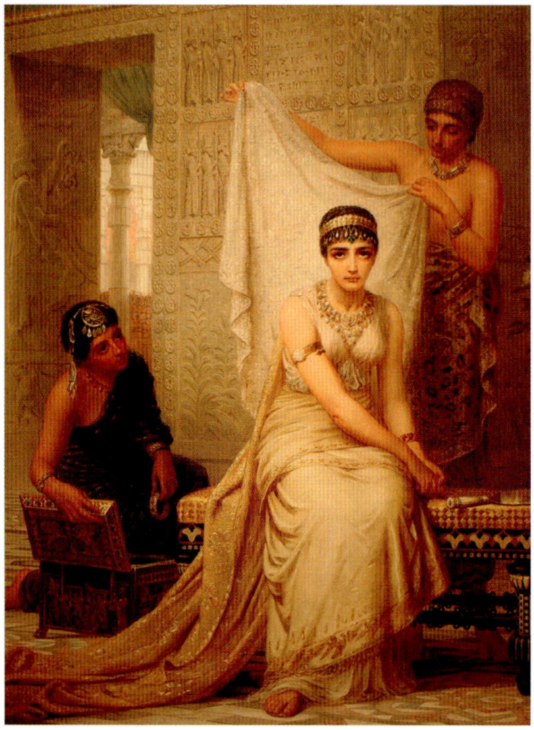

Figure 7.5. Edwin Long, *Queen Esther*, 1878. Oil on canvas, 213.5 × 170.3 cm. National Gallery of Victoria, Melbourne. Purchased 1879 (accession no. p.307.1-1).

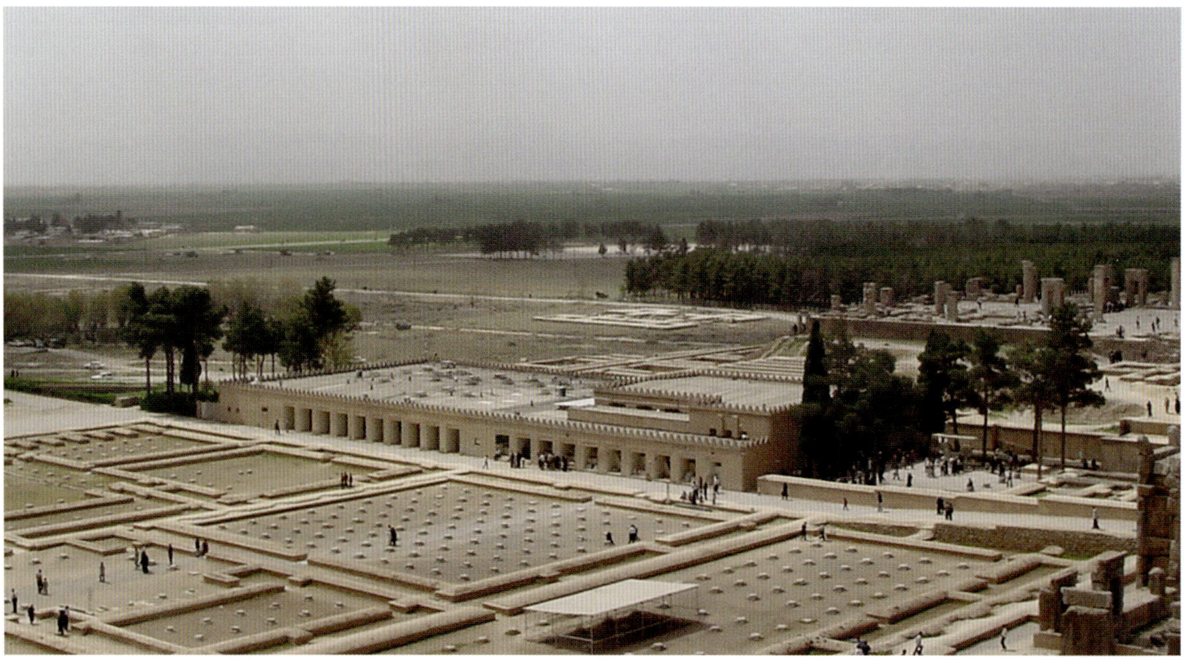

Figure 7.6. The building known as the "Harem" at Persepolis. Photo by M. Zare.

Persepolis Archives

One of the monumental discoveries at Persepolis was the Persepolis administrative archives, which contained some thirty thousand clay tablets. The archives comprise two groups of clay tablets and tablet fragments: several hundred pieces from the Treasury (the Treasury Archive) and tens of thousands of pieces found in a gatehouse in the fortification wall (the Fortification Archive) (fig. 7.7). The Fortification Archive texts date from 509 to 493 BCE (the thirteenth to the twenty-eighth regnal year of Darius I). They record transfers of food products in Fars and locations between Persepolis and Susa, especially rations for workers, travelers, and officials. Many of the texts were written at way stations and subcenters, then sent on to Persepolis. A smaller number were written at Persepolis periodically to compile the information from incoming texts into larger accounts or summaries.

The Treasury Archive texts, dating from 492 to 457 BCE (spanning the reigns of Darius I and his successors, Xerxes I and Artaxerxes I), were written at Persepolis. They deal with silver paid from the Persepolis treasury, especially to support laborers and craftsmen building the structures on the terrace.

Most of the Persepolis texts are written in cuneiform in Elamite, the language spoken and written in southwestern Iran for thousands of years before speakers of Iranian languages arrived there. As Persians lived among the Elamites and gained ascendancy, Persian rulers adopted Elamite recording techniques and incorporated many Persian names, titles, and administrative terms transcribed with Elamite spellings. The few tablets written in other languages reflect the scope and diversity of the empire's provinces. The fact that almost all the Persepolis tablets were written in Elamite testifies to the continuation of Elamite civilization at the Persian court and in Persian society.

In the international realm, the Aramaic alphabet and language were used for administration, legal recording, and official communications in Anatolia, Egypt, Syria-Palestine, Babylonia, and Iran itself. The Fortification Archive included hundreds of administrative texts in Aramaic, and hundreds of the Elamite tablets also contain short Aramaic notations. The Aramaic was written either in ink with a brush or pen (when the clay tablet was mostly dry and hard) or incised with a stylus (while the clay was still soft).

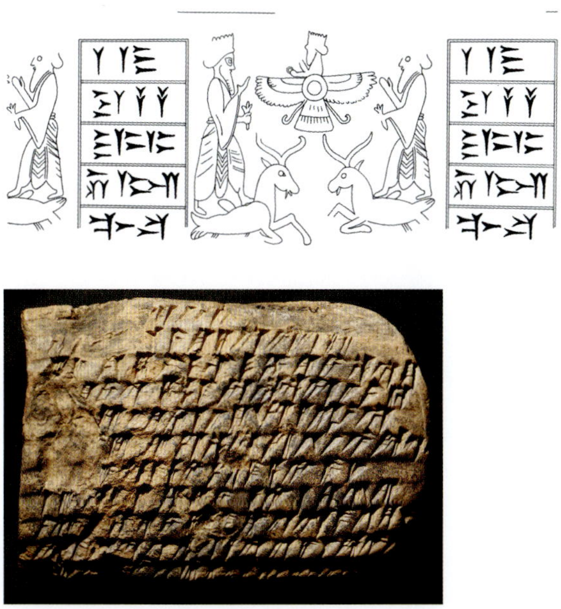

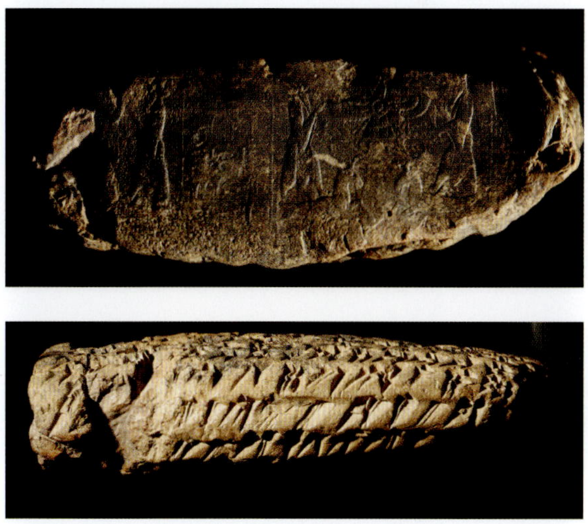

Figure 7.7. Line drawing and photographs of Persepolis Fortification Archive tablet 12 (ISACM A23259). Images courtesy of the Persepolis Fortification Archive Project.

Column Capitals and Shafts

Most of the column capitals that supported roof beams at Persepolis had double protomes in the shape of bulls, bulls with human heads, or griffins (figs. 7.8 and 7.9). Archaeological studies have shown that the columns and sculptures were all originally painted. **Cat. no. 66**, a double-bull capital, probably belonged to a portico of the Hall of a Hundred Columns at Persepolis. Although standing today at just under 3 meters, it shares elements of the taller columns of the main halls at Persepolis. The fluted shaft, which at full height rose 16.5–19.5 meters, is topped by a flower-like capital emerging from a wreath of leaves that hang like petals. The front parts (protomes) of two bulls rest on top. The open space between the bulls was designed to support a wooden beam. Most elements of the column were inspired by other cultures. The fluted shaft is Greek in style. The flower-like capital has Phoenician and Urartian parallels and ultimately originated in Egypt. The double-protome capital, however, is purely Achaemenid in style. Like all architectural elements at Persepolis, this column was originally gilded and painted, as figure 7.8 shows.

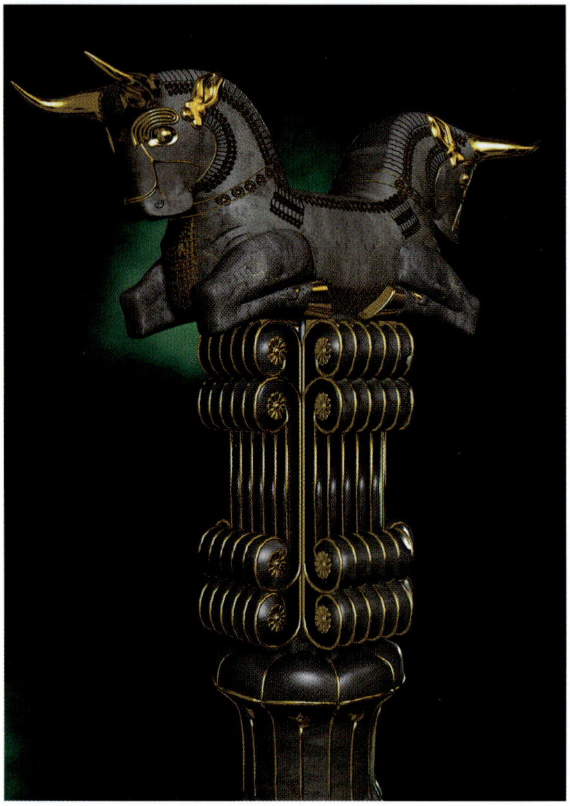

Figure 7.8. Digital reconstruction of Persepolis column. Image courtesy of F. Rezaeian.

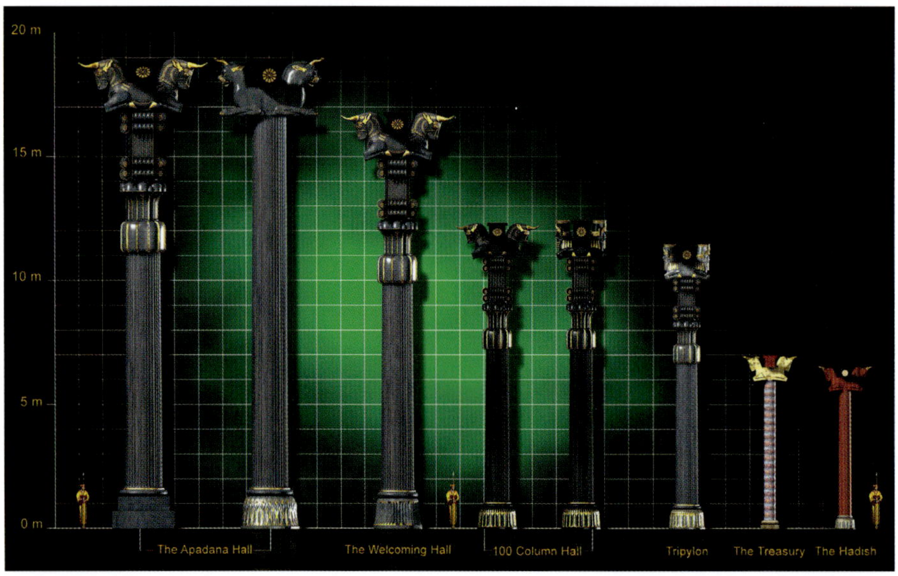

Figure 7.9. Digital reconstructions of various types of columns and capitals used in buildings at Persepolis. Image courtesy of F. Rezaeian.

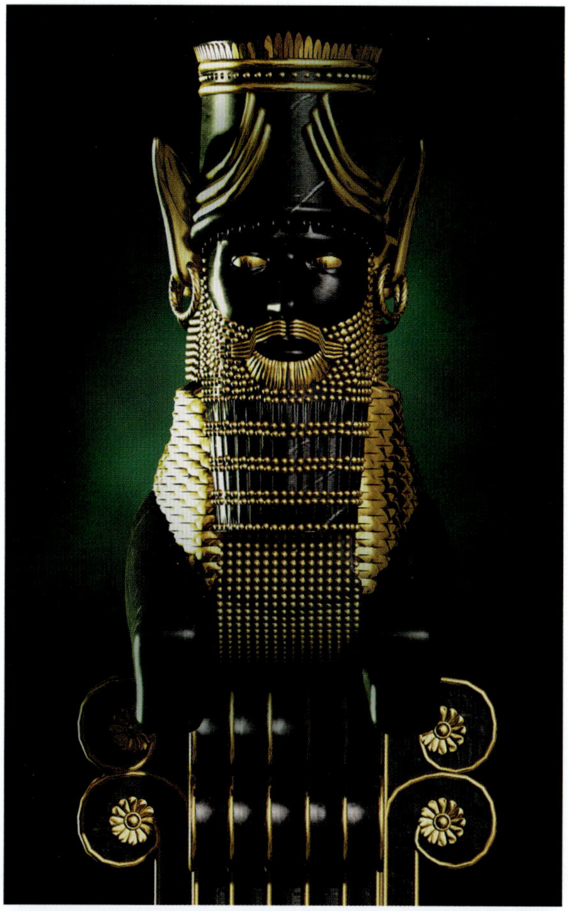

Figure 7.10. Digital reconstruction of capital with human-headed bull. Image courtesy of F. Rezaeian.

Cat. no. 67 (fig. 7.10) represents one side, or protome, of a type of human-headed bull capital used exclusively in the Tripylon (Council Hall). The divine crown with triple horns, along with other features of this sculpture, has Assyrian origins. The facial details, as well as the bird feathers on its shoulders, were delicately rendered even though the capital would have soared at a considerable height above the ground.

A colossal pair of striding, human-headed bulls also flanked the entrance of the Gate of All Nations. The architects of Persepolis installed such colossal guardian figures at the entrances of important buildings as protection against evil spirits. **Cat. no. 68**, a highly polished stone bull's head, derives from one of two guardian bulls that flanked the portico of Persepolis's Hall of a Hundred Columns. The bull is rendered in the Achaemenid court style. The huge, plain surface of its naturalistically rendered face is divided into schematic zones of massive veins, sharp-edged eyelids, and tightly curled hair.

This colossal bull's head confronting the visitor at the center of the gallery now lacks its ears and horns, which were made separately to ensure they did not break when the sculpture was transported to the site. Like many carvings and sculptures of the ancient Near East, this specimen must have been painted, and the ears and horns may have been covered with gold, as the reconstruction in figure 7.11 suggests.

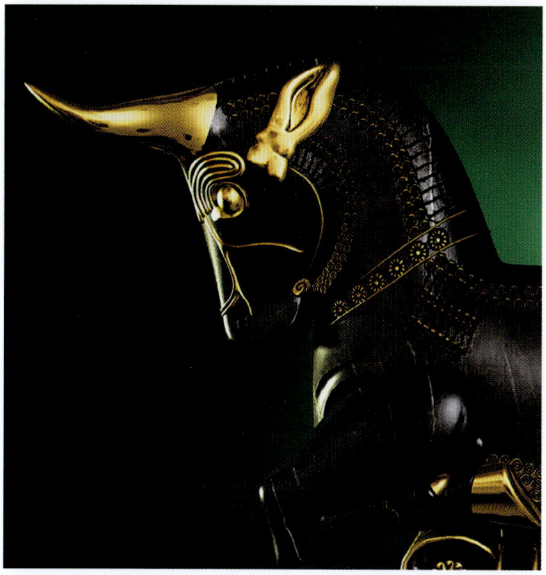

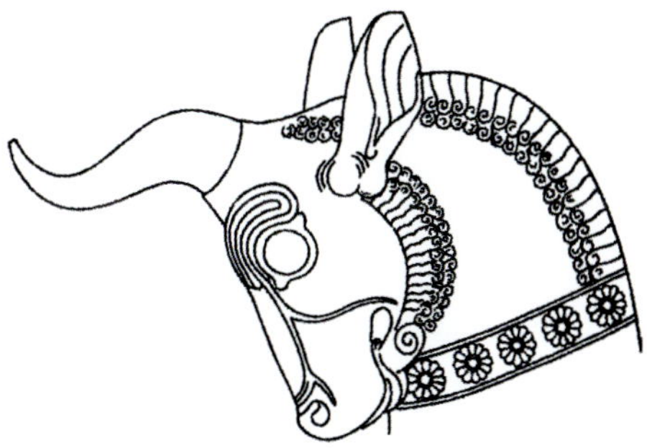

Figure 7.11. Digital econstruction and drawing of bull capital. Images courtesy of F. Rezaeian.

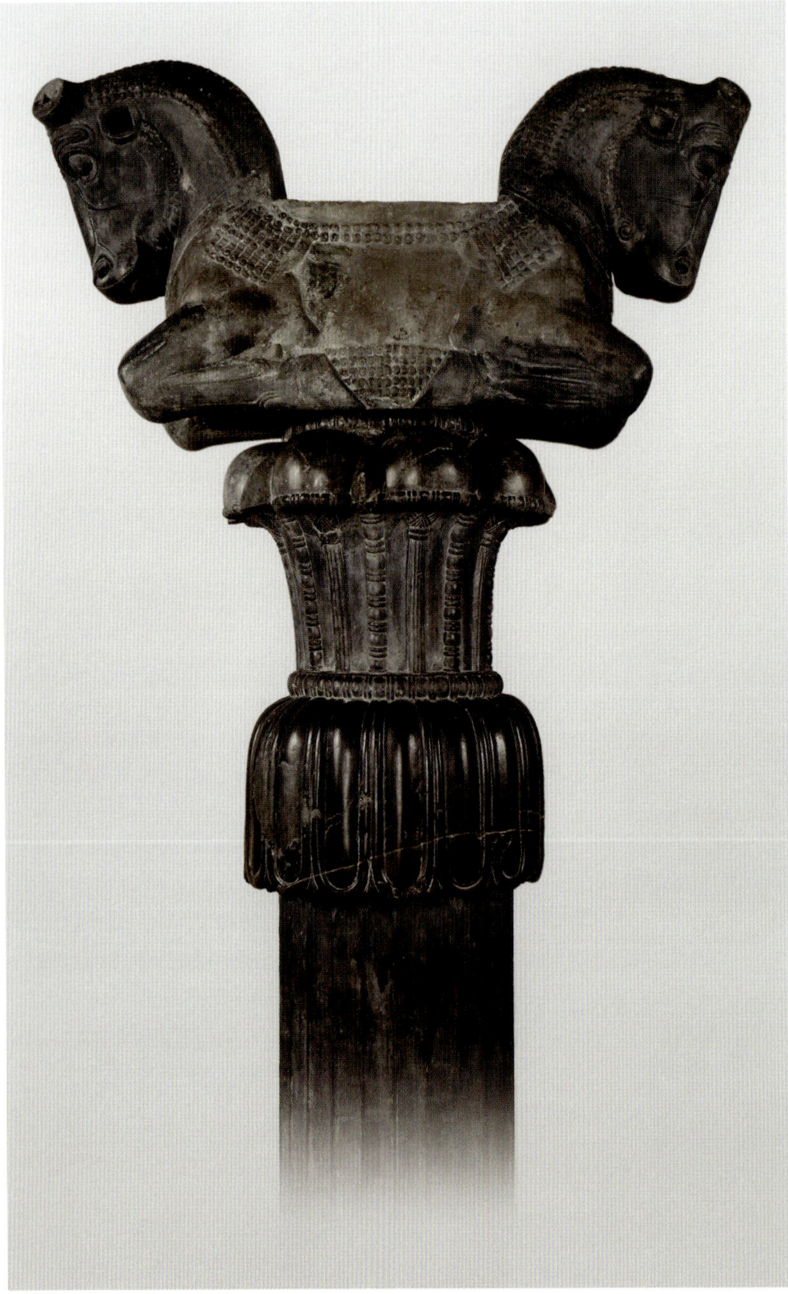

66. Composite Capital

Limestone (with modern restoration)

Iran, Persepolis, Apadana, southern portico

Achaemenid period, reigns of Darius I and Xerxes I (522–465 BCE)

Excavated in 1933–1934

ISACM A24069 (column), A24070 (capital)

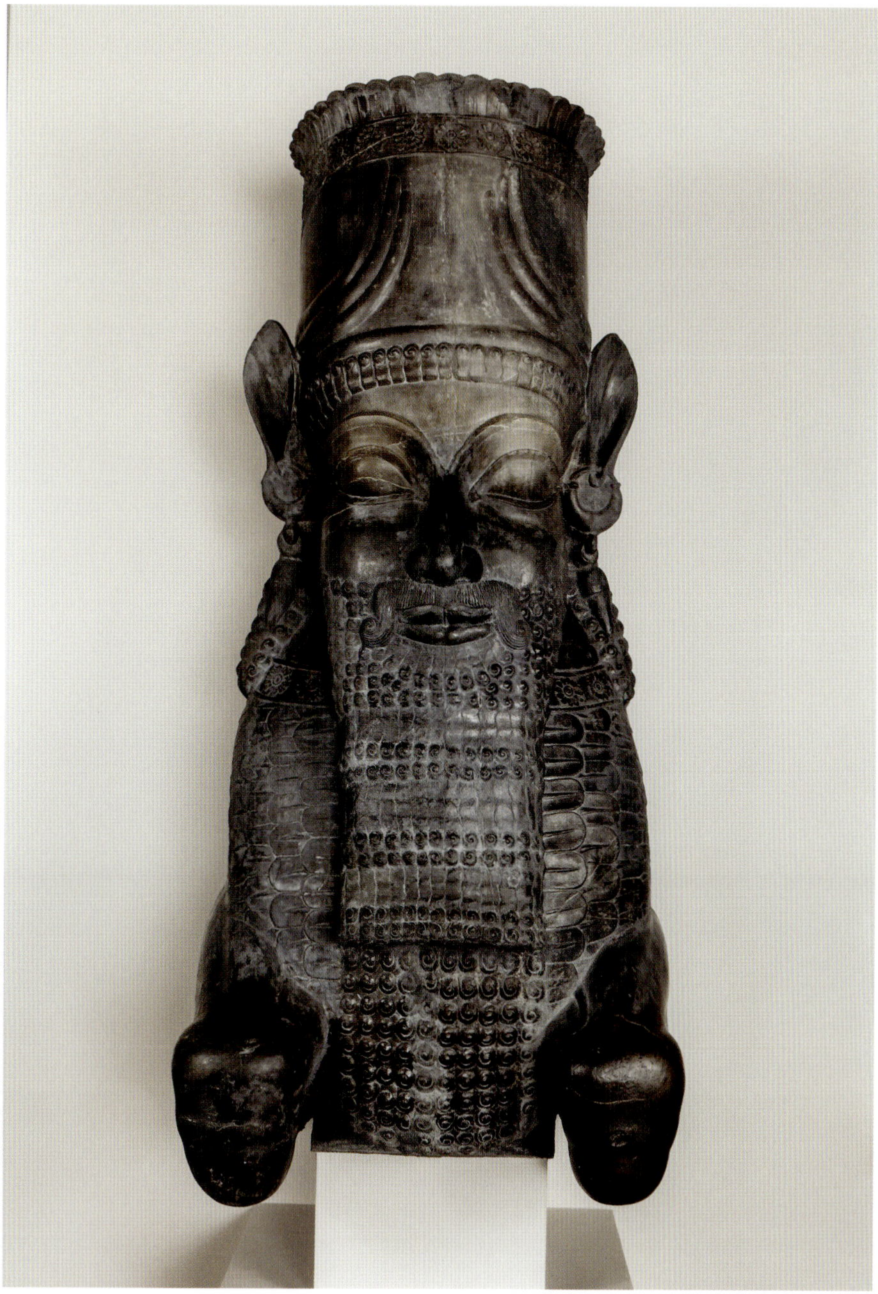

67. Capital Fragment

Limestone (with modern restoration)

Iran, Persepolis, Central Building

Achaemenid period, reign of Xerxes I (486–465 BCE)

Excavated in 1932–1934

ISACM A24066

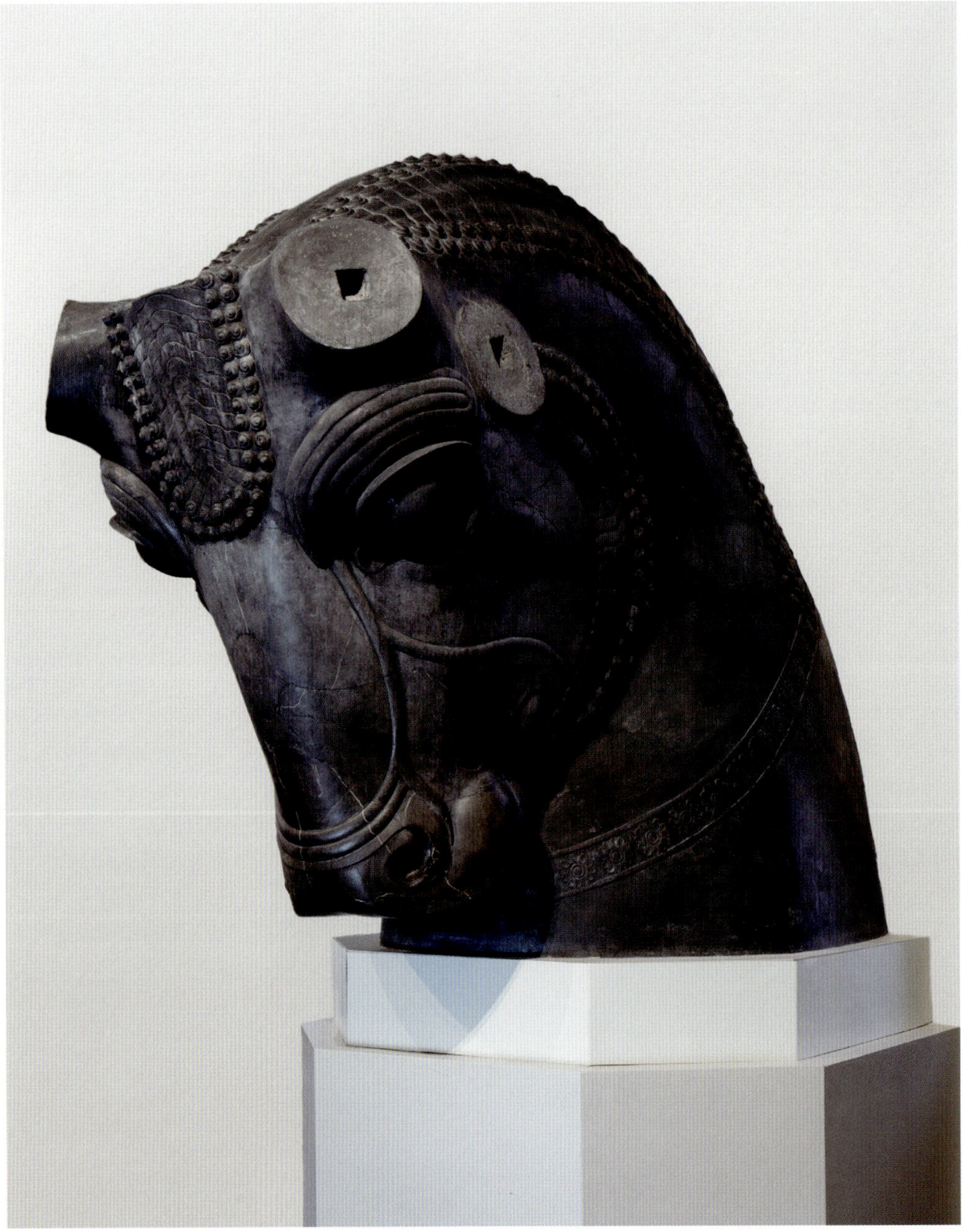

68. Colossal Bull Head

Limestone (with modern restoration)

Iran, Persepolis, Hall of a Hundred Columns, east anta of portico

Achaemenid period, reigns of Xerxes I and Artaxerxes I (486–424 BCE)

Excavated in 1932–1933

ISACM A24065

Reliefs and Inscriptions

Cat. no. 69 is an architectural element known as a "cavetto cornice," a concave shape decorated with vertical leaves. The idea was borrowed directly from Egypt. Some Persepolis tablets mention Egyptian artisans working at Persepolis, and this lintel may well have been carved by an Egyptian stonecutter at the Achaemenid court. All preserved lintels at Persepolis are of this type.

Cat. no. 70, a masterfully carved frieze, may have belonged to the lower part of a lintel or to part of an audience scene from a palace wall at Persepolis. With its exquisitely carved striding lions, the frieze is probably an imitation in stone of a cloth canopy under which the king gave audience. The tasseled fringe at the base consists of knotted cords clearly inspired by woven materials. The upper register represents the canopy's roof and is decorated with large, twelve-petaled rosettes. Below are two registers of smaller rosettes that frame a file of striding lions rendered in the typical Achaemenid court style. The lions' highly stylized cheek muscles resemble two leaves; the wrinkles of their noses are represented by smoothly carved low ridges; their manes have stylized tufts divided into rows; and their shoulder muscles resemble figure eights. Striding rows of lions had long symbolized power and protection in much of the ancient Near East.

The lion–bull combat scene on **cat. no. 71** has very ancient origins. The earliest example is on a stamp seal from Susa dating to about 4200 BCE; later, during the Protoliterate period, the theme became popular in both Iran and Mesopotamia, and during the Early Dynastic period in the third millennium BCE, various compositions of the combat scene populated glyptic art (fig. 7.12).

The lion–bull iconography has generated several interpretations, ranging from the astronomical and seasonal (depicting the equinox) to the symbolic (as a representation of the day-and-night cycle, with the lion representing the sun and the bull the night).

While this motif may well have had different meanings and significance throughout its long history, what is certain is that these two animals represent power and majesty, fit for royal iconography. Achaemenid monumental art is formal, symbolic, and devoid of any attempt at narrative. In contrast to the art of Assyrian palaces, which had vivid scenes of war, torture, and beheading, Achaemenid art typically portrays calm, stability, and peace. The lion–bull combat stands as the exception, where fear and rage are clearly and successfully rendered.

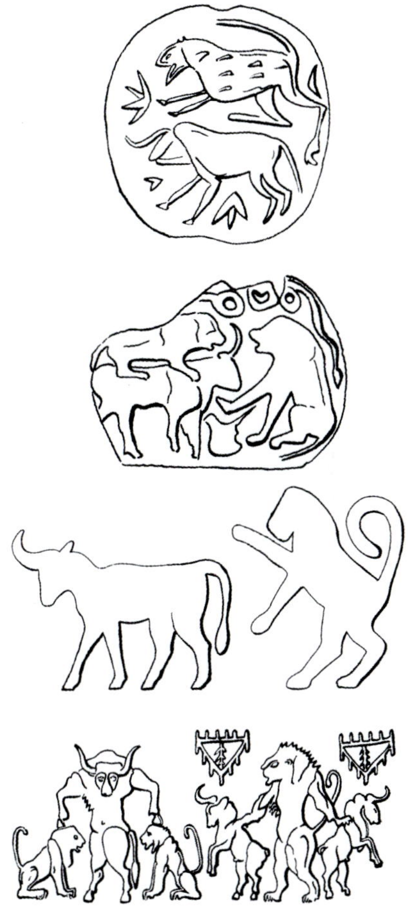

Figure 7.12. Drawings of glyptic scenes. Top to bottom: Susa (ca. 4200 BCE), Gawra (ca. 3600 BCE), Chogha Mish (ca. 3200 BCE), Susa (ca. 3000 BCE). After Amiet 1961, no. 144; Amiet 1961, no. 55; Delougaz and Kantor 1996, pl. 140; Amiet 1961, no. 588.

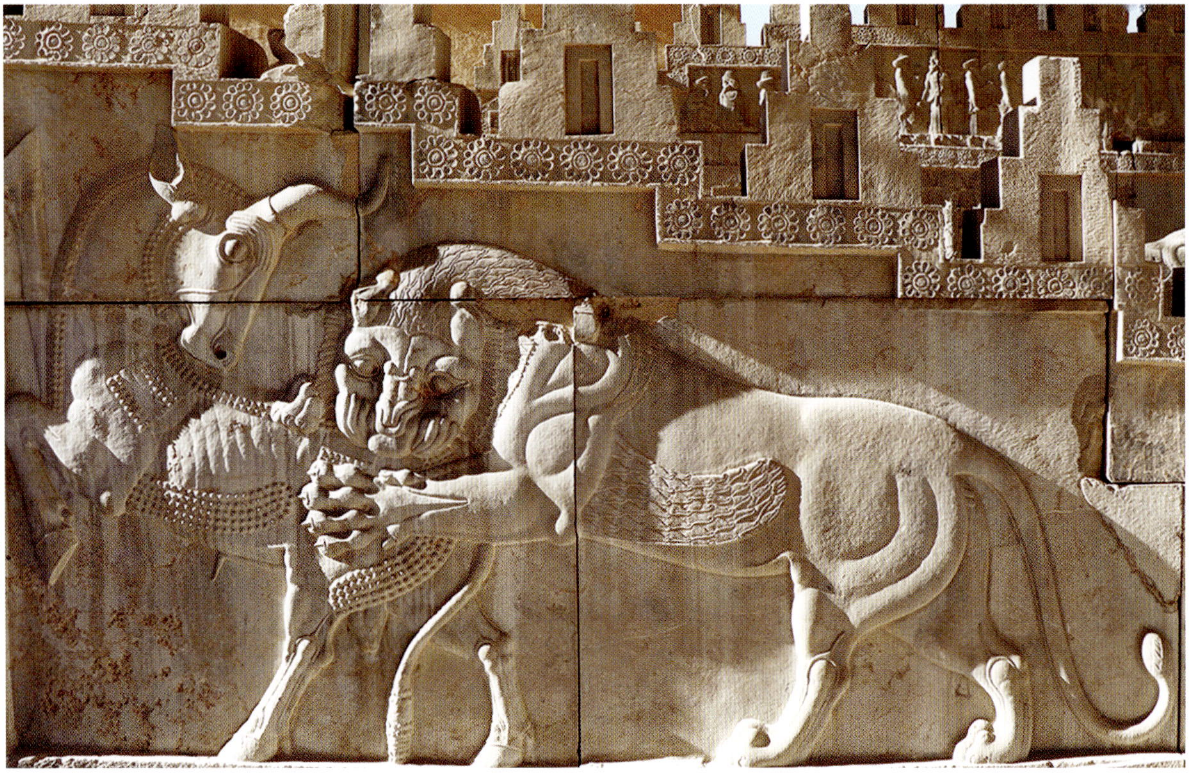

Figure 7.13 Relief of the lion–bull combat scene at Persepolis. Photo by A. Alizadeh.

Whatever the symbolic significance of this combat scene at Persepolis, it is used exclusively on the facade of the staircases of the various palaces, where the scene's triangular shape is perfectly suited to the staircases' triangular space (fig. 7.13).

The dedication of a newly constructed building to a deity through an inscribed object, statuette, or metal plaque was long practiced in ancient Mesopotamia and Iran. **Cat. no. 72**, a stone slab inscribed during the reign of Xerxes I, was used as a foundation stone in the corner of one of the buildings of that king. It was removed by a successor and used, along with six others, in a bench inside the garrison. The seven slabs bear cuneiform inscriptions in Old Persian, Babylonian, and Elamite that record versions of two texts. This slab, in Babylonian, gives the titles and attributes of Xerxes I, lists vassal lands that brought tribute to him, and tells how he suppressed disorder and the worship of "evil ones," or *daiva* ("demons") in Old Persian.

ISAC archaeologists excavated many objects of blue frit, or "Egyptian blue," at Persepolis, including fragments of composite sculptures, tableware, and architectural elements. This composite material—made of quartz, calcite, and a copper compound—imitates the intense blue of lapis lazuli, a precious stone of Afghanistan. Its rarity made it a status symbol in the ancient Near East. **Cat. no. 73**'s trilingual inscription, written in Old Persian, Elamite, and Babylonian, reads: "Knobbed peg of precious stone [or lapis lazuli] made in the house of Darius the King."

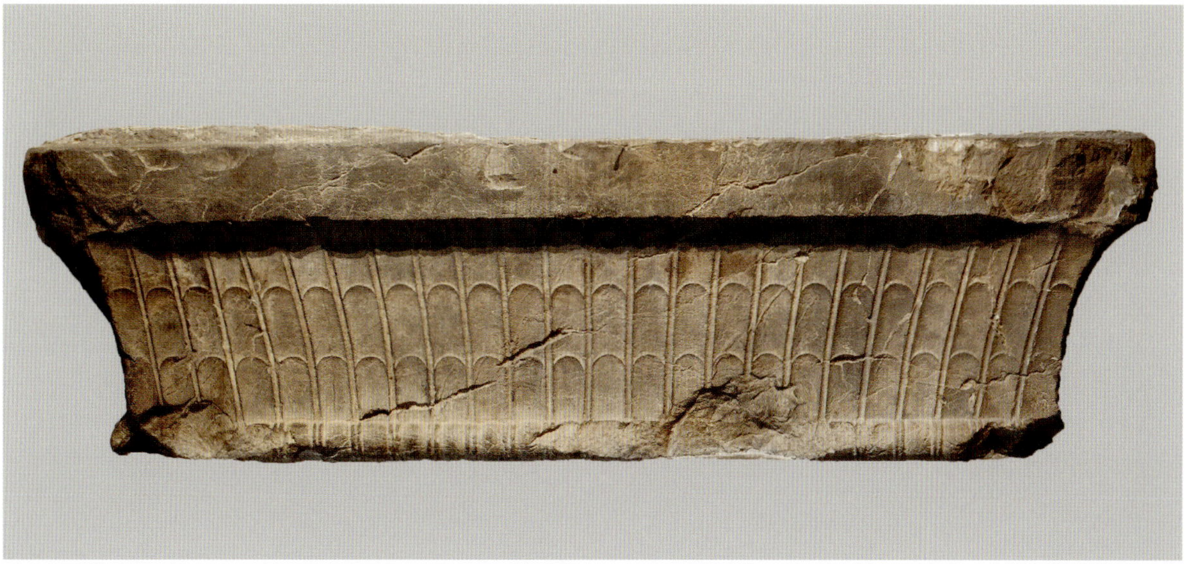

69. Lintel

Limestone

Iran, Persepolis, "Harem"

Achaemenid period, reign of Xerxes I (486–465 BCE)

Excavated in 1933–1934

ISACM A24074

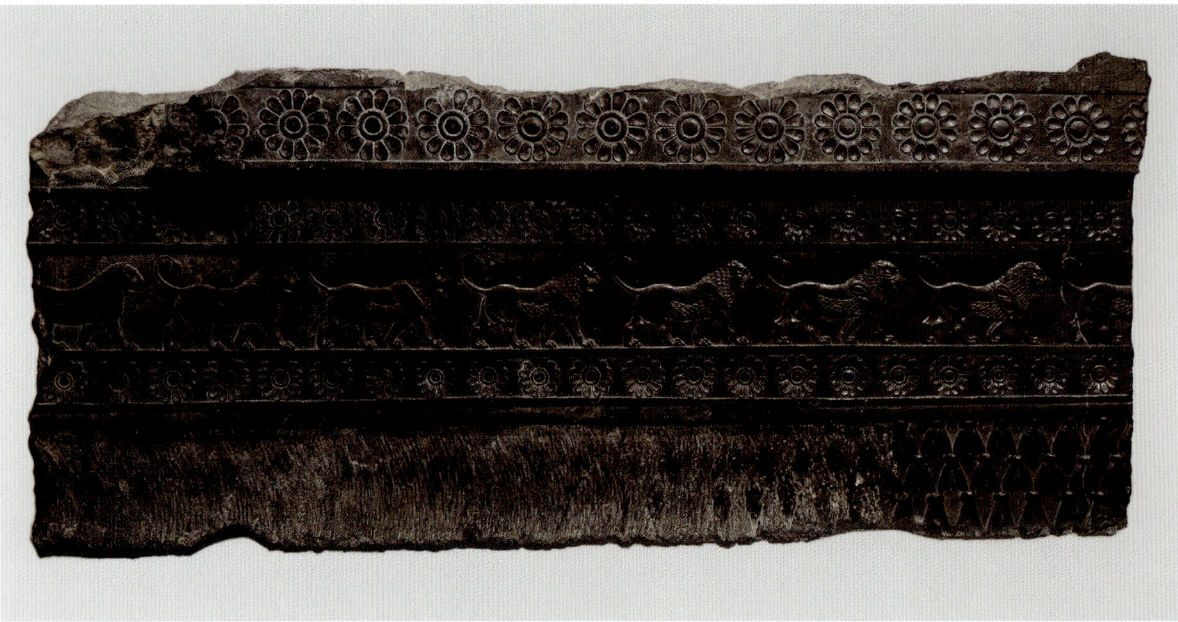

70. Frieze

Limestone

Iran, Persepolis, Palace G

Achaemenid period, reigns of Darius I and Xerxes I (522–465 BCE)

Excavated in 1933–1934

ISACM A24068

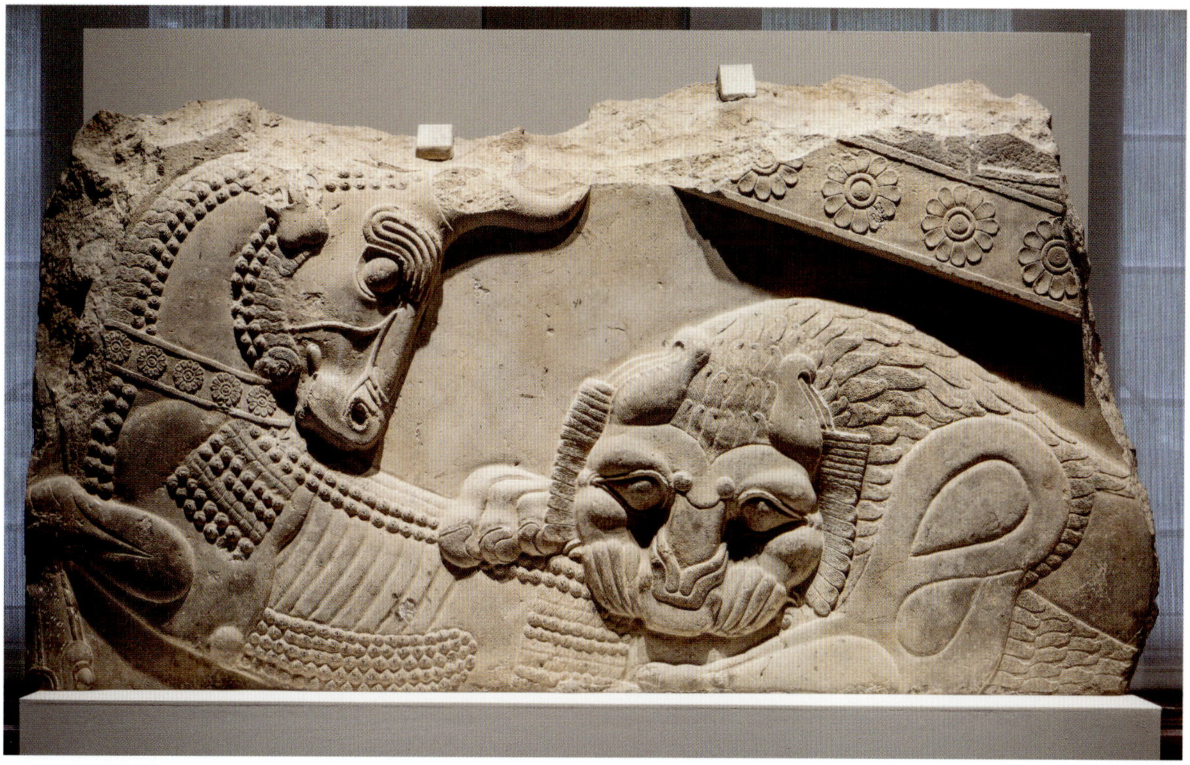

71. Relief

Limestone

Iran, Persepolis, Palace H, west end of facade (probably reused from Palace G)

Achaemenid period, probably reign of Artaxerxes III (358–338 BCE)

Excavated in 1933–1934

ISACM A73100

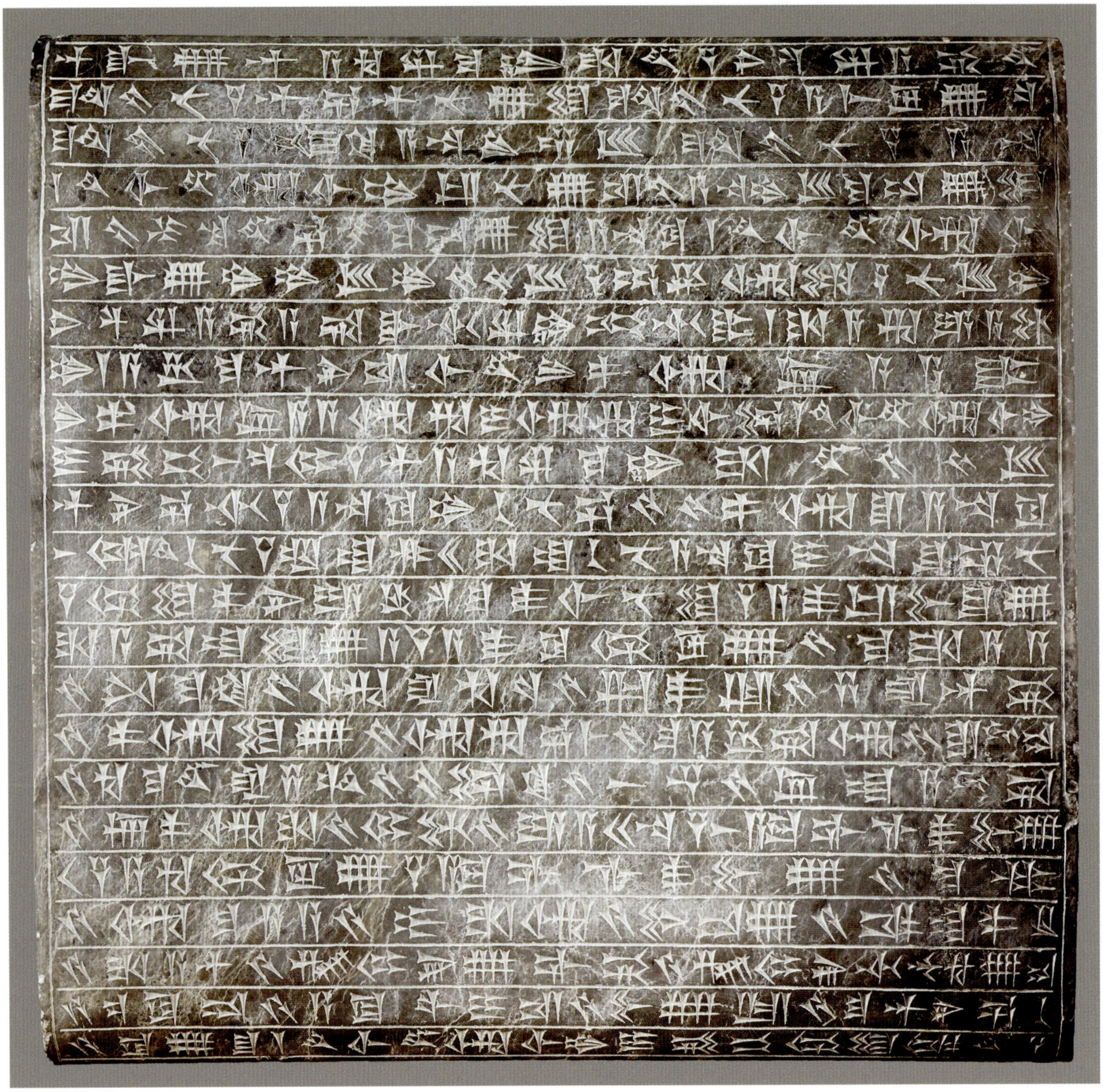

72. Foundation Slab

Limestone

Iran, Persepolis, garrison quarters

Achaemenid period, reign of Xerxes I (486–465 BCE)

Excavated in 1935

ISACM A24120

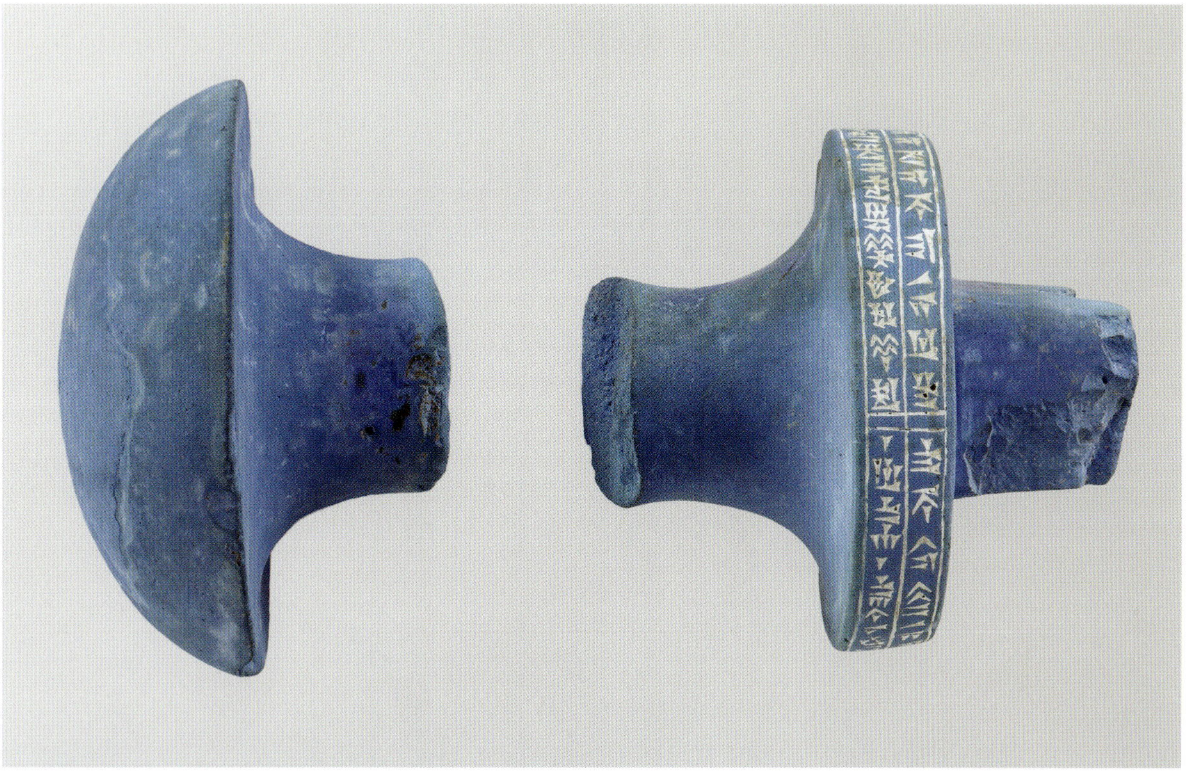

73. Wall Peg with Trilingual Text

Egyptian blue, paint

Iran, Persepolis, west passage of the "Harem"

Achaemenid period, reign of Darius I (522–486 BCE)

Excavated in 1931–1932

ISACM A29808A–B

Jewelry and Amulets

A spectacular roundel showing a winged lion is thought to come from Hamadan, ancient Ecbatana, a summer residence of the Achaemenid court (**cat. no. 74**). Close examination of the roundel reveals the artist's mastery, as described by ISAC art historian Helene Kantor (1957, 11–12):

> Restrained within the circuit of a slender, twisted cord, a lithe-bodied lion, transfigured by the glory of a great upsweeping wing, turns as if in snarling defiance of pursuers. The forelegs are still stretched in the stride of a walk just ceased, while the hind-quarters seem already tensed for possible battle; the curious small horns and the ear are bent back suddenly and threateningly; the tail lashes.

Such roundels were either suspended or sewn on garments worn by wealthy, possibly royal, individuals. One can envisage the dazzling contrast between the gold and a fabric of strong color, such as purple, a favorite hue of the royal Achaemenids.

Stone necklaces from Persepolis are rare. The individual beads of **cat. no. 75** and the reconstructed necklace shown in figure 7.14 demonstrate the high craftsmanship of the Achaemenid period. Given that the extremely narrow (1 millimeter), curving holes of the crescent-shaped central beads were made without modern drills, these exquisite necklaces testify to the jewelry-making skills of artisans in the Achaemenid period.

Stone eyes were first used around 2600 BCE in Sumerian and Elamite statues, such as the statue in figure 7.15 displayed in the ISAC Museum's Mesopotamian Gallery. While the statue's oval-shaped stone types continued to be used as eyes, the circular glass and stone eyes found at Susa and Chogha Zanbil were primarily used on decorative wall tiles and doorknobs, either to ward off the evil eye or to represent the watchful eyes of deities (**cat. no. 76**; fig. 7.16). Such superstition continues to this day. The stones eyes from Persepolis may have been used in a similar fashion.

Evil-eye protection amulets or paintings were used in ancient Egypt, Mesopotamia, and Iran, as well as in the classical world. They still exist in some form in Jewish, Christian, Muslim, Buddhist, and Hindu cultures (fig. 7.17). Terms for the evil eye in various cultures include Arabic *ayin harsha*, Hebrew *ayin ha'ra*, French *mauvais oeil*, German *böser Blick*, Italian *mal occhio,* Latin *oculus malus*, Persian *bla band*, Scottish *droch shuil*, Spanish *mal ojo / el oja*, and Turkish *nazar boncuğu*.

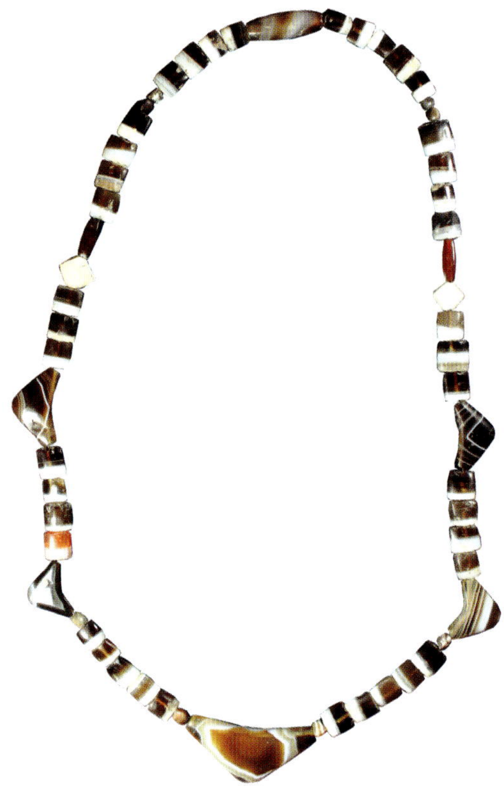

Figure 7.14. Necklace of semiprecious stone beads from Persepolis (ca. 500–350 BCE), National Museum of Iran, Tehran. Photo by A. Alizadeh.

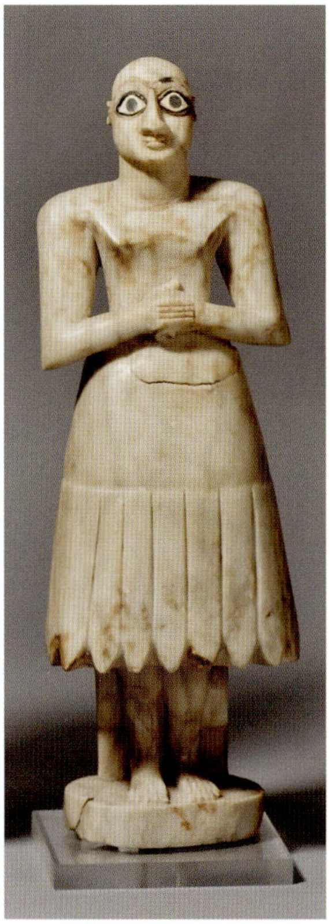

Figure 7.15. Gypsum standing male figure (with modern restoration) from the Abu Temple at Eshnunna, Iraq, Early Dynastic period (ca. 2900–2600 BCE) (ISACM A12332).

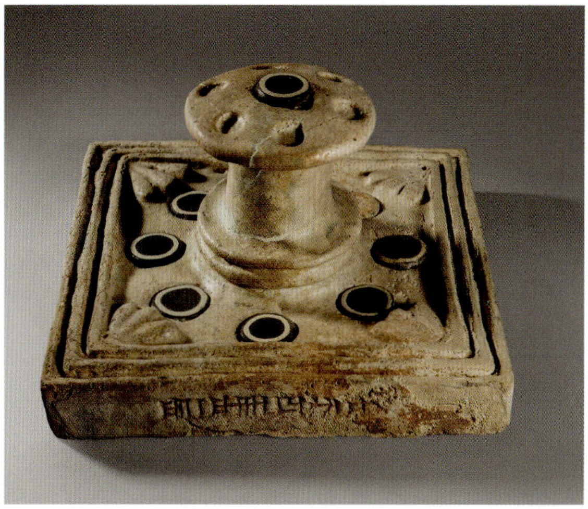

Figure 7.16. Doorknob / wall peg with nine glass eyes from Chogha Zanbil, Khuzestan, Iran, Middle Elamite period (ca. 1400–1000 BCE), National Museum of Iran, Tehran. Photo by N. Fakurzadeh.

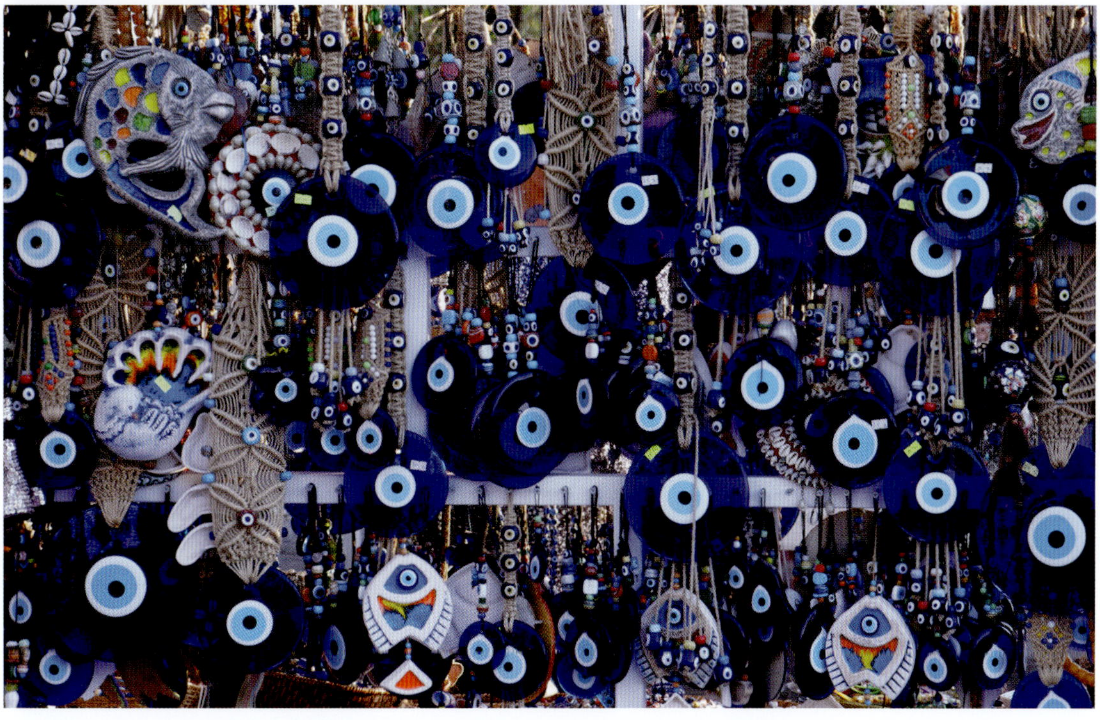

Figure 7.17. Evil-eye amulets shop in Istanbul, Turkey. Photo by V. Walker, Wikimedia Commons.

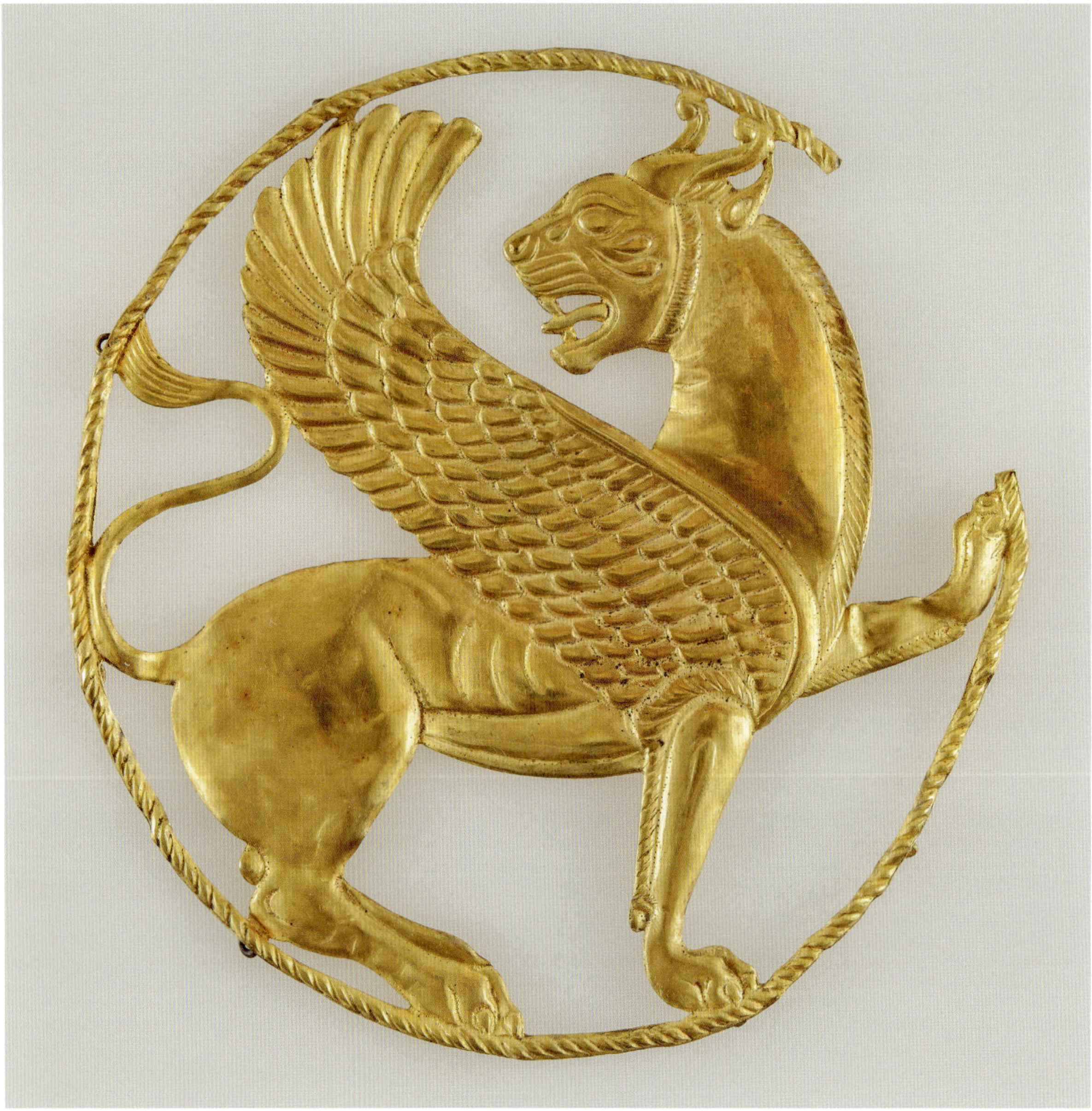

74. Roundel with Winged Lion

Gold

Iran

Achaemenid period (ca. 550–330 BCE)

Purchased in New York, 1948

ISACM A28582

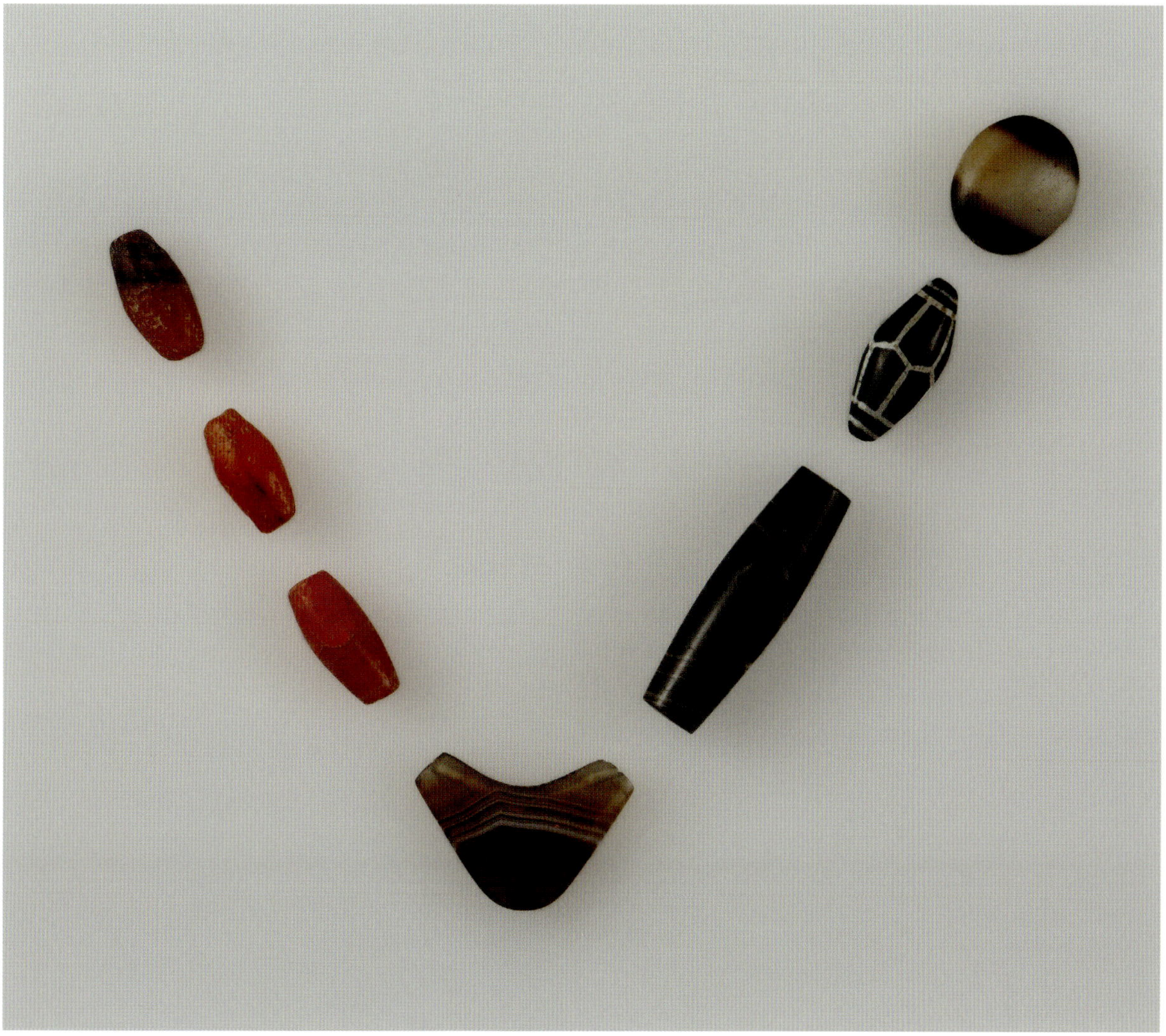

75. Variously Shaped Beads

Stone

Iran, Persepolis

Achaemenid period (ca. 550–330 BCE)

Excavated in 1931–1935

ISACM A19576M–N, A22949, A19580–19581, A19583, A19586

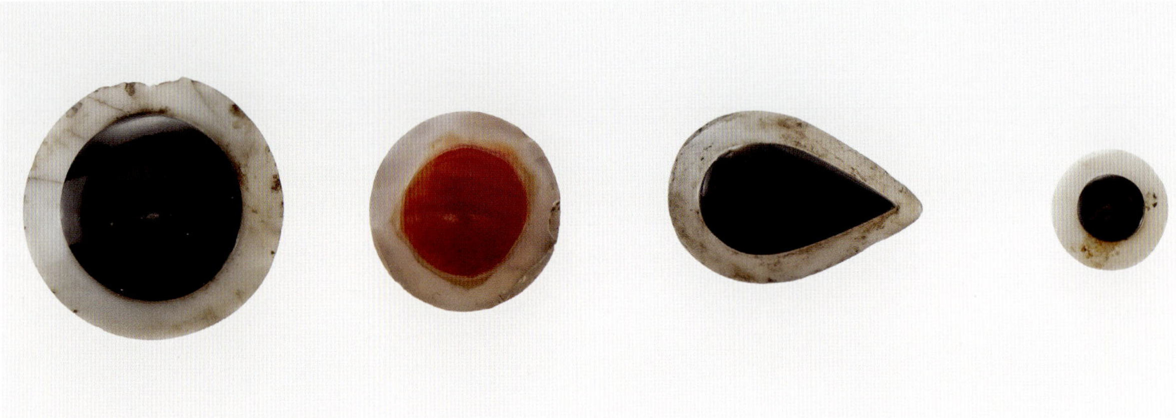

76. Eye Stones

Onyx/sardonyx

Iran, Persepolis, Treasury and Terrace

Achaemenid period (ca. 550–330 BCE)

Excavated in 1933–1934, 1936

ISACM A22944, A23289, A23349, A19434A

Tableware and Furniture

More than fifty vessels inscribed with the king's name were found in the Treasury at Persepolis. The name, wherever legible, is that of Xerxes I (486–465 BCE). Almost all the fragments came from shallow, footed or footless plates (**cat. no.** 77). Originally the vessels bore an inscription in four languages—Old Persian, Elamite, Babylonian, and Egyptian—written in one continuous line encircling the exterior surface. The name and title in Old Persian, Elamite, and Babylonian is "Xerxes, the Great King." In Egyptian, the inscription reads "Xerxes, the Pharaoh."

The griffin, a composite creature, is one of the most popular and long-lasting ancient images in the Near East, North Africa, and Europe. It appears on sealings and sculpture and in architecture, folklore, heraldry, and fiction from the fourth millennium BCE until today, including among the gargoyles that adorn buildings on the University of Chicago campus.

The image of the mythological griffin first appears on late fourth-millennium BCE seal impressions from Susa (fig. 7.18). The griffin is also prominent in Iranian mythology, where it is called *Shirdal*, "lion-eagle." Like the typical mythological griffin, the winged griffins on the plaques forming the bronze band of **cat no. 78** have the beak and head of an eagle; the neck, body, and front legs of a lion; and prominent ears. The ancients considered the griffin to be especially powerful and majestic because it combines the power of the lion, king of the beasts, and of the eagle, king of the sky.

Cat. no. 78 has many nail holes and may originally have decorated a door or encircled a wooden pole. There is no record of the bronze band's origins; it was found in storage in the 1970s exactly as it had been packed after its excavation. However, the style leaves little doubt that the band comes from Persepolis.

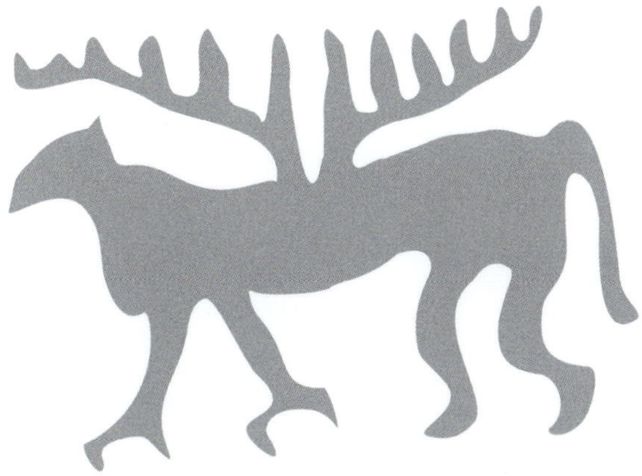

Figure 7.18. Drawing of a griffin from seal impressions, Susa, fourth millennium BCE. After Amiet 1961, no. 587, redrawn and reconstructed by A. Alizadeh.

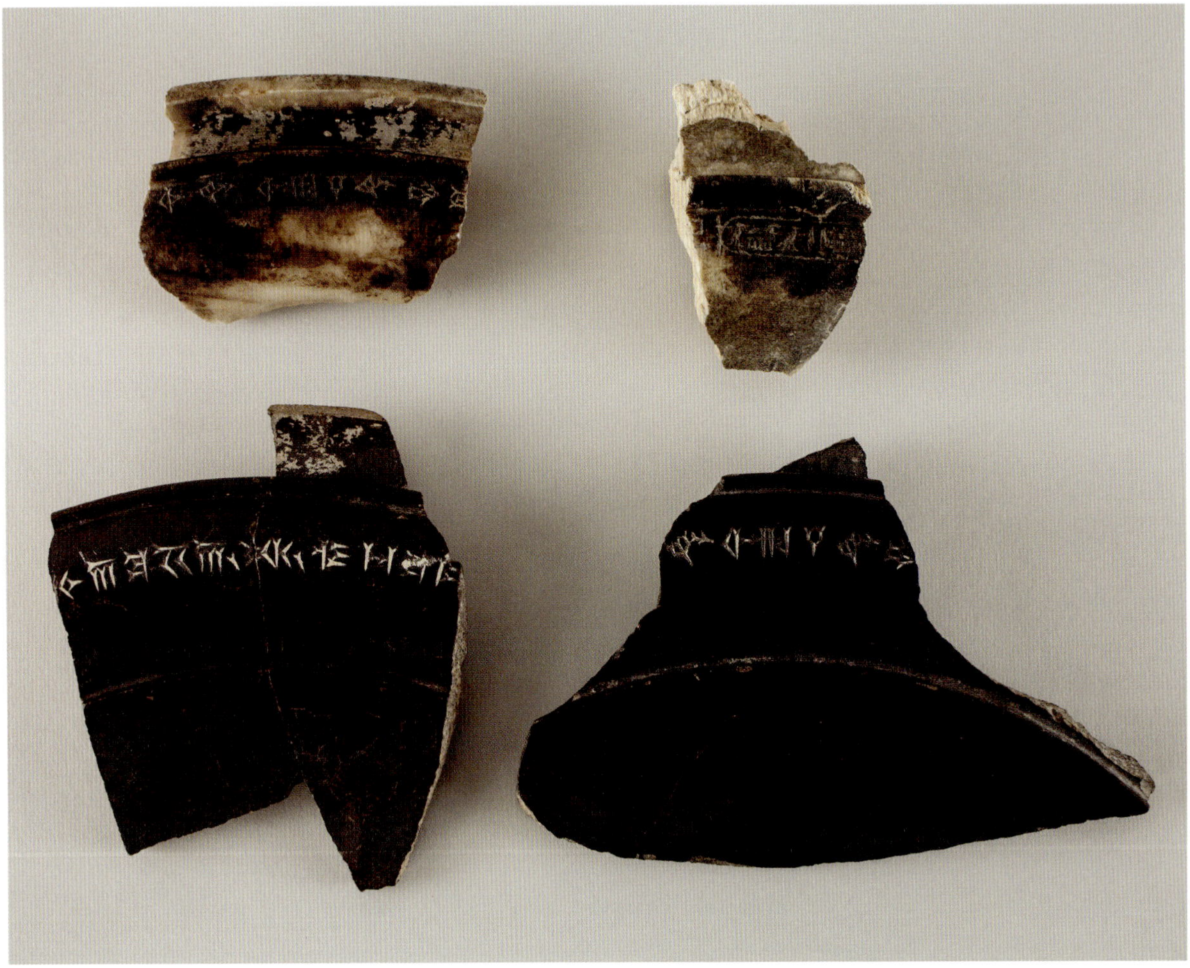

77. Plate Fragments with Inscriptions

Stone

Iran, Persepolis, Treasury

Achaemenid period, reign of Xerxes I (486–465 BCE)

Excavated in 1936

ISACM A23372, A23381, A23222A, A23221
(clockwise from top left)

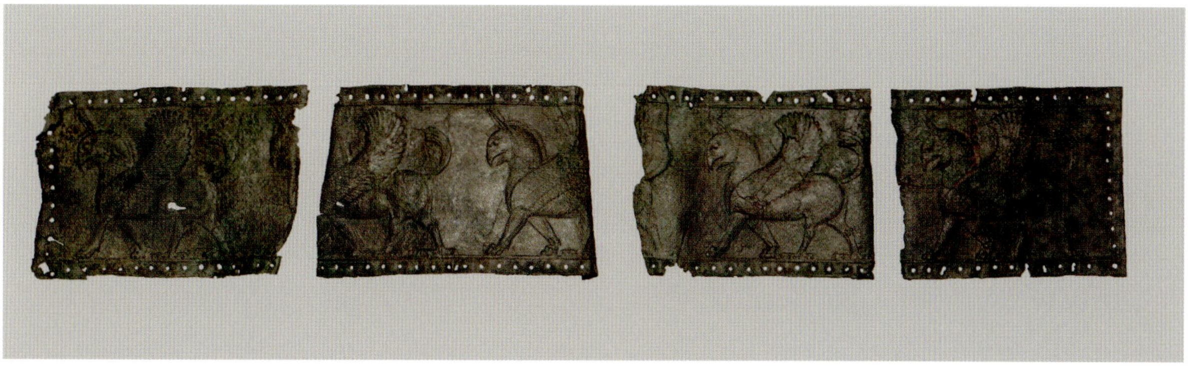

78. Plaques with Striding Griffins

Copper alloy

Iran, attributed to Persepolis

Achaemenid period (ca. 550–300 BCE)

Acquired before 1935

ISACM A35138A–D

List of Catalog Objects

Catalog number	Description	ISAC Museum registration number(s)
1	Sherd	A51141
2	Fragmentary bowl	A34785
3	Cylindrical bowl	A34802
4	Tortoise-shaped ritual vessel	A64641
5	Deep bowl with ibexes	A35278
6	Jar	A58299
7	Sherds from goblets	A51205, A51208, A51210
8	Figurine fragment	A64643
9	Lip or ear studs	A32494, A33008, A64642
10	Bottle with drooping spout	A33157
11	Cup with twisted handle	A38699
12	Spouted jar	A32412
13	Miniature jar	A33062
14	Beveled-rim bowl	A32404
15	Double-spouted jar with applied decoration	A32842
16	Jar sealing fragment	A64653
17	Envelopes	A32566, A64606
18	Complex tokens	A32507, A64602, A64608, A64619, A64622, A64623, A64625, A181472
19	Numerical tablet	A32620A–B
20	Bowl	A20136
21	Fragmentary bowl	A39940
22	Sherd	A39941
23	Conical cup	A20116
24	Fragmentary stand	A20104
25	Beaker	A20097
26	Beaker	A20164
27	Conical cup	A20089
28	Conical cup	A20117
29	Fragmentary bowl	A20217

Catalog number	Description	ISAC Museum registration number(s)
30	Bowl	A20218
31	Bowl	A20137
32	Bowl	A20114
33	Human figurine	A19780
34	Human figurine	A19781
35	Human figurine	A19783
36	Human figurine	A19779
37	Human figurine	A19786
38	Seated human figurine	A19784
39	Seated human figurine	A24847
40	Dagger	A38695
41	Copper stamp seal	A38694
42	Door sealing	A20242
43	Stone weight	A27931
44	Jar	A28726
45	Jar	A28731
46	Glazed pottery flask	A27939
47	Glazed pottery jar	A27940
48	Kernos	A28709–28712
49	Seated bear	A27919
50	Miniature bird vessel	A28675
51	Molded female figurine	A27967
52	Molded female figurine	A163150
53	Proto-Elamite tablet fragment	A27921
54	Disk-headed pin	A25293
55	Open-work pinhead with a "mistress of animals"	A24177
56	Cylinder seal and modern impression: two dancing figures accompanied by a boar, monkeys, a bird, and a cross	A25231, C1573
57	Standard finial with a "master of animals"	A7276
58	Standard finial with a "master of animals"	A24181
59	Standard finial with ibexes	A7285

Catalog number	Description	ISAC Museum registration number(s)
60	Pin with decorative head showing a feline attacking an ibex	A24178
61	Horse bit with winged mouflon figures	A7272
62	Horse bit with horse figures	A7278
63	Situla with human-headed winged ibexes flanking a sacred tree	A24179
64	Spike-butted axe head	A7275
65	Crescent-shaped battle-axe head	A7330
66	Composite capital	A24069–24070
67	Capital fragment	A24066
68	Colossal bull head	A24065
69	Lintel	A24074
70	Frieze	A24068
71	Relief	A73100
72	Foundation slab	A24120
73	Wall peg with trilingual text	A29808A–B
74	Roundel with winged lion	A28582
75	Variously shaped beads	A19576M–N, A19580–19581, A19583, A19586, A22949
76	Eye stones	A19434A, A22944, A23289, A23349
77	Plate fragments with inscriptions	A23221, A23222A, A23372, A23381
78	Plaques with striding griffins	A35138A–D

Concordance of ISAC Museum Registration Numbers

ISAC Museum registration number(s)	Catalog number	Description
A7272	61	Horse bit with winged mouflon figures
A7275	64	Spike-butted axe head
A7276	57	Standard finial with a "master of animals"
A7278	62	Horse bit with horse figures
A7285	59	Standard finial with ibexes
A7330	65	Crescent-shaped battle-axe head
A19434A	76	Eye stone
A19576M–N	75	Beads
A19580–19581	75	Beads
A19583	75	Bead
A19586	75	Bead
A19779	36	Human figurine
A19780	33	Human figurine
A19781	34	Human figurine
A19783	35	Human figurine
A19784	38	Seated human figurine
A19786	37	Human figurine
A20089	27	Conical cup
A20097	25	Beaker
A20104	24	Fragmentary stand
A20114	32	Bowl
A20116	23	Conical cup
A20117	28	Conical cup
A20136	20	Bowl
A20137	31	Bowl
A20164	26	Beaker
A20217	29	Fragmentary bowl
A20218	30	Bowl
A20242	42	Door sealing
A22944	76	Eye stone

ISAC Museum registration number(s)	Catalog number	Description
A22949	75	Bead
A23221	77	Plate fragment with inscriptions
A23222A	77	Plate fragment with inscriptions
A23289	76	Eye stone
A23349	76	Eye stone
A23372	77	Plate fragment with inscriptions
A23381	77	Plate fragment with inscriptions
A24065	68	Colossal bull head
A24066	67	Capital fragment
A24068	70	Frieze
A24069–24070	66	Composite capital
A24074	69	Lintel
A24120	72	Foundation slab
A24177	55	Open-work pinhead with a "mistress of animals"
A24178	60	Pin with decorative head showing a feline attacking an ibex
A24179	63	Situla with human-headed winged ibexes flanking a sacred tree
A24181	58	Standard finial with a "master of animals"
A24847	39	Seated human figurine
A25231	56	Cylinder seal: two dancing figures accompanied by a boar, monkeys, a bird, and a cross
A25293	54	Disk-headed pin
A27919	49	Seated bear
A27921	53	Proto-Elamite tablet fragment
A27931	43	Stone weight
A27939	46	Glazed pottery flask
A27940	47	Glazed pottery jar
A27967	51	Molded female figurine
A28582	74	Roundel with winged lion
A28675	50	Miniature bird vessel
A28709–28712	48	Kernos
A28726	44	Jar

ISAC Museum registration number(s)	Catalog number	Description
A28731	45	Jar
A29808A–B	73	Wall peg with trilingual text
A32404	14	Beveled-rim bowl
A32412	12	Spouted jar
A32494	9	Lip or ear stud
A32507	18	Complex token
A32566	17	Envelope
A32620A–B	19	Numerical tablet
A32842	15	Double-spouted jar with applied decoration
A33008	9	Lip or ear stud
A33062	13	Miniature jar
A33157	10	Bottle with drooping spout
A34785	2	Fragmentary bowl
A34802	3	Cylindrical bowl
A35138A–D	78	Plaques with striding griffins
A35278	5	Deep bowl with ibexes
A38694	41	Copper stamp seal
A38695	40	Dagger
A38699	11	Cup with twisted handle
A39940	21	Fragmentary bowl
A39941	22	Sherd
A51141	1	Sherd
A51205	7	Sherd from goblets
A51208	7	Sherd from goblets
A51210	7	Sherd from goblets
A58299	6	Jar
A64602	18	Complex token
A64606	17	Envelope
A64608	18	Complex token
A64619	18	Complex token
A64622	18	Complex token
A64623	18	Complex token
A64625	18	Complex token

ISAC Museum registration number(s)	Catalog number	Description
A64641	4	Tortoise-shaped ritual vessel
A64642	9	Lip or ear stud
A64643	8	Figurine fragment
A64653	16	Jar sealing fragment
A73100	71	Relief
A163150	52	Molded female figurine
A181472	18	Complex token
C1573	56	Cylinder seal impression: two dancing figures accompanied by a boar, monkeys, a bird, and a cross

Bibliography

Alizadeh, Abbas

2003 *Excavations at the Prehistoric Mound of Chogha Bonut, Khuzestan, Iran, Seasons 1976/77, 1977/78, and 1996.* Oriental Institute Publications 120. Chicago: Oriental Institute.

2008 *Chogha Mish.* Vol. 2, *The Development of a Prehistoric Regional Center in Lowland Susiana, Southwestern Iran: Final Report on the Last Six Seasons of Excavations, 1972–1978.* Oriental Institute Publications 130. Chicago: Oriental Institute.

2014 *Ancient Settlement Systems and Cultures in the Ram Hormuz Plain, Southwestern Iran: Excavations at Tall-e Geser and Regional Survey of the Ram Hormuz Area.* Oriental Institute Publications 140. Chicago: Oriental Institute.

2017 *Selected Objects from the Reorganization of the National Museum Storage Areas.* Tehran: National Museum of Iran.

Amiet, Pierre

1961 *La glyptique mésopotamienne archaïque.* Paris: Éditions du CNRS.

Delougaz, Pinhas, and Helene Kantor

1996 *Chogha Mish.* Vol. 1, *The First Five Seasons of Excavations, 1961–1971,* edited by Abbas Alizadeh. Oriental Institute Publications 101. Chicago: Oriental Institute.

Feller, Barbara

2013 "Die Anfänge der Bürokratie: Funktion und Einstaz von Siegeln im 4. und 3. Jahrtausend v. Chr." In *Uruk: 5000 Jahre Megacity,* edited by Nicola Crüsemann, Margarete van Esse, Markus Hilgert, and Beate Salje, 159–65. Berlin: Vorderasiatisches Museum.

Kantor, Helene

1957 "Achaemenid Jewelry in the Oriental Institute." *Journal of Near Eastern Studies* 16: 1–23.

Langsdorff, Alexander, and Donald E. McCown

1942 *Tall-i-Bakun A: Season of 1932.* Oriental Institute Publications 59. Chicago: University of Chicago Press.

Moorey, P. R. S.

1971 *Catalogue of the Ancient Persian Bronzes in the Ashmolean Museum.* Oxford: Ashmolean Museum.

1974 *Ancient Persian Bronzes in the Adam Collection.* London: Faber.

Roaf, Michael

1990 *Cultural Atlas of Ancient Mesopotamia and the Ancient Near East.* Oxford: Facts on File.

Schmidt, Erich F.

1939 *The Treasury of Persepolis and Other Discoveries in the Homeland of the Achaemenians.* Oriental Institute Communications 21. Chicago: University of Chicago Press.

Schmidt, Erich F., Maurits N. van Loon, and Hans Curvers

1989 *The Holmes Expeditions to Luristan.* Oriental Institute Publications 108. Chicago: Oriental Institute.

Trümpelmann, Leo

1988 *Persepolis.* Mainz: von Zabern.